Effective Color Displays

Theory and Practice

Computers and People Series

Edited by

B. R. GAINES and A. MONK

Monographs

Communicating with Microcomputers: An introduction to the technology of man–computer communication, *Ian H. Witten* 1980
The Computer in Experimental Psychology, *R. Bird* 1981
Principles of Computer Speech, *I. H. Witten* 1982
Cognitive Psychology of Planning, *J-M. Hoc* 1988
Formal Methods for Interactive Systems, *A. Dix* 1991

Edited Works

Computing Skills and the User Interface, *M. J. Coombs and J. L. Alty (eds)* 1981
Fuzzy Reasoning and Its Applications, *E. H. Mamdani and B. R. Gaines (eds)* 1981
Intelligent Tutoring Systems, *D. Sleeman and J. S. Brown (eds)* 1982 (1986 paperback)
Designing for Human–Computer Communication, *M. E. Sime and M. J. Coombs (eds)* 1983
The Psychology of Computer Use, *T. R. G. Green, S. J. Payne and G. C. van der Veer (eds)* 1983
Fundamentals of Human–Computer Interaction, *Andrew Monk (ed)* 1984, 1985
Working with Computers: Theory versus Outcome, *G. C. van der Veer, T. R. G. Green, J-M. Hoc and D. Murray (eds)* 1988
Cognitive Engineering in Complex Dynamic Worlds, *E. Hollnagel, G. Mancini and D. D. Woods (eds)* 1988
Computers and Conversation, *P. Luff, N. Gilbert and D. Frohlich (eds)* 1990
Adaptive User Interfaces, *D. Browne, P. Totterdell and M. Norman (eds)* 1990
Human–Computer Interaction and Complex Systems, *G. R. S. Weir and J. L. Alty (eds)* 1991

Practical Texts

Effective Color Displays: Theory and Practice, *D. Travis* 1991

EACE Publications

(Consulting Editors: *Y. WAERN and J-M. HOC*)

Cognitive Ergonomics, *P. Falzon (ed)* 1990
Psychology of Programming, *J-M. Hoc, T. R. G. Green, R. Samurçay and D. Gilmore (eds)* 1990

Effective Color Displays

Theory and Practice

David Travis
British Telecom Research Laboratories,
Human Factors Division,
Ipswich, UK

ACADEMIC PRESS
Harcourt Brace Jovanovich, Publishers
London   San Diego   New York
Boston   Sydney   Tokyo   Toronto

ACADEMIC PRESS LIMITED
24/28 Oval Road
LONDON NW1 7DX

U.S. Edition Published by
ACADEMIC PRESS INC
San Diego, CA 92101

A catalogue record for this book is available from the British Library

ISBN 0-12-697690-2

Printed in Great Britain at the University Press, Cambridge

PREFACE

Electronic displays are ubiquitous as the interface between people and computers. They are used to present information in the form of text, numbers and graphics. Over the last five years, computer systems have grown considerably in sophistication and one of the main areas of change has been the increasing use of color on visual display units. The standard IBM personal computer can now display 256,000 colors and a Sun workstation can display 16.8 million. Hence, hardware is no longer a limiting factor in the decision to use color on a visual display and users perceive its absence as old-fashioned. As a consequence, computer interfaces that fail to use color may not be endorsed by users.

Color can be a most effective way of conveying information and it has important uses in tasks where identification, coding and response times are important. Moreover, there is no question that in most contexts users prefer color to monochrome displays: color interfaces sell and succeed. But when color is used inappropriately it can be very counter productive and few software designers have much experience with the use of color. The aim of this book is to synthesize our current knowledge in the area and specify guidelines so that programmers, engineers and psychologists can use color effectively.

This book has been written for managers, human factors engineers, computer scientists and anyone else involved in the design process. A small amount of experience with computers and the use of visual displays is assumed but no knowledge of color science, psychology or physiology. The book can be used as a reference text or as the basis of a course on color displays, for example in degree courses in Computer Science, Ergonomics, Electronic Engineering or Psychology.

The author's strategy has been to introduce tutorial material where this is necessary to grasp fundamental principles and to understand the limitations of both the display device and the perceptual system.

Technical terms are defined in a glossary; and in order to place each chapter squarely within the context of color display use, each is preceded by an overview. Also provided at the end of each chapter is a summary of guidelines for the design of color displays drawn from the arguments in the text. This structure is intended to provide the student with the necessary information to begin display design without burdening him or her with excessive and unnecessary information. Ancillary sections at the end of each chapter provide annotated bibliographies that are intended to guide the student towards those areas that he or she may wish to explore in greater depth.

In order that the book may be understood by non-specialists, the first two chapters contain introductory material. Chapter 1 considers the design of color displays: this includes a discussion of how such displays work and how they may be effectively controlled by microcomputer. This includes reviews of all the major display technologies, and cathode-ray displays in particular. Frame buffer systems are covered in some depth. The concepts introduced in this chapter are required in succeeding chapters where readers may use the information to evaluate their own color display.

Chapter 2 presents a model of color vision that considers each stage in the perceptual process from eye to brain. This chapter also considers color deficiency: it describes the incidence of color deficiency, the common color confusions and the probable causes. It also describes how to test for color deficiency. Finally, the chapter considers the relevance of color vision and color deficiency to the design of color displays. It shows that an understanding of color vision puts designers and engineers in a better position to use color properly on color displays.

Chapter 3 describes methods of color specification. Although the number of applications that use color are many and varied, it is generally the case that color is used on visual displays for one of four reasons. First, color may be used on displays to represent color *qua* color, that is for realism. This includes applications such as computer-aided design, where products are "built" and may be shown to customers as an example of the finished version; or for example in the printing industry, where precise color specification and color judgements must be made. This is the substance of Chapter 3. This chapter describes eight color spaces, including the internationally agreed standards, and provides the information required to transform to them from computer RGB color specifications. Students frequently find these transformations needlessly difficult; to simplify the procedure as much as possible a simple introduction to matrix algebra is provided in one appendix, and another appendix lists a set of computer functions (written in 'C') that carry out these transformations.

Chapter 4 considers the other three reasons why color is used on displays: for formatting, coding and aesthetic purposes. For aesthetic purposes, what matters is simply that the final display looks appealing. To achieve this, the rules of color harmony are reviewed. But color may also be used for coding or formatting purposes: for example, this would be the case in applications where it was important to segregate or group different types of visual information, or to signify meaning by use of color. Methods for achieving this are reviewed in this chapter, and the final section shows how the model of color vision can be used to answer specific design problems.

Finally, Chapter 5 presents practical suggestions for ways in which the designer may assess a display system that uses color. This chapter supplies readers with the necessary information required to evaluate the display system, the working environment of the user, the system hardware and the software. This chapter is complemented by an appendix that synthesizes the environmental guidelines into a simple checklist.

Color displays in the work environment will soon become as commonplace as the microcomputer. This book provides the reader with the necessary intellectual tools to make their introduction effective.

Acknowledgements

The following people contributed in small or large ways to the content and style of this book: Steve Emmott, Robert Down, Joyce Farrell, John Fletcher, Alex Healey, Tanya Heasman, Gret Higgins, John Krauskopf, Darren van Laar, Nick Milner, Andrew Monk, Alan Whitmore and John Wilson. I would particularly like to thank Gret Higgins for her help in researching Chapter 5 and for producing some of the color plates; Steve May who helped program the Munsell Book of Color on a Sun SparcStation; and Malcolm Silburn who took and re-took the photographs of screens to provide the colored plates. At Academic Press, Andrew Carrick tolerated a number of missed deadlines, yet still maintained an infectious enthusiasm for the project; and David Atkins was a great help in my efforts to produce this book camera-ready. This book developed from an idea that initially belonged to Andrew Monk: I thank him for giving me the idea and for encouraging its execution so vigorously.

David Travis

For Denise and Joshua

CONTENTS

1

THE DISPLAY SYSTEM

1   Overview

This chapter describes the technology used to produce images on color displays. The first section is concerned with the cathode ray display. The screen of a cathode ray tube (crt) is made up of a number of discrete picture elements or pixels. In the limiting case, each pixel of a color display screen consists of three phosphors each driven by separate electron guns. Ideally, activation of one of these guns causes a single class of phosphor to luminesce.

In raster displays, the digitized picture is initially written in a specialized area of computer memory known as the frame buffer. *This is dealt with in the second section of this chapter. The frame buffer contains three values (one for each electron gun) with each value monotonically related to the luminance of each pixel. These values may be used to directly alter the voltage of the electron guns in the display, and hence the color of each pixel. Look-up tables may be interposed between the frame buffer and the electron guns for compensation purposes (such as gamma correction).*

Cathode-ray displays are generally bulky, and the crt/frame buffer system may introduce unwanted elements into the final image. Hence, the cathode-ray display is far from an ideal system, and alternative, non-crt-based display technologies are available that avoid some of these problems. The final section reviews some of the competing technologies.

2   The cathode-ray display

Although the cathode ray display is approaching its centenary, and although a number of alternatives have been proposed, it is still the most widely used method for the electronic display of information. Compared with other types of display device (see Section 4) it is inexpensive, reliable, durable and versatile. As a consequence of this its common place in the home and office is unlikely to be usurped in the near future, nor indeed in the not-so-near future. As a consequence, a disproportionate amount of this chapter is devoted to a consideration of the cathode ray display. How are pictures generated on a cathode ray tube? And what limits the display side of the display system? Answers to these questions will help the designer produce more effective displays.

2.1   The cathode-ray tube

The cathode-ray tube or picture tube is a quite simple device, comprising about half-a-dozen components (see Figure 1.1). Electrons produced by a heated cathode are fired at a controled rate through control grids. The accelerating plates increase the velocity of the electron beams, and the focusing structures act to sharpen the fuzzy beam of electrons. The deflection structure aims the beam of electrons at the phosphor coating. These components are seated in what is known generically as the 'neck' of the tube. Finally, the phosphors fluoresce liberating the high-energy of the electrons.

The deflection structure may comprise deflection coils or deflection plates, depending on whether the focusing system is electromagnetic or electrostatic, respectively. Both systems have the problem that the electron guns need to be situated some distance from the face of the cathode-ray tube in order that the beam of electrons can be adequately focused. A consequence of this is that the cathode ray tube is usually as long as the screen is wide (measured diagonally). This bulk may be significant where electronic displays are required in cramped conditions (such as aircraft, see below), and it is mainly for this reason that alternative display techniques have been investigated (see Section 4). One problem with flattening the conventional crt is that the electron beams must be deflected through larger angles as the electron guns are moved closer to the face of the crt, and this causes focusing problems. Flat-panel crts using alternative technologies are extremely difficult to manufacture.

2.1.1 The electron guns

Electrons emitted from the cathode of the crt are focused and deflected electro-optically so that they impinge on the phosphor screen. The apparatus involved in the generation, focusing and deflection of the electron beam is collectively referred to as the *electron gun* (although this is not strictly accurate: see Figure 1.1). Monochrome crts contain only one electron gun; color crts contain three. The three guns in a color system are universally referred to as 'red', 'green' and 'blue' guns; this is despite the fact that each electron gun in a color crt and the stream of electrons produced by each gun is physically identical. The color names refer to the set of phosphors at which the gun is notionally aimed. However, it should be borne in mind that the 'red' electron gun (for example) could just as easily drive the green-emitting phosphor as the red-emitting.

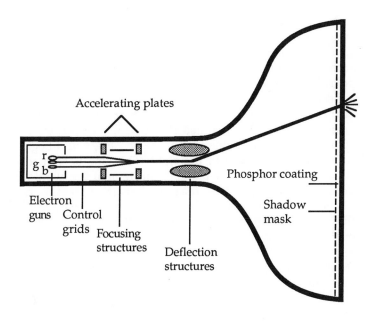

Figure 1.1: The elements of a cathode ray tube. For details see text.

2.1.2 *Principles of scanning*

The image on a cathode ray display is generally produced by one of two methods. In the first method, known as *vector scanning*[1], the screen image is drawn very much as we would draw an image with a pencil, except that it is traced out by an electron beam. The passage of the electron beam is deflected in the x and y directions by the electro-optical focusing system. Laboratory oscilloscopes are examples of vector displays and figures drawn in this way are termed Lissajous figures. For example, when a square is drawn as a Lissajous figure by vector scanning, only four lines will be scanned by the electron beam, those being the four sides of the square. In the second method, known as raster scanning, every pixel in the display is drawn whether or not it plays a part in the required figure. Consequently, the same square drawn by raster scanning involves scanning all the lines of the display: over 1000 for a high-quality graphics workstation.

At first sight, it looks as if vector scanning is to be preferred over raster scanning, but this is really only the case when the image comprises straight lines or curves. When an image includes a large amount of detail (for example, an image of a face) the raster method is more suitable because the image is less subject to flicker. Vector scanning may be too slow to get from the first to the final point of the image, since the image is stored as a set of vector commands (for example, draw line from x_1, y_1 to x_2, y_2). Since raster scanning is vastly more popular, and lends itself to color graphics, it is considered in the rest of this section.

Raster scanning is a feat of electronic timing. If you were able to slow down an electron beam as it scanned the screen, the spot (as it would appear if you were looking at the face of the screen) would begin at the top left and scan horizontally to the right. This line is termed a *scan line*. The scan line would not be perfectly horizontal but would deflect downwards to the right. The reason that it deflects gradually downwards is because it is easier to generate a voltage to do this than to deflect the beam suddenly downwards. The spot would then momentarily disappear and then reappear at the left of the screen, a fraction below where it began (see Figure 1.2). The process of the beam turning off (or 'blanking') and then returning to scan another line is termed the *horizontal retrace* or *flyback*. It is quick (several microseconds) and, under normal viewing, it is effectively instantaneous.

This scanning procedure continues until the electron beam is at the bottom right of the screen. After each line has been scanned, the beam is again blanked and it returns to the top left of the screen. This process is known as the *vertical retrace* or flyback. The complete screen area on which the lines are drawn is known as the *raster*.

The frequency with which the screen is re-drawn is designed to match the frequency of the AC mains. Hence in the UK it is 50 Hz; in the United States, 60 Hz. Interestingly, visitors from the US to the UK frequently complain of flicker in television pictures, whereas UK viewers rarely find television flicker disturbing. One theory for this is that the visual system becomes adapted to the particular refresh frequency of the display; this causes a reduction in sensitivity to flicker at just this frequency. Evidence to support this comes from the finding that subjects are least sensitive to flicker from displays that scan from the top to the bottom: when the television set is placed on its side (hence altering the scan direction) subjects become more sensitive to its flicker[2]. So if you find television flicker annoying, the solution appears to be: watch more television!

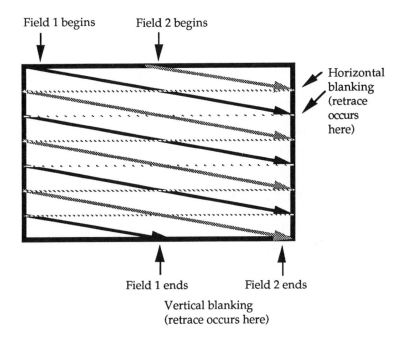

Figure 1.2: Principles of television scanning for an interlaced system. The dark lines show the path of the first field; the lighter lines show the path of the second field. The dotted lines represent the horizontal retrace. A real system would have many more horizontal lines than are shown here.

Just as with a motion film, a television image is really a sequence of static frames. But unlike a motion film, the rate at which new frames are presented is not necessarily the same as that at which the screen is re-drawn: indeed, with television transmission it is not. In the description of the path of the electron beam (above) a progressively scanned display was described. Some displays (such as conventional color televisions) are interlaced: that is, the electron beam scans only the odd horizontal lines before returning to scan the even horizontal lines. Hence each frame consists of two sets of interleaved lines (see Figure 1.2). Each set of lines is termed a *field*, and the field rate is hence twice the frame rate. A field rate of 50 Hz is not always sufficiently high to remove traces of flicker, especially since our threshold for detecting flicker is dependent on the luminance of the display. However, interlacing is favored in broadcast transmission because the frame rate can be halved and yet smooth movement can still be seen without picture flicker. Also, halving the frame rate causes a 50% reduction in the bandwidth of information that needs to be transmitted.

2.1.3 *Understanding some technical specifications of crts*

Among the wealth of technical information supplied with display systems are buried some of the following technical terms. This section is intended to explain some of the jargon.

• Frame rate (also called vertical frequency or vertical scanning) is the rate at which one complete image is drawn. For most applications 50 Hz is a minimum, but up to 100 Hz is to be preferred to eliminate flicker.

• Interlaced/non-interlaced. Interlacing is a method of reducing the frame rate whilst keeping flicker to a minimum. On an interlaced system, each frame consists of two fields that comprise every other line of the image. If each frame contained 525 lines and the system was interlaced (as with television in the UK) then the first field would contain lines 1, 3, 5 ...525 and the second field would contain lines 2, 4, 6 ...524. Non-interlaced systems are to be preferred for close geometric work (for example, computer-aided design), else lines that are only one or two pixels in width will appear to flicker.

• Video frequency (also called the dot clock) is the speed at which the electron beam can be turned on or off.

• Line rate (also called horizontal frequency or horizontal scanning) is simply the rate at which each line of the display is scanned. Line rate is given by the product of the frame rate, the number of fields per frame and the number of lines per field. For example, for a frame rate of 50 Hz on an interlaced system with two fields per frame displaying 320 lines per field the line rate is 50 x 2 x 320 or 32 KHz. Line rate increases significantly when high definition televisions are considered. Such displays need to maintain the same field rate, but each complete field may consist of over 1000 scan lines. Dividing the line rate by the frame rate yields the vertical resolution in lines; dividing the video frequency by the line rate yields the horizontal resolution in dots.

- Pitch is defined as the centre-to-centre distance between adjacent holes or slots in the shadow mask. A typical value for a high quality crt would be 0.31 mm.
- Resolution is the number of separately addressable pixels[3].

2.2   The display screen

A color television picture consists of a single spot of light of varying luminance which scans the screen striking three types of phosphor that each emit only a single hue. Yet despite this we appear to see hundreds of different colors on the screen, objects appear to move smoothly and we get a fine impression of pattern and texture. In order to understand how this illusion is perpetrated, it is necessary to look closely at the structure of a display system.

2.2.1 Pixels

Each separately addressable part of the display is termed a pixel: this is a (rough) acronym for 'picture element'. In the limit, each pixel of a color display consists of three separate phosphors; but without the aid of a magnifying glass, it is not possible to resolve these individual elements, especially at normal viewing distances. The phosphors are sometimes arranged in small circular triads (for example, the delta arrangement[4]); and sometimes as stripes that extend over the vertical height of the television screen (for example, the Sony Trinitron)[5]. Magnified examples of some different types of pixel arrangements are shown in Plate 1.

A simple way to understand the way images are produced from dots on the screen is to look at a magnified black-and-white photograph from a newspaper, or study a pointillist painting (Plate 2). Image pixelation is especially useful for producing alphanumeric characters. For example, the same pixel cell matrix can be used to produce the same letter in a number of different fonts[6].

2.2.2 Phosphor characteristics

When struck by a beam of electrons, each phosphor emits its own characteristic radiation by a process known as *cathodoluminescence*. Essentially, this means that the kinetic energy in the fast stream of electrons is converted into light energy. If the image is to be maintained then the phosphor needs to be continually fed with electrons because the rate at which the phosphor fades (its persistence) is short. Different phosphors with different persistences are available: these can range from around 40 μs for a P-4 phosphor to over 3 seconds for a P-26 phosphor[7]. Long persistence phosphors have the advantage that flicker is reduced[8]; but where it is necessary to produce moving images, short persistence phosphors are to be preferred, since image smear is reduced.

The variety of colors that may be produced on an electronic display is ultimately constrained by the spectral characteristics of the three phosphors. In order to produce the widest gamut of colors, the phosphors need to be highly saturated and appropriately positioned in color space (see Chapter 3). In practice the phosphors are positioned so that most colors of everyday interest may be reproduced, although some highly saturated colors cannot be generated.

Why just three phosphors? With certain minor qualifications[9], all colors can be matched by a mixture of three suitably chosen 'primaries' (see Chapters 2 and 3). The word 'primary' is used by lay-persons and experts alike, but it is a misnomer because it implies the 'primary' colors are somehow fundamental. Yet we could choose almost any three phosphors for a crt: the only constraint is that the color produced by one of them should not be able to be matched by mixing the other two. But no matter how saturated the three phosphors are made, there will still be a number of colours that cannot be produced (see Figure 3.5 in Chapter 3). These colors are said to be 'out of gamut'. They can be brought within gamut by introducing a fourth or fifth 'primary' color. Display manufacturers have not been concerned with introducing these extra primaries; one reason for this is that we rarely see highly saturated colors in the real world and hence their absence is not noticed.

2.2.3 The shadow mask

In theory, each class of phosphor is separately driven by an individual stream of electrons. In practice, the electron beams are broader than a single phosphor and the beams may be slightly misaligned or badly focused: it is consequently possible that a phosphor may be driven by the 'wrong' gun. This problem may be reduced by using a mask, known as the *shadow mask*. The shadow mask is a thin metal screen placed about a centimeter from the phosphor coating. It is really no more than a filter, allowing the beam from the red gun to pass only to the red phosphor, the beam from the green gun to pass only to the green phosphor, and the beam from the blue gun to pass only to the blue phosphor. The other phosphors are 'shadowed' from the wrong electron beams by the mask (see Figure 1.3).

The shadow mask consists of a number of holes or slots, with (in principle) each slot corresponding to a single pixel. The three electron beams are aligned so that they come to a sharp focus just as they pass through this slot; they then diverge and head for their 'own' phosphor. Any electron beams that are poorly aligned will be lost in the shadow mask. If the beams are slightly larger than the slot, electrons will be wasted heating up the shadow mask: one estimate of the percentage of electrons transmitted (the 'transparency') is 23%[10]. This is in good agreement with the fact that only about one-quarter of the total mask area is comprised of holes. Monochrome screens do not require a shadow mask of course, and this is the main reason why they are generally brighter than color screens: because four times the number of electrons are reaching the phosphor coating.

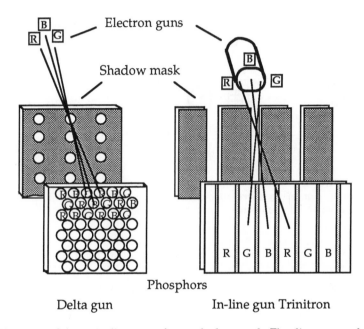

Figure 1.3: Schematic diagrams of a crt shadow mask. The diagram on the left shows the delta gun arrangement; the diagram on the right shows the Trinitron. The Trinitron uses an in line gun arrangement: this simply means that the electron guns are lined up horizontally and are not spatially displaced, as with the delta gun arrangement.

The center-to-center spacing of dots in the shadow mask is known as the *pitch*. Although it is tempting to equate the pitch of the shadow mask with the resolution of the display, an electron beam usually passes through more than one slot of the shadow mask, and hence the resolution of the crt is more fundamentally limited by factors such as the electro-optical focusing system.

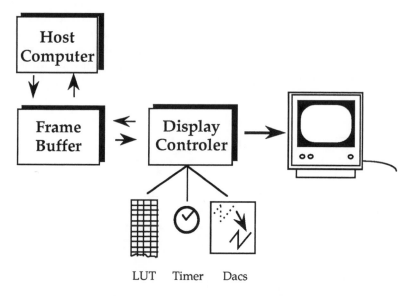

Figure 1.4: The salient components in a display system. The display controler comprises three elements: look-up tables (luts), a timing mechanism and digital-to-analog convertors (dacs).

Because the shadow mask is continually absorbing electrons, with time it becomes heated and highly magnetized. This causes the shadow mask to dome and in turn modifies the position of the shadow mask slots relative to the phosphors. This results in a lack of resolution, since the electron guns may drive the 'wrong' phosphors. The magnetic build-up can be removed by degaussing the shadow mask. Virtually all high quality cathode ray tubes automatically degauss at power on, but on some you will also find a separate 'degauss' button. This is clearly a useful feature that should be looked for by the purchaser of any high quality display if the display is not frequently powered down.

3   The frame buffer and display controler

In order to use color displays effectively, it is useful to know how images are generated and controled by computer. Figure 1.4 shows the important elements in the chain of events from computer program to color picture. The salient components are the frame buffer controler and the display controler.

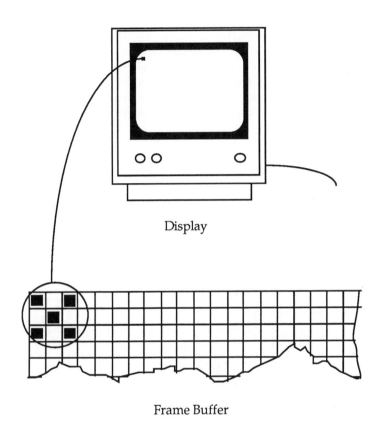

Display

Frame Buffer

Figure 1.5: The relationship between the frame buffer and the display screen. Note that the mapping is one-to-one

3.1   Frame buffer

The frame buffer, sometimes referred to as the *display* or *video buffer*, is simply a section of high-speed computer memory (hence you might also see it referred to as picture or image memory). It contains a description of one frame of the image in digitized form. The spatial resolution of the image is determined by the spatial resolution of the frame buffer. Hence each (x, y) location in the frame buffer memory should be thought of as corresponding to an individual pixel at the same (x, y) screen position (see Figure 1.5).

3.1.1 Black-and-white system

Consider the black and white frame buffer system depicted in Figure 1.6. Each bit in the frame buffer memory can be either on (1) or off (0), and hence each pixel in the final image will be either lit or unlit. Any given spatial position in the frame buffer matches an analogous spatial position on the screen. Hence, to generate a picture that is 200 pixels high by 320 pixels in width, the frame buffer needs a memory capacity of 200 x 320 or 6400 bits. This type of frame buffer would be described as 'bit mapped' since it has only one bit plane.

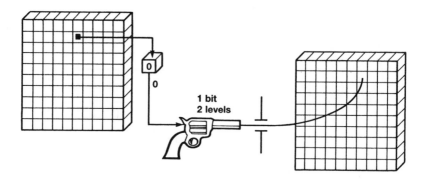

Figure 1.6: A frame buffer system for a black-and-white display. The frame buffer, shown on the left, can take on binary values 0 or 1 at each spatial location. These in turn switch the electron gun (symbolized by a revolver) either on or off at the corresponding spatial position on the display (shown on the right). Because only one electron gun is used in this system, only two colors (black and white) may be produced.

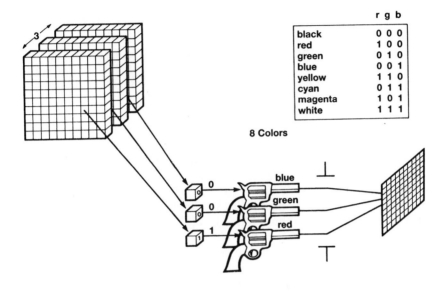

	r g b
black	0 0 0
red	1 0 0
green	0 1 0
blue	0 0 1
yellow	1 1 0
cyan	0 1 1
magenta	1 0 1
white	1 1 1

8 Colors

Figure 1.7: A frame buffer system for a simple color display. Because this system has three electron guns that may be individually controled, eight (2^3) different colors may be produced (see insert).

3.1.2 Simple color system

A simple frame buffer system capable of displaying chromatic information is shown in Figure 1.7. This frame buffer has three bit planes, with each plane driving one of the three color guns. The spatial resolution of the screen is once again determined by the two dimensions of spatial resolution in the frame buffer memory; color resolution is determined by the bit depth or 'bits per pixel' (in this case, 2^3). Different colors are produced by different combinations of the three guns at each pixel. For example, white is produced by having all the guns on, and yellow by having the red and green guns switched on and the blue switched off (see Figure 1.7)[11].

3.1.3 Advanced color system

The number of colors may be increased by introducing a display controler. The display controler reads pixel values from the frame buffer and outputs them to a digital-to-analog convertor (usually abbreviated to dac). For example, a system with 12 bit planes could devote four planes to each gun; the output to each dac would therefore be a four bit word with digital values between 0 and 15. The dacs (one for each gun) could hence control the voltage of each gun over 16 levels, instead of the gun being simply 'on' or 'off'. This type of 'byte mapped' system is shown in Figure 1.8.

Once again, the number of different colors that may be produced is governed by the bit depth, and in this example is 2^{12} or 4096. Note here that the word "color" is being used in a loose sense: two colors are defined as being different merely if they have different R, G and B dac values associated with them. Indeed, such a system might be used simply to provide a gray scale, and not for color at all. Moreover, when the steps between the different dac voltages are very small, the 'colors' may not all be discriminable. The different voltages may result in slightly different intensities, but the eye may be unable to distinguish them. Hence a system able to produce 16.8 million different colors (that is, a system with 8-bit dacs for each gun) is not necessarily 16.8 times as good as one able to produce only a million different colors, since some of the improvement will be lost to our eyes.

3.1.4 How to get more colors from your display

How can you produce more colors from an existing display? Two simple ways of increasing the number of available colors are to interleave colors spatially or temporally. Imagine you have the simple eight color system detailed in Figure 1.7 and you want to produce an image midway in color between green and yellow. You could simply increase the 'grain' of your pixel system by drawing the image with half the pixels painted yellow and the other half painted green (of course, they would need to be appropriately interleaved). For this to work effectively, either the display device needs to be of relatively high spatial quality or the viewing distance needs to be relatively large since you are essentially swopping spatial resolution for intensity resolution. Then, except under very close inspection, the human eye should not be able to resolve the individual elements (the 'supra-pixels'). Depending on your particular system you may be able to exploit this further: for example, you could mix the pixels in the ratio of 2:1 or even 3:1. This technique, analogous to halftoning in printing, is known as 'dithering'[12].

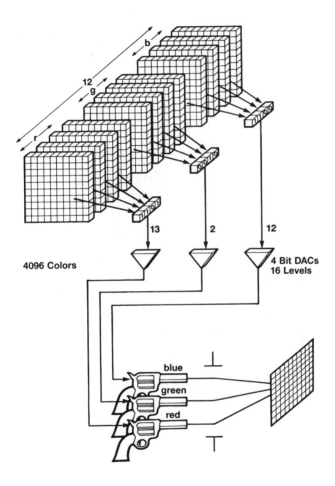

Figure 1.8: A frame buffer system for an advanced color display. Because this system has four bit planes for each gun, each gun can take on one of 16 (2^4) intensity levels at each spatial location. Hence a grand total of 4096 (2^4 x 2^4 x 2^4) colors may be produced with this system.

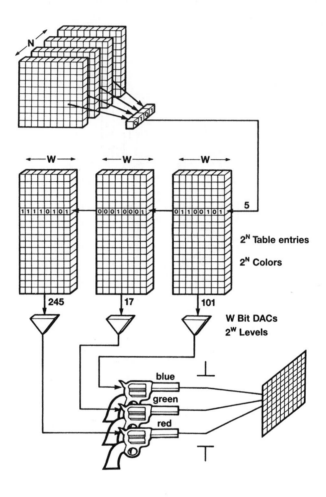

Figure 1.9: A frame buffer system for a color display using look-up tables. In this system, the frame buffer has four bit planes as in Figure 1.8, but now the value at each spatial location is taken as an address to a table. The number of intensity levels that may be controled by each dac is determined by the width of the look-up table. For the general case where the frame buffer has N bit planes and W bit dacs, the number of different colors that may be produced at any one time in 2^N; the intensity range for each gun is 2^W; and the total number of colors that can be produced (the palette) is $2^W \times 2^W \times 2^W = 2^{3W}$.

A second technique for increasing the number of colors available is by temporal dithering. To produce the same image as before, draw a green and a yellow image on alternate frames. In order to avoid screen interference, you will need to detect when the vertical retrace occurs and change the picture in this interval. When the color difference between the two colors you wish to temporally mix is too great you will be able to detect the screen flicker because you are essentially halving the frame rate. So with this method you are swopping temporal resolution for intensity resolution. Consequently, this technique is really only suitable for systems with fast frame rates, or optionally with at least 6 bit digital-to-analog convertors (see below) so that the colors you dither between are perceptually close. As before, depending on your display system you may be able to dither in other ratios (for example, 2:1).

You could of course use both the spatial and temporal techniques simultaneously and increase the number of colors still further. The limit of this technique is when the 'illusion' of television fails.

3.2   Display controler

The display controler acts as a timer to provide synchronization pulses for the monitor. It also contains the circuitry to convert RGB values into voltages for transmission by digital-to-analog converters. However, from a programmer's perspective, probably the most useful feature of the display controler is the use of look-up tables.

3.2.1 Look-up tables: what are they?

One disadvantage of the system shown in Figure 1.8 is that to change colors, the image planes must be rewritten. This is a slow process relative to the blanking interval of the electron beams within which period all computations must be done to eliminate screen interference. This type of system would be unsuitable in any applications where fast screen changes are required, as in some forms of animation. An alternative way of changing color quickly is to use a look-up table (frequently abbreviated to lut) in the display controler. With this type of system, the value from the frame buffer may be used as an index into three tables, one table for each color. The table value, and not the frame buffer value, is then passed to the dac and onto the electron gun. Consequently, a single number in the frame buffer can produce very different effects on the three electron guns (see Figure 1.9).

3.2.2 A color system using look-up tables

One great advantage of look-up tables as far as changing color is concerned is that the image planes do not require rewriting. Instead, the look-up table serves as a 'color map' of the screen, and all that is required to change the colors in the picture is to change the appropriate numbers in the color table. Take as an example a picture of a set of traffic lights. This is shown schematically in Figure 1.10.

The grid composed of small squares represents a portion of the frame buffer. Each small square in the frame buffer corresponds to a pixel at the same (x, y) position on the display screen. Although only one of the image planes is pictured here, the figure should be thought of as having 'depth' corresponding to the number of bits per pixel. (For example, if there are 8 bits per pixel, there would be eight image planes and each cell in the grid can take on a number between 0 and 255). The first step is to draw a color map of the image. Each frame buffer cell must be given a value. This is shown schematically in the figure: the background cells all contain color number 1; the traffic light frame comprises cells with color number 2; the stem of the traffic lights comprises cells with color number 3; and the lights comprise cells with color numbers 4, 5 and 6 (see Table 1.1).

So far there are no actual colors, there are only color numbers. Confusingly, color numbers bear absolutely no relationship to color: a color number is merely an address to a table, just as a street number can be thought of as an address to a house. Color number 4 could be black, or white, or blueish-green or in fact any color that could be produced by the display system. Similarly, a house with number 4 might be terraced, semi-detached or a bungalow. An appropriate analogy is to think of painting by numbers: the number itself gains a color only by association in a reference table with a particular colored crayon.

So how might we produce an image of a set of traffic lights signaling 'Stop', presented on a gray background frame with a blue stem, all set against a white background? Take, for example, the color number of the background, color number 1. We want to set this to white. This is quite simply achieved by setting the contents of the first address of all three look-up tables equal to (say) 128. Another way of saying this is that the RGB triplet should be (128,128,128). Similarly, we want color number 2 to correspond to gray. This is achieved by setting the contents of the second address of all three look-up tables equal to 32 (RGB triplet: 32, 32, 32; this should give a passable gray). To obtain a blue (for color number 3) the contents of the third address in the look-up table for the blue dac could be set to 255; the contents of the third addresses in the red and green look-up tables should be set to zero (RGB triplet: 0, 0, 255). To get the red traffic light, color number 4 requires the RGB triplet (255, 0, 0). Color numbers 5 and 6 are both set to black (RGB triplet 0, 0, 0; see Table 1.1).

Let us now assume that we wish to change the traffic lights to signal 'Go'. All that is required is to set the top light (currently red) to black

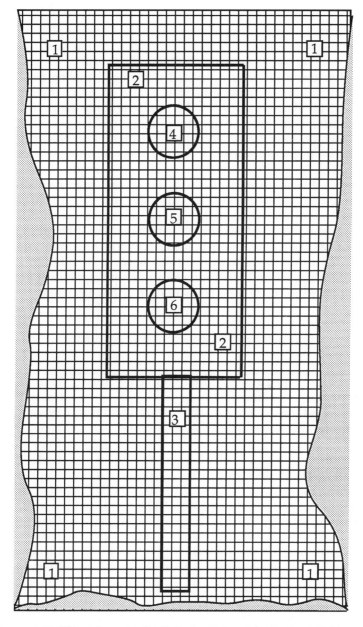

Figure 1.10: This schematic diagram shows how a color map might be represented in computer memory (the frame buffer). Only a small part of the complete frame buffer is shown. Each square on the background grid represents a pixel in the frame buffer's memory.

and the bottom light (currently black) to green. This involves changing two elements in the look-up table (see Table 1.1). The RGB triplet for color number 4 needs to be changed from (255, 0, 0) to (0, 0, 0); and that for color number 6 changed from (0, 0, 0) to (0, 255, 0).

Note that the color map remained unchanged during this piece of simple animation. The image itself was altered by changing a small number of tabulated values (in this example, only two). This would occupy a trivial amount of computing time. If we had not used look-up tables, it would have been necessary to change more values because it would have been necessary to rewrite the relevant portions of the frame buffer. In practice, for the very simple example given here, the difference between using a look-up table and rewriting the image planes might be barely noticeable. This is because the critical constraint is that all the values (whether they are in look-up tables or in the image planes) must be changed within the vertical retrace interval (about 1.25 milliseconds). With the more realistic scenario of more complicated displays, or where large areas of color need to be altered, changing many individual frame buffer values can occupy significant computing time, compared to changing a few values in a look-up table.

Table 1.1: Color numbers and look-up tables. For details, see text and Figure 1.10.

Image Description	Color number	Red	Green	Blue	Perceived Color
Background	1	128	128	128	White
Frame	2	32	32	32	Gray
Stem	3	0	0	255	Blue
Top light	4	255	0	0	Red
Middle light	5	0	0	0	Black
Bottom light	6	0	0	0	Black
Background	1	128	128	128	White
Frame	2	32	32	32	Gray
Stem	3	0	0	255	Blue
Top light	4	0	0	0	Black
Middle light	5	0	0	0	Black
Bottom light	6	0	255	0	Green

One example might be where you wish to see separate layers of a printed circuit board (pcb). This can be quite simply achieved by giving the contents of each layer a different color number: for example, layer 1 could be set to color number 1 and layer 2 set to color number 2. If the user wishes to see the first layer of the pcb, then color number 2 (the second layer of the pcb) should be set to be the same as the background; color number 1 (the first layer of the pcb) could be set to, say, red. When the user wishes to switch to the second layer of the pcb, color number 1 should be set to the background, and color number 2 could be set to, say, green.

Because so few elements of computer memory are being changed, it is evident why look-up tables are so useful when speed is an important constraint. Indeed, the entire image can be changed if the look-up table can be rewritten during a vertical retrace. For example, the traffic lights could be made to disappear by setting color numbers 2 to 6 equal to the background (RGB triplet: 128, 128, 128). Look-up tables enable global color changes to be made with ease.

When many elements of computer memory are being changed, interference ('snow') may appear on the screen. This occurs because an attempt is being made to change the video display at the same time the computer is updating it. By detecting the appropriate synchronization pulses, the blanking intervals (see Section 2.1.2) may be used to access the host computer without causing screen interference. This technique is most useful when the displayed image needs to be rapidly changed: for example during animation. Some graphics systems get around this problem by incorporating 'video RAM' chips. Essentially these allow the programmer to make a copy of the video display and alter this copy while the screen is being drawn. The copy and the original can then be switched, and the procedure continued.

The length of the look-up table (*i.e.* the number of bits in) is determined by the bit depth of the frame buffer. But importantly, the number of bits per pixel is determined by the width of the look-up table (*i.e.* the number of bits out); these two values need not be the same. For example, the system depicted in Figure 1.9 would be described as having 4 bits in and 8 bits out. The number of different colors that can be shown at any one instant is determined by the length of the look-up table. This is determined by the bit depth of the frame buffer (in this case, $2^4 = 16$). But the total number of intensity levels (bits per pixel) that may be produced by an individual gun is determined by the width of the look-up table (*i.e.*, the dac width, in this case $2^8 = 256$). The total number of colors available (*i.e.* the 'palette') is found by multiplying the three dac widths (in this example, $2^8 \times 2^8 \times 2^8 \cong 16.78$ million).

4   Alternatives to cathode ray displays

Consider some characteristics of an ideal color display[13]. Here, these are divided into two groups, the first broadly concerned with image reproduction, and the second concerned with manufacturing and application considerations.

Image reproduction
- High spatial and temporal resolution.
- High luminance and chromatic contrast.
- Wide color gamut.
- Uniform in space, time and color.
- Independence of the color channels.
- Insensitive to ambient illumination.

Manufacturing and application
- Versatility.
- Cheapness.
- Reliability
- Durability.
- Able to be mass produced.
- Compatible with existing display drivers.
- Thin and lightweight.
- Efficient with energy.
- Safe.

How does the cathode ray display perform against these attributes? Image reproduction is generally good. Crts are now commonly available with a large number of addressable pixels (1024 pixels by 1280 pixels), fast frame rates (up to about 100 Hz) and short-persistence phosphors: for all but the most demanding applications, these are sufficient to fool the human eye into thinking that an image is neither digitized nor flickering. Although a substantial amount of energy is wasted heating up the shadow mask, the luminous efficiency of crts is high and adequate for most viewing conditions; and crts are well suited to producing colored images. The gamut of television phosphors is not wide enough to reproduce all possible colors, especially highly saturated ones, but it can reproduce virtually all colors of everyday interest. The main disadvantages of the crt are that it is non-uniform, the three color guns are rarely independent, and it is sensitive to ambient illumination. For example, consider an electronic display used in the cockpit of a fighter aircraft. It might be used to signal status reports on the engines or be used for navigation. When the aircraft is flying above clouds, the ambient illumination in the cockpit reaches very high levels; at such light levels the crt display becomes 'washed out' and impossible to read. When sunlight streams through a window at home and disturbs television viewing we are able to draw a curtain or reposition the television set, options not open to the fighter pilot.

The large number of crts in use suggest that it performs well against manufacturing and application considerations. Indeed, the crt is versatile: it can produce alphanumerics and graphics, reproduce photographs, and it can be made in small (hand-held) and large versions. It is cheap, in that it can produce more information per unit time than any competing display device. It is reliable and durable (the sheer number of crts in existence testify to this). The crt is easily mass produced and since it is commonly found in homes and offices around the world, it would be inconvenient and expensive to replace with new technology. However, the crt is bulky and has a high power consumption. Consider the aircraft display mentioned above. The pilot's cockpit is small and space is at a premium; hence a bulky crt is a significant cost, and depth may need to be added to the display console, and even to the plane itself, simply to incorporate it. Whether or not crts are entirely safe is a contentious issue; this is considered in Chapter 5, Section 4.1.7.

Alternative display devices are required not to replace the crt in the home and office but to replace the crt in very particular applications. For example, where depth and power consumption are important considerations (such as in portable computers or television sets), or where screen uniformity, independence of the color channels and insensitivity to ambient illumination are considered crucial. Three competing display technologies are reviewed: liquid crystal displays; plasma displays; and electroluminescent displays[14].

4.1   Liquid crystal displays

4.1.1 Description

Liquid crystal displays have been used for some time as the displays in digital watches, and they have recently come to prominence as the technology used in small, hand-held televisions. As their name suggests, liquid crystals may have either liquid or crystal properties: they can be poured, yet they retain an ordered molecular structure typical of crystals. The most common variety used in displays are known as 'twisted nematic'. The molecules in liquid crystals can be considered to be arranged in layers. Liquid crystals of the twisted nematic variety have the molecules on the top layer oriented at right-angles to the molecules in the bottom layer. When an electric field is applied, the molecules align parallel to each other. Hence, the liquid crystal can be considered to be in one of two states: twisted on or twisted off. When the liquid crystal is twisted on it has the useful property of changing the polarization of polarized light through 90° when twisted off it reflects the incident light.

Now, consider the operation of a liquid crystal sandwiched between a pair of crossed polarizers. When it is twisted on, the light polarized by the front polarizer passes through the liquid crystal, which rotates the plane of polarization, and is then absorbed by the back polarizer. To an observer, the cell appears black. When it is twisted off, light that passes through the front polarizer is simply reflected off the liquid crystal. To an observer, the cell appears gray. Figure 1.11 attempts to represent this procedure pictorially[15].

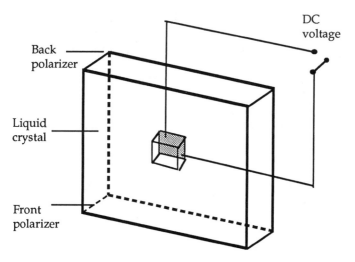

Figure 1.11: The essential components of a liquid crystal display system. The shaded cube represents a single pixel.

We now have the building blocks of a visual display, with color displays made by using colored polarizers[16]. A matrix of such cells can be constructed to produce an addressable display, with each cell representing a pixel. Such displays hence have the advantage, from a manufacturing viewpoint, of matrix addressability.

Returning to our list of 'ideal' characteristics, what are the main advantages and disadvantages of liquid crystal displays?

4.1.2 Advantages

Image reproduction

• High spatial resolution.
• Uniformity in space, time and color: because each pixel is directly and separately addressable, with no contamination by neighboring pixels, the liquid crystal display is perfectly uniform.

• Independence of the color channels.
• Relative insensitivity to ambient illumination so long as the display is backlit. However, image quality often depends on viewing angle, although this can be improved by controling the thickness of the liquid crystal[17].

Manufacturing and application

• Thin and lightweight: they average about 1-2 cm in thickness.
• Efficient with energy: they operate at very low power.
• Safety: they do not use the high voltages typical of cathode ray tubes and they are non-emissive.
• Matrix addressability.

4.1.3 Disadvantages

Image reproduction

• Low temporal resolution: smear is a problem when dynamic images are produced on a liquid crystal display.
• Low luminance and chromatic contrast.
• Color gamut is lower than crts, mainly because of the problem of producing a saturated blue primary.

Manufacturing and application

• Quality displays are expensive.
• Incompatible with existing display drivers.

4.2   Plasma displays

4.2.1 Description

An example of a plasma, or gas discharge, display with which we are all familiar is the neon displays used in advertising. Their mode of operation is quite simple. For a gas to emit radiation it must be ionized by applying a high voltage. In practice this is achieved by bathing a pair of electrodes within the gas. An addressable display is produced by building the electrodes as a matrix of intersecting rows and columns: applying a voltage causes the gas to glow orange. The applied voltage can be either AC or DC; AC displays have the advantage that they do not require refreshing. See Figure 1.12 for a visual summary of this description.

4.2.2 Advantages

Image reproduction

• High luminance contrast for monochrome displays.
• When used in conjunction with a circular polarizer to reduce light scatter, plasma displays are quite insensitive to ambient illumination.

Manufacturing and application
- Fairly cheap to produce.
- Durable; plasma panels are tolerant to harsh environments.

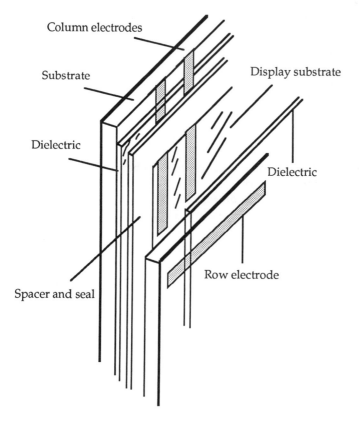

Figure 1.12: The essential components of a plasma display system.

4.2.3 Disadvantages

Image reproduction[18]

- Gray scale capabilities only. Color displays have been produced (using phosphors or different gas mixtures), but these are of low luminance and short lifetime.
- Crosstalk may occur between adjacent pixels.

Manufacturing and application

• Incompatible with existing display drivers.
• Screens require high voltages.
• Although some plasma displays are reported to have lifetimes of around 50000 hours[19], color plasma displays suffer from the problem that phosphor lifetime can be very short.

4.3   Electroluminescent displays

4.3.1 Description

In the presence of an alternating electric field, phosphors emit light. This process is known as *electroluminescence*. Electroluminescent (EL) material is generally constructed from a high-purity zinc sulfide activated with manganese sandwiched between a pair of electrodes. EL displays hence address pixels of EL material by passing an alternating current between a pair of orthogonal (row and column) electrodes. A schematic diagram is shown in Figure 1.13.

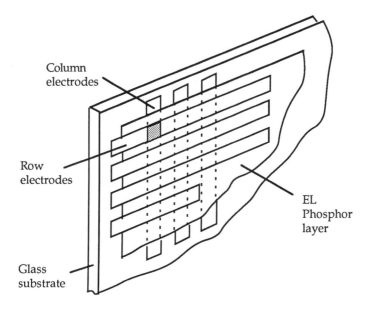

Figure 1.13: The essential components of an EL display system.

4.3.2 Advantages

Image reproduction

• Uniformity in space and time: because each pixel is directly and separately addressable, with no contamination by neighbouring pixels, EL displays are perfectly uniform.
• Good luminance contrast with no dependence on viewing angle.
• Image does not wash out under high ambient illumination.

Manufacturing and application

• Solid-state construction: there is no requirement to sandwich gases or liquids between glass plates.
• Extremely thin: the display itself approximates a micron in thickness.
• Matrix addressability.
• Safe, because they have a low driving voltage and are non-emissive.

4.3.3 Disadvantages

Image reproduction

• Little color capability due to the problem of designing a blue phosphor with appropriate saturation. EL displays are currently offered in monochrome varieties only.

Manufacturing and application

• Incompatible with existing display drivers.
• The currents that result from the applied voltage are relatively high and may be difficult to control.

4.4   Summary

It is unlikely that the cathode ray tube will be totally replaced in the near future. The impetus behind the research effort is to design displays that may be used in harsh environments where space is at a premium. Currently, the new generation of supertwist liquid crystal displays look to be the best alternative to the cathode ray tube, and one of the main reasons for this is that color reproduction is possible on such displays.

5   Display guidelines: key points

• *With a crt display, aim for a field rate of at least 70 Hz, non-interlaced. At values less than 70 Hz, screen flicker may become noticeable.*
• *If good image quality is a premium, consider 1000 x 1000 pixels as a benchmark.*
• *Aim for a display with saturated primaries in order to increase the color gamut of the display system.*
• *A degauss button on a crt display will reduce the magnetic build-up in the shadow mask and improve image quality.*

• *For accurate color reproduction the system should have at least 8 bits per pixel.*
• *A system that uses look-up tables will help speed up screen changes in application programs, and is crucial for animation sequences.*
• *In confined spaces, or where power consumption is an issue, a crt may be unsuitable. Consider LCD displays as a first alternative.*

6   Further reading

Catmull, E. (1979) A tutorial on compensation tables. *Computer Graphics*, **13**: 1-7.

A useful introduction to creating and using look-up tables. Additionally, it shows you how to compensate for the non-linearities introduced when turning a computer image into a photographic one.

Foley, J. D., Van Dam, A. (1982) *Fundamentals of Interactive Computer Graphics*. London: Addison Wesley.

Packed with useful programming tips.

Mulligan, J. B. (1986) Minimizing quantization errors in digitally-controled CRT displays. *Color Research and Application*, **11**: S47-S51.

Provides "halftoning" algorithms that you might find useful for increasing the capabilities of your display if it has dacs with a resolution of 8 bits or less.

Tannas, L.E. (1985) *Flat-Panel Displays and CRTs*. New York: Van Nostrand Reinhold Company.

A comprehensive review of crts and their alternatives.

7   Notes and References

1 You may see this method of scanning alternatively referred to as random scanning or calligraphy. For a comparison of vector and raster methods of drawing, see Eastman, C. M. (1990) Vector versus raster: a functional comparison of drawing technologies. *IEEE Computer Graphics and Applications*, **10** (5): 68-80.

2 The first evidence for this comes from the study of Corbett, J. M. and White, T. A. (1976) Visibility of flicker in television pictures. *Nature*, **261**: 689-690. For a contradictory study, see Ostberg, O., Shahnavaz, H. and Stenberg, R. (1987) CRT flicker and scan-line direction. *Displays*, **8**: 75-78.

3 For a paper comparing display resolution with visual resolution see Murch, G. M., Beaton, R. J. (1988) Matching display resolution and addressability to human visual capacity. *Displays*, **9**: 23-26.

4 So called because the center of the three phosphors form a Δ.

5 For more information see Doi, K. (1983) Cathode ray tubes: recent trends for character-graphic display. *Displays*, **4**: 197-200.

6 For an excellent review of typography and computers see Collins, J. (1989) The ABCs of digital type. *Byte*, **14** (November): 403-408.

7 These times are the spectral peak decay time to the 10% point. A useful list of phosphor characteristics can be found on page 82 (Table 2.1) of Sherr, S. (1979) *Electronic Displays*. New York: Wiley.

8 Bauer, D. (1987) Use of slow phosphors to eliminate flicker in VDUs with bright background. *Displays*, **8**: 29-32.

9 The main qualification is that certain, highly saturated colors cannot be matched unless one of the three primaries is itself mixed with the light to be matched.

10 Spronson, W. N. (1983) *Colour Science in Television and Display Systems*. London: Adam Hilger.

11 For the issues involved in the question: how many bits are enough? see Cowlishaw, M. F. (1985) Fundamental requirements for picture presentation. *Proceedings of the Society for Information Display*, **26**: 101-107.

12 Algorithms for dithering may be found in Foley, J. D., Van Dam, A. (1982) *Fundamentals of Interactive Computer Graphics*. London: Addison Wesley; and Iizuka, M., Ohe, Y., Kimata, N., Suzuki, T. (1987) Generation of quasi-fine colour images by random dither techniques and photographic multiple exposure techniques. *Displays*, **8**: 79-86.

13 Some of these criteria have been collected from Tannas, L.E. (Ed.) (1985) *Flat-Panel Displays and CRTs*. New York: Van Nostrand Reinhold Company.

14 For a short review of recent developments in crt technology, see Infante, C. (1988) Advances in crt displays. In *Conference Record of the 1988 International Display Research Conference*, IEEE: New York, pp 9-12.

15 For recent developments see Green, B. J. (1989) Developments in full-colour liquid crystal displays. *Displays*, **10**: 181-184.

16 This is a simplification, since producing colored polarizers is not an easy task. See Mizoguchi, R., Kobayashi, K., Shimomura, T. and Kobayashi, S. (1983) Evaluation and optimization by colorimetry of polarizers for liquid crystal display. *Displays*, **4**: 201-206.

17 So called supertwisted nematic liquid crystals help to reduce this problem; see Raynes, E. P. and Waters, C. M. (1987) Supertwisted nematic liquid crystal displays. *Displays*, **8**: 59-63.

18 In exciting new developments, some of these disadvantages may be obsolete; see Friedman, P. S., Peters, E. F., and Soper, T. J. (1989) Improved ac plasma displays: achievement of large-area, multicolour and high-altitude panels. *Displays*, **10**: 17-20.

19 Weber, L. F. (1985) Plasma displays. In Tannas, L.E. (ed.) (1985) *Flat-Panel Displays and CRTs*. New York: Van Nostrand Reinhold Company.

2

THE VISUAL
SYSTEM

1   Overview

This chapter describes how we see color. In the first section, a model of color vision is described based on psychophysical and physiological measurements. The model has three broad stages. The first stage is trichromatic since it is based on the quantum catches in three types of cone photoreceptor. These three classes of cone have broad and overlapping spectral sensitivities but may be loosely referred to as long-wave sensitive (L), medium-wave sensitive (M) and short-wave sensitive (S). Each class is effectively color blind: it is unable to distinguish a change in chromaticity from a change in luminance (or, loosely, brightness). To extract chromatic information from these signals, the outputs of the different classes of cone must be compared. This occurs at a second, 'opponent', stage of color processing. Two classes of opponent pathway have been isolated: one that differences the output of M and L cones; and a second that differences the output of S cones with some combination of M and L cones. Luminance information is multiplexed with the chromatic information carried in the M and L opponent pathway. In the third stage of color vision the two chromatic signals and the luminance signal are transformed to produce the world of color.

The second section of the chapter considers color deficiency. It describes the incidence of color deficiency, the common color confusions and the probable causes. It also describes how to test for color deficiency.

2   Color vision and color displays

2.1   Introduction

Because color is such a natural part of our world, it is difficult to convince people that there is something about our color vision that needs to be explained. Color truly appears to be a physical property of objects to which we passively respond. It takes quite a leap of the imagination to realize that color is not a fact of physics but a fact of psychology: in a very real sense, we actively construct the color in our world. Our visual system presents us with analysed snapshots of the environment, and these snapshots, just like those from a camera, are affected by optical properties, by the level of surrounding illumination and by the type of 'film' we are using. Our eyes are simply sensors that transduce light; and like all sensors, there are particular radiations to which our eyes are sensitive. In the case of human vision, these particular radiations are those from the visible spectrum. So we are all color blind because there are physical radiations in the world that we are unable to detect: these begin in the ultra-violet and the infra-red ends of the visible spectrum, and some fish, birds and insects make a much better job of detecting them than we do.

Yet the physiological mechanisms by which we see color are still not fully understood. Indeed, how the brain analyses color is currently an area of active research from which a clear pattern is still yet to emerge. The structure of this chapter approximately reflects the weight of knowledge in this area: more space is given to first-stage than second-stage mechanisms, and there is comparatively little discussion of third-stage mechanisms. Because our perception of hue is ultimately limited by these early stages, they are of most interest to the designer, programmer or engineer who wishes to choose colors that take account of the human factor in software design. Sufficient information should be provided to filter displays through a model of color vision. In fact, the aim of this chapter is to illustrate the importance of color vision in designing color displays. General principles are drawn together in the last section of this chapter.

In this chapter we draw on two lines of evidence on which a theory of color vision has been based. The first line of evidence is *physiological*, generally obtained from monkeys but sometimes obtained from human material. The second line of evidence is *psychophysical*, and is obtained from human subjects only. Physiological data is obtained by inserting a probe in some part of the system and recording activity at that site. Psychophysics is non-invasive and investigates the complete system by the study of psychological responses to physical stimuli. The physics refers to the measurement of the stimulus; the psychology refers to the measurement of the sensation. This chapter deals exclusively with color vision and color displays; the more general area of vision and visual displays is dealt with elsewhere[1]. Specific design issues that may be generated from the model of color vision described here are covered in Chapter 4.

2.2   First-stage mechanisms

2.2.1 Photoreceptors: rods and cones

The initial stage of vision is the incidence of light quanta on light sensitive cells or *photoreceptors* at the back of the retina. Photoreceptors are specialized nerve cells that transduce light energy (quanta) into electrical energy (a graded nerve potential). The photoreceptor contains a light-sensitive pigment termed a *visual pigment* because of its obvious role in vision. There are two kinds of photoreceptor, and hence the retina is frequently described as duplex.

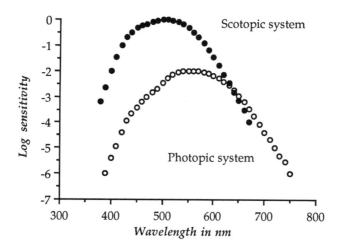

Figure 2.1: Photopic (V_λ) and scotopic (V'_λ) sensitivity functions. The x-axis plots wavelength in nm; the y-axis plots log sensitivity. Both functions have been normalized so that their maximum occurs at 555 nm and 507 nm, respectively. The scotopic function has been displaced by two log units to reflect its greater absolute sensitivity.

The two classes, known as rods and cones because of their structural appearance under the light microscope, are the start of the process of seeing but we use the two classes of receptor for different kinds of vision. Indeed, we do not use our rods for color vision. Color vision is solely the domain of the cone receptors[2]. The reason why vision is colorless with rod vision is because there is only one visual pigment common to all the rod receptors; and a single visual pigment can identify only the number of quanta absorbed, it cannot identify the wavelength of those quanta. This has been termed the Principle of Univariance[3] (see Section 2.2.3.1). As you will see, in order to generate a chromatic signal the eye needs to compare the outputs from more than one class of visual pigment.

Instead, we use our rods for vision in twilight. Hence, the duplex anatomical organization of our retina underlies a similar duplicity in the nature of our sensitivity to light. It is as if we have in our retinae two carefully interleaved 'films', one with high sensitivity used in low light levels that yields a black-and-white sensation (the scotopic system); a second with lower sensitivity that operates under brighter light levels and that yields a color sensation (the photopic system). Figure 2.1 shows the relative sensitivity of these two systems.

Physiological evidence shows that the rods are most sensitive to light radiation around 500 nm (what would be perceived in photopic vision as a bluish-green, see Figure 2.1), whereas the cones fall into three separate classes (see Figures 2.5 and 2.6). The single photopic function shown in Figure 2.1 is actually an amalgam of the three classes of cone (see Section 2.2.3). These three classes have maximal sensitivity around 420, 530 and 560 nm[4]. However the actual sensitivity curves of the rod and cone photopigments are broadband, and although the cone receptors are often referred to as 'blue', 'green' and 'red' sensitive (corresponding to the appearance of the spectral regions where they are approximately, but not exactly, most sensitive) their actual sensitivities overlap. Because of the broadness of their sensitivity, some authors have taken issue with the description of the different cones as blue-, green- and red-sensitive, and prefer instead the description short- (S), middle- (M) and long- (L) wave sensitive. This description is preferred because both the M and L cones respond to light that appears red and green to us; and the M cones are actually more sensitive than the S cones to light that appears blue to us. Unfortunately, the description of the cones as short-, middle- and long-wave sensitive is not ideal either because it implies that the three classes of cone are regularly spaced in the spectrum, and clearly (see Section 2.2.3 and Figures 2.5 and 2.6) they are not; indeed, the M and L cone sensitivity functions are strikingly similar.

2.2.2 *Retinal topography*

2.2.2.1 Visual angle

Before discussing the arrangement of photoreceptors in the retina, we need to come to some agreement as to how visual distances should be measured. One description might be to say simply "an object of size h metres is d metres from the eye". However, this description is object centered and not viewer centered. This is a problem because a whole family of objects, identical except for their size, could yield the same pattern of light on the retina (see Figure 2.2a). In the absence of other cues these objects would be indistinguishable. Researchers in vision use their own particular metric for describing visual distances. Since the stimulus to vision is the pattern of light on the retina, the metric used is the angle (expressed as a tangent) subtended by an object (see Figure 2.2b).

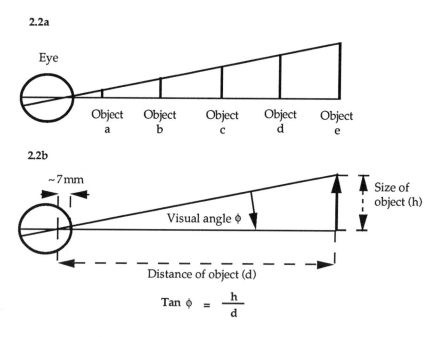

2.2a

Eye

Object a   Object b   Object c   Object d   Object e

2.2b

~7 mm

Visual angle ϕ

Size of object (h)

Distance of object (d)

$$\text{Tan } \phi = \frac{h}{d}$$

Figure 2.2: The upper Figure (2.2a) shows an object-centeredd description of visual stimuli; note that an infinite number of objects can give rise to the same pattern of light on the retina. The lower Figure (2.2b) shows how to compute the visual angle using a viewer-centered description.

2.2.2.2 Photoreceptor arrangement

In any one eye there are about 6.8 million cones and about 115 million rods[5]. However, the relative densities of both classes of receptor change quite dramatically as the retina is crossed: indeed, there is one area, about 0.2 degrees in diameter, where the rods are entirely absent (Figure 2.3).

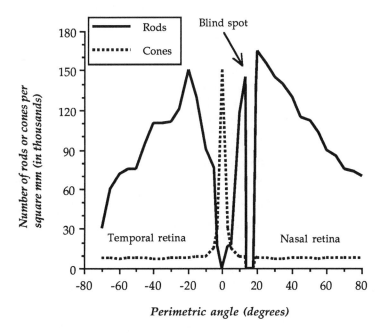

Figure 2.3: The relative densities of rod and cone photoreceptors as a function of visual angle (adapted from Cornsweet, T. N. (1970) *Visual Perception*. New York: Academic Press). The visual field may be vertically divided into two broad areas, nasal and temporal. The nasal visual field is that half of the visual field from central vision towards the nose; temporal visual field is the remaining half, from central vision towards the ear. Similarly, nasal and temporal retina refer to those areas of retina from the fovea towards the nose and ear, respectively.

This is part of a slightly larger retinal area where the cone density is maximal. This covers an area of about 5 degrees and is termed the fovea: a section through the fovea reveals that it is a pit (indeed, fovea is Latin for pit) because the blood vessels and neural machinery that usually lie on top of the photoreceptors are pushed aside helping to improve image quality. The fovea is the retinal region that yields our best acuity. Whenever you fixate a letter on this page it is being imaged right on top of this region of receptors.

As the retina is traversed, moving out from the foveal region, the density of cone receptors decreases markedly having a density of some 1% of their foveal value just 2 mm from the foveal centre[6]. On the other hand, the density of rod receptors increases to a maximum density some way out from the central foveal region. This is why astronomers sometimes find it easier to detect stars when they fixate them off center.

2.2.3 Cone spectral sensitivity functions

2.2.3.1 The Principle of Univariance

An important feature of each individual class of cone is that it is color blind: no single class of cone is able to make color discriminations. It can identify only the number of quanta absorbed; it cannot identify the wavelength of those quanta. This has been termed the Principle of Univariance. Put simply, this states that any individual class of cone is unable to disambiguate changes in intensity from changes in wavelength. It means that if it were possible to point a single cone at (say) either a red or green light source and monitor its response, the response of the cone would be identical to both lights so long as the intensity of one of them could be adjusted. This adjustment is necessary so that an equal number of quanta are caught by the cone, but clearly the wavelength of those quanta is irrelevant. Changing the wavelength merely changes the probability that an individual quantum will be caught. Until recently, this was a theoretical concept only; it has now been given the status of experimental fact[7].

The rod and cone cells have a characteristic spectral signature: as wavelength is varied, sensitivity varies. These sensitivities provide the visual system with a window on the electromagnetic spectrum. The reason why the part of the electromagnetic spectrum labeled "visible" is visible (Figure 2.4) is simply because this is where evolution has considered it optimal to place our visual pigments. The windows of visibility of insects, birds and fishes are very different to our own, and the reason is because their visual pigments differ.

These signatures are generally referred to as *spectral sensitivities*. For each class of cone, the spectral sensitivity is approximately identical and a large number of researchers have set out to establish the different sensitivities of the cones. The purpose behind such measurements is that they are able to answer the question: what limits color vision? With such a database, models of color vision can be constructed and predictions about color discrimination can be made.

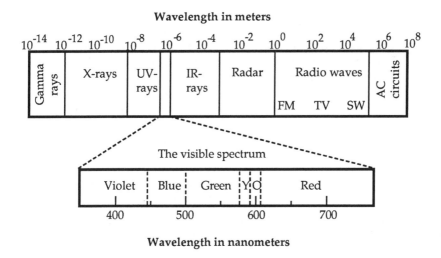

Figure 2.4: The electromagnetic spectrum. The upper half of the Figure shows wavelength in meters. Only a small fraction of this is visible; this fraction is shown in the expanded, lower, section. The color names associated with the spectral regions are approximate only.

2.2.3.2 Physiological evidence

A direct way of estimating cone spectral sensitivities is to extract a cone cell from a retina and measure its spectral sensitivity. In practice this is very difficult to achieve, and it is only in the last 20 years or so that such measurements have been technically possible. Two separate physiological techniques have been used.

In the first method, known as *dual-beam microspectrophotometry*, a sample of retina is placed on a microscope slide and an individual cone cell is identified. One of a pair of very small light beams, each about only 2 μm in diameter, is oriented so that it passes through the pigment-containing part of the cell; the other light beam is placed in a neighboring, but clear, area of the slide. The wavelength of the light beams is then varied through the spectrum and the absorbance of the pigment, relative to the absorbance of the neighboring area, is computed.

Because of the very small size of photoreceptors and the low signal-to-noise ratio of microspectrophotometers, individual records are invariably of poor quality and they need to be averaged with other records obtained from the same cone class. Averaged results obtained from human tissue[8] are shown as the symbols in Figure 2.5.

In the second method[9], individual cells are sucked into a micropipette and a minute electrical current is measured. This current would normally travel in the fluid around the cell, but the micropipette forces the current to travel by a different route by which it can be measured. Variations in current output from the cell are produced by varying the wavelength or intensity input, and these variations are taken as a measure of sensitivity. Although the measured current is small, the signal-to-noise ratio is better than with microspectrophotometry: the latter is really only sufficient for estimating the peaks of the spectral sensitivity functions (that is, the top two logarithmic units of sensitivity, a factor of 100), whereas the former can estimate reliably over six logarithmic units (a factor of one million). Averaged results obtained from monkey tissue[10] are also shown in Figure 2.5 as the solid lines. Given the differences by which the two sets of data are collected, it is satisfying that the two sets of data are in good qualitative agreement.

2.2.3.3 Psychophysical evidence

Given the accurate physiological estimates of the sensitivities of the cones, one might question the necessity of estimating their sensitivities psychophysically. After all, when a physiologist measures responses from the visual system he can point at some physical structure from which his measurements were obtained. On the other hand, the psychophysicist needs to treat the whole nervous system as a black box. The experimenter sends in a input (for example, a flash of light) and measures the output (for example, a button press). But what is being measured in this experiment? The sensitivities of the cones? Or the brain? Might the measurements be contaminated by some later part of visual processing (for example, inhibition)? Or an earlier part (for example, the lens filtering the spectral properties of the light sent into the black box)? In short, psychophysicists must make assumptions about whether or not a particular hypothetical mechanism has been 'isolated'. So why do psychophysical experiments when it is possible to do physiological experiments?

There are a number of answers to this. First of all, physiological experiments cannot always be performed. Physiological measurements of isolated cone cells have become possible only within the last couple of decades. Yet psychophysical measurements of putative cone sensitivities have been available for over a century[11]. Second, psychophysical measurements are invariably more precise than physiological measurements. The suction electrode technique of estimating cone sensitivities is an exception to this rule, but generally physiological sensitivities cannot be obtained over as great a range of sensitivity as psychophysical measurements. Third, psychophysical measurements may be obtained from Man, whereas this is rarely the case with physiological measurements.

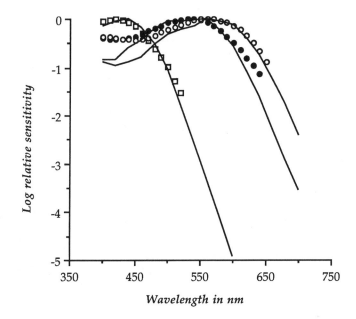

Figure 2.5: Physiological estimates of cone sensitivities. Microspectrophotometric measurements of the visual pigments in the cone cells of human eyes (symbols) are here compared with the spectral sensitivities of cone cells in monkeys measured by recording photocurrents using a suction electrode (solid lines). The suction electrode technique enables measurements to be made over a much wider range of sensitivities than the microspectrophotometric technique. All data sets have been normalized to have maximal sensitivity at zero log relative sensitivity. Note that the two sets of data are in qualitative agreement; the quantitative differences remain unexplained, although they are probably due to measurement error rather than species differences.

Psychophysical estimates of the fundamental spectral sensitivity functions (the 'fundamentals') may themselves be 'direct' or 'indirect'. One example of direct estimates comes from the considerable work of Stiles[12]. In Stiles' technique, the visual system is probed with a small test flash (typically 1-deg of visual angle and flashed for about one-fifth of a second), the wavelength of which is chosen to maximally excite one of the cone fundamentals relative to the other two. Sensitivity is then measured to variations of a background field (typically 10-deg of visual angle) upon which the test flash is superimposed. As an example, take the S cone fundamental. To isolate this fundamental, Stiles chose a test flash of 434.8 nm[13] (perceptually, this appears violet). First, he measured a subject's absolute sensitivity to this test flash, that is with no background field present; and then he measured the intensity (specifically, the radiance) of various background fields that, when superimposed on the test flash, raised threshold by a factor of ten. Fields of a wavelength close to the maximum sensitivity of the S fundamental required less intensity to raise threshold by this amount than fields of a longer or shorter wavelength. Plotting the reciprocal of these values yields a sensitivity function. By following the same procedure for the M and L cones the fundamental sensitivities of color vision should result.

Unfortunately, Stiles' methods led to a total of seven sensitivity curves: three candidates for the S fundamental, and two each for the M and L fundamentals. In order to clearly distinguish these from cone fundamentals, Stiles was careful to call them 'Π mechanisms'. Over the years, a number of researchers have been engaged in attempting to find out which of the Π mechanisms, if any, represent the S, M and L fundamentals. The weight of evidence favours Π_1, Π_4 and Π_5 respectively as the best candidates of the seven (see Figure 2.6), although it is generally recognized these are not the absolute truth. Part of the reason for this is that Stiles' technique assumes that each class of cone is independent in both its detection of the test flash and in controling its state of adaptation; it turns out that this is true only under certain conditions, and indeed it now appears that interactions between the cone types are what led to the "spurious" Π mechanisms and certain features of some of the more realistic functions (for example, the long-wavelength plateau or lobe of Π_1). Stiles' technique has been honed by other researchers to yield functions which more closely obey these assumptions and are probably closer to the fundamental sensitivities of color vision[14]. Even so, the essential technique is due to Stiles' pioneering work.

There is also an indirect method of estimating the cone sensitivities from psychophysical measurements based on color matching functions. Since an understanding of this is required for some of the color space manipulations described in the next chapter, a brief summary is provided here.

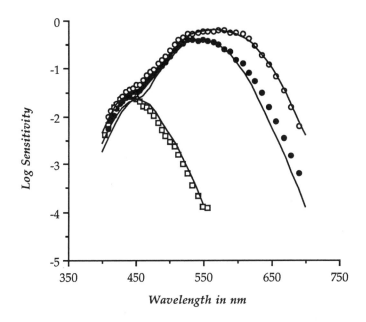

Figure 2.6: Psychophysical estimates of cone sensitivities. Stiles π mechanisms (π_1 π_4 and π_5 symbols) are here compared with the Smith-Pokorny fundamentals (solid lines). Stiles' data have been adjusted so that the maximum sensitivity of each π mechanism agrees with the Smith-Pokorny fundamentals. For Stiles π mechanisms, the curves represent the sensitivity of observers to background fields of different wavelength when subjects were required to detect a 435 nm (π_1), 500 nm (π_4) or a 667 nm (π_5) test stimulus. The data for π_1 above 555 nm is not shown. Of all Stiles' π mechanisms, these are the best candidates for the cone fundamentals. However, certain features of these curves (for example, a long-wavelength plateau on π_1, not shown here) suggest that these are not the complete truth. (see text for more details). These psychophysical functions appear quite different from the physiological functions shown in the previous figure; this is partly because the physiological data are normalized at their peak sensitivity, and partly because the physiological data ignores the screening effects of inert pigments in the eye, and indeed by the visual pigment itself. When appropriate corrections are made, the two sets of data are in good agreement[15].

Color matching functions are simply plots of the relative amounts of three primary lights required to match a monochromatic light. In other words, for any color, C_λ, color matching functions plot the values of $r(\lambda)$, $g(\lambda)$ and $b(\lambda)$ that satisfy the expression:

$$C_\lambda \equiv r(\lambda) + g(\lambda) + b(\lambda)$$

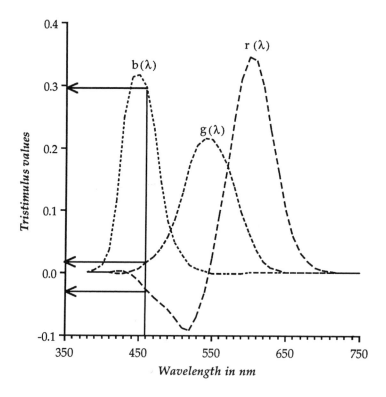

Figure 2.7: CIE (1931) RGB color matching functions.

An example of a set of color matching functions is shown in Figure 2.7. Three curves are shown in Figure 2.7, labeled $r(\lambda)$, $g(\lambda)$ and $b(\lambda)$, based on color matching by three primary lights selected from the blue (435.8 nm), green (546.1 nm) and red (700 nm) parts of the spectrum. The x-axis represents the wavelength of a test light, C_λ, that a subject was required to match with these three primary lights; and if a vertical line is drawn from any particular wavelength it is possible to read from the y-axis what amounts of the three primaries would be required to match this light. So for example, 460 nm (a wavelength that perceptually appears deep blue) could be matched with 0.298 of the blue primary, 0.015 of the green primary and -0.026 of the red primary. These three numbers are known as *tristimulus values*.

Why was a 'negative' amount of red light required to match 460 nm? The reason is that, in experiments such as this, subjects are rarely able to match the standard light without mixing it with one of the primaries. So a 'negative' amount of red light simply means that the algebraic expression above is transformed to:

$$C_\lambda - r(\lambda) \equiv g(\lambda) + b(\lambda)$$

At first inspection, this looks like a failure of trichromacy since the chosen standard light could not be matched by a mixture of three primary lights. In fact, the reason why this happens in color matching experiments is simply because the standard light is monochromatic and so causes dramatically unequal rates of absorption in the three classes of cone. This can be appreciated by glancing at the cone spectral sensitivities presented in Figures 2.5 and 2.6. These unequal rates of absorption cannot be matched with the primary lights (except in the trivial case where the wavelength of the standard light is the same as one of the three primaries), and hence to achieve a match the standard light must first be desaturated by mixing in one of the primaries. Incidentally, this is why a television set with three display primaries will *never* be able to represent all the colors that we can see in the world (see Chapter 3, Figure 3.5).

Because colorimetric calculations were performed by hand in the 1930s, it was considered a disadvantage that one of the tristimulus values in the r(λ), g(λ), b(λ) set was frequently negative. It was thought that the negative sign could easily go astray and result in computational errors. Consequently, in the CIE XYZ standard of colorimetry described in Chapter 3, a different set of color matching functions are used. The data in Figure 2.7 were transformed as if the color matching had been carried out with unreal or imaginary primaries; it might help to think of these imaginary primaries as super-saturated colors. There are three standard sets of color matching functions in circulation: the CIE 1931 set, the Judd (1951) modification of these (shown in Figure 2.8) and the Stiles and Burch (1959) set[16]. In this book, the Judd (1951) set of color matching functions are used, although all these sets of color matching functions are essentially the same[17]. Figure 2.8 shows that in this transformed system, all tristimulus values are positive.

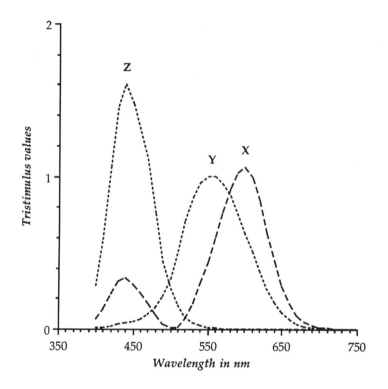

Figure 2.8: The Judd (1951) set of color matching functions. (For details, see text).

These color matching functions can be used to derive tristimulus values for any spectral power distribution, and it is a fact that two colors with the same tristimulus values will match precisely. This is despite the fact that they may have very different spectral power distributions[18]. Color matching functions provide an objective definition of color in terms of three standard primary lights, and it is for this reason that the CIE standard of colorimetry is based upon such measurements (see Chapter 3).

Now, there is a fundamental law of color vision[19], which states that the cone fundamentals must be expressible as linear combinations of these color matching functions. In matrix form:

$$\begin{bmatrix} S \\ M \\ L \end{bmatrix} = \begin{bmatrix} k_1 & k_2 & k_3 \\ k_4 & k_5 & k_6 \\ k_7 & k_8 & k_9 \end{bmatrix} \begin{bmatrix} X \\ Y \\ Z \end{bmatrix}$$

where S, M and L are the modulations of the three classes of cone, and X, Y and Z are the color matching functions. In order to derive the fundamentals it is necessary to determine the nine coefficients of transformation in the k-matrix.

The k-matrix can be derived only by making certain assumptions about color vision. One assumption is that a form of color deficiency known as *dichromacy* (see Section 3) is a reduced form of normal color vision. This assumption is known as the *Helmholtz-König reduction hypothesis*, and fundamentals derived using this hypothesis are consequently known as Helmholtz-König fundamentals. Specifically, three assumptions are made about dichromats: first, they lack one of the normal classes of cone pigment; second, the remaining two classes of cone pigment are exactly the same as those of normal observers; and third, the cones themselves are the same in all respects as those of normal trichromats. This is a rather bold set of assumptions, but good evidence exists for the first two. The last assumption is rather difficult to test and so is implicitly assumed.

If we accept the Helmholtz-König reduction hypothesis, we can solve the k-matrix quite simply[20]. Because dichromats can use only two classes of cone to discriminate colors, any lights that cause equal ratios of activity in those two classes will not be discriminated. Hence, straight lines that represent equal ratios of the two cone activities in a trichromatic color space will describe a locus of colors that are confused by dichromats; and these loci will converge on the point where both of the cone contributions are zero.

It is these points, known as 'co-punctal points', that help solve the k-matrix above. The co-punctal points (x_p, y_p, and z_p for the protanope, x_d, y_d and z_d for the deuteranope and x_t y_t, and z_t for the tritanope) are related to the color matching functions (X, Y and Z) and the cone fundamentals (S, M and L) by the following expression:

$$\begin{bmatrix} X \\ Y \\ Z \end{bmatrix} = \begin{bmatrix} x_p & x_d & x_t \\ y_p & y_d & y_t \\ z_p & z_d & z_t \end{bmatrix} \begin{bmatrix} n_1 S \\ n_2 M \\ n_3 L \end{bmatrix}$$

By inverting the co-punctal point matrix, the k-matrix can be derived and hence so too can the fundamentals, apart from the normalization constants n_1, n_2 and n_3.

There are a number of different sets of fundamentals. These arise from combinations of different assumptions about the co-punctal points, and/or the use of different sets of color matching functions, and/or different assumptions about the normalization constants (the normalization constants determine the relative heights of the functions). The set of fundamentals used in this book is that of Smith and Pokorny (see Chapter 3 and Figure 2.6), since these have been most widely adopted by researchers in vision; indeed, it has been proposed that a system of colorimetry based on these fundamentals should replace the CIE XYZ system[21].

Since our color vision depends in the first instance on three classes of receptor, it is said to be *trichromatic*. The color matching experiment, where three lights are mixed to match a standard light, is a classic demonstration of this. The history of the theory of trichromacy is a long one[22], and the facts were certainly known as long ago as 1719[23]. In some general psychology textbooks it is occasionally stated that the trichromatic theory is wrong. It is not. It is, however, true that the trichromatic theory is an incomplete description of how we see color and it needs to be modified to account for other phenomena in color vision (see Section 2.4). The theory of trichromacy merely states that at some stage our color vision depends on three variables. We now know these three variables to be the quantum catches of the three classes of cone receptor in our eye.

2.2.4 Incidence of the three classes of cone

The three classes of cone are neither equally numerous nor equally distributed over the retina. Firstly, L cones outnumber M cones by about 2:1, although there are some individual differences in the exact proportions[24]. Moreover, S cones appear to be significantly less numerous than L and M cones. Anatomical and psychophysical estimates suggest that S cones account for only 10% of the total number of cones[25]. This means our spatial vision should be comparatively poor when it relies solely on activity in S cones. A considerable literature testifies to this[26].

Secondly, whereas L and M cones have their highest incidence in the fovea, S cones are virtually absent in the central foveal region[27], having maximal incidence within an annulus of 1 degree eccentricity[28]. This suggests that our color vision should be atypical when it relies on receptor activity in the very central foveal region: in particular, it should resemble the color vision of the rare kind of dichromatic observer who lacks the S cones (the tritanope; see Section 3).

Experimental evidence supports this notion[29], and the phenomenon has been christened *small field tritanopia*. The practical consequences of this are that fine detail should not be represented by deep blues or violets. This includes not simply text but also such things as mouse cursors. The visual system processes signals from S cones more slowly than signals from L and M cones[30] and hence a deep blue or violet mouse cursor exploits the poor spatial *and* temporal resolution of the S cone system of the eye. Yet it is astonishing that such cursors are often encountered in application programs. Color boundaries that rely on S cones for discrimination should similarly be avoided[31] (see Chapter 4).

There is one area where both rod and cone receptors are absent: this area is known as the optic disk or the blind spot (for obvious reasons), and it is where the neural machinery from the photoreceptors leaves the eyeball, forms the optic nerve and travels to the brain. The blind spot is about 18 degrees of visual angle from the fovea in the nasal visual field (see Figure 2.3). It is easy to detect your own blind spot by placing two crosses on a piece of paper about two inches apart, closing one eye, and then moving the piece of paper towards you. If the left eye is closed, you should fixate on the left cross, and *vice versa*. Next time you are in tedious company you might want to take a leaf out of Charles II's book and 'decapitate' the person by imaging his or her head on your blind spot[32].

It is astonishing that we go around with fairly large blind spots in both our eyes and yet remain completely unaware of their presence, except when we do a test like this. It's obviously not because the blind region of each eye is covered by a good region in the other eye since we would become suddenly aware of the blind spot when we close one eye. The fact that we are not means that there is some "filling in" process in vision. Indeed, this is the reason why some insidious diseases of the eye (for example, glaucoma and optic neuritis) that cause localized blind spots or "scotomata" may go unnoticed by their victim: the brain 'paints over' areas of the visual image that have no retinal representation.

2.3   Second-stage mechanisms

2.3.1 Chromatic pathways

The Principle of Univariance states that any individual class of cone is color blind. Hence, in order that we may discriminate changes in intensity from changes in wavelength, the outputs from the photoreceptors must be compared.

This stage of processing, which has been termed 'opponent', was first qualitatively suggested in the nineteenth century by Ewald Hering and vigorously promoted by his twentieth century disciples, Hurvich and

Jameson[33]. One argument long in its favor stems from the psychological links between red and green, on the one hand, and blue and yellow on the other. For example, most people would describe colors as being composed of combinations of four 'primary' colors (red, green, blue and yellow), and not three as might be expected if the three photoreceptors in the trichromatic theory had direct lines to the brain. Moreover, we do not use the opposing hues (red-green, blue-yellow) in conjunction to describe colors (for example, we can see bluish-greens but not reddish-greens): this has been taken as evidence to support the notion that there is a neural mechanism that can signal (say) either red or green but not both simultaneously. Indeed, early physiological measurements[34] lent credence to this view: neurones were found that, qualitatively at least, seemed to obey these canonical forms.

Because there are three classes of cone there are a number of different ways they can interact with each other; but the evidence from recent physiology[35] and psychophysics[36] is that there are only two classes of second-stage mechanism: one that differences the outputs of the L and M cones (often called a 'red/green' pathway); and a second that differences the S cone output with the sum of the L and M cone outputs (often called a 'blue/yellow' pathway). This yields two color difference channels (see Figure 2.9). If we difference the outputs from the classes of cone using any likely set of cone fundamentals (for example, the Smith-Pokorny set shown in Figure 2.6) we would find that the maximum sensitivity of a pathway that differences the L and M cone outputs is at 460 nm and 700 nm; and one that differences the S cone output with the sum of the L and M cone outputs is at about 420 nm and about 580 nm (see Figure 2.9).

These wavelengths respectively correspond to perceptions of blue/red and violet/red, not red/green and blue/yellow. Although the precise locations of the peaks and valleys of these functions can be adjusted by adjusting the assumed cone weights at the opponent site, this adjustment cannot reasonably be made: measurements of the opponent channels show that, certainly for the "red/green" class, each class of cone contributes about equally[37]. Since it is almost certainly these cone differences that are being computed by the second stage mechanisms, neither the 'red/green' nor the 'blue/yellow' opponent pathway seem to correspond to our perceptual intuitions.

This is rather unfortunate because it contradicts the anecdotal evidence suggesting there is something unique about red, green, blue and yellow. This conflict between color perception and color-coding by the second-stage mechanisms is curious and has yet to be fully explained. After all, there *is* something unique about red, green, blue and yellow, as established by a number of experimenters[38]; but perhaps we should not expect early visual processing to carry that uniqueness.

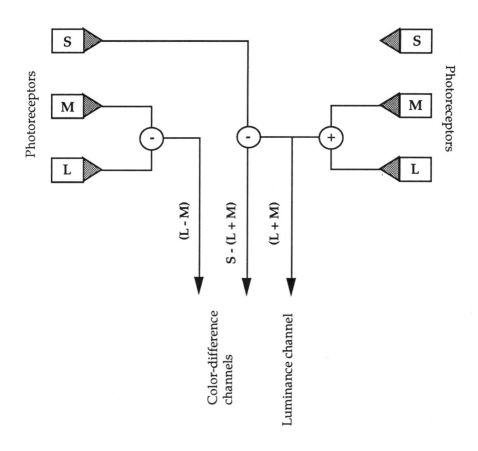

Figure 2.9: Schematic wiring diagram of the visual system. S, M and L represent the short-, medium- and long-wave photoreceptors, the first-stage mechanisms; the circles represent second-stage mechanisms. The luminance channel is formed by summing the outputs of the M and L photoreceptors; and the color-difference channels are formed by differencing the outputs of the photoreceptors in the ways shown in the figure. This figure is incomplete in three respects: (i) for the L&M channel, S cones may or may not contribute (but if they do their contribution is very small); (ii) for the L-M channel, S cones may also provide an input (although once again if they do their contribution is very small)[39].

Perhaps at a subsequent level these color difference signals are themselves differenced and compared. For now the weight of evidence unequivocally points to a second stage of chromatic processing having the features shown in Figures 2.9 and 2.10.

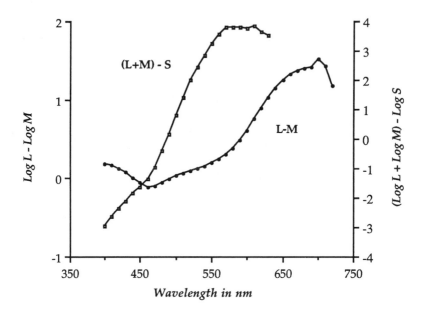

Figure 2.10: Quantitative model of the chromatic opponency of the two color difference channels. The plotted values were computed from the Smith-Pokorny fundamentals. Note the change of scale for the two data sets.

Studies of the genetics of color vision in animals suggest that, in terms of evolution, the 'blue/yellow' chromatic pathway was the first color difference channel to develop. At some later stage in primate evolution, the 'red/green' chromatic pathway was grafted on top of this. It has been further suggested that these two chromatic channels divide our world into cold and warm hues respectively[40].

2.3.2 Luminance pathway

What happens to the luminance information? Hering himself suggested a 'black/white' pathway in addition to the two chromatic ones. The spectral sensitivity of this channel is generally considered to represent the sum of activity in the L and M cone receptors. Some informal evidence in favor of the hypothesis that S cones do not contribute to the luminosity system is that short-wavelength light adds much chromatic information to a scene whilst leaving the brightness relatively unaffected. (This is why, on a crt, yellow text on a white background is hard to read. The default 'yellow' and 'white' on a crt usually differ only in the fact that the white contains the blue primary whereas the yellow does not. Since the blue primary generally has relatively low luminance, the yellow text has little luminance contrast with the white background; see Chapter 4, Section 6.5). More direct evidence comes from the fact that the standard luminosity[41] function (the function labeled 'photopic' in Figure 2.1), V_λ, can be modeled as the sum of the L and M cone responses only[42]. In fact, the relative heights of the M- and L-cone sensitivities of Smith and Pokorny given in Figure 2.6 are based on their assumed relative contributions to V_λ (about 2:1 respectively).

Psychophysical evidence[43] suggests that the luminance channel is better equipped for many visual tasks than the chromatic channel. For example, the luminance channel outperforms the chromatic channels on tests of spatial vision (form perception, acuity) and temporal vision (motion perception). Hence, designers should try to include luminance information within screen design (see Chapter 4).

Intriguingly, there is a paucity of physiological evidence for the existence of separate chromatic and luminance channels, and it may well be the case that the physiological channel that carries the M and L cone difference signals also transmits their sum: that is, the two signals are multiplexed[44].

2.4 Third-stage mechanisms

The issue of how the signals from the luminance channel and the color difference channels are subsequently transformed to yield the multi-colored world in which we live is currently unanswered. This short section is intended to convey the flavor of the problem; because a successful solution has not yet been proposed, a model is not proposed.

2.4.1 Color constancy

If you were asked to report the color of the paper on which this text is printed, you would almost certainly describe the color as white. This is despite the fact that you may be reading the book in your garden on a summer's day; or under the yellow, tungsten illumination of your study; or under the blue, fluorescent illumination of a lecture theatre. Despite these gross changes in illumination, the paper still looks white. Yet the retinal cone cells (Figures 2.5 and 2.6) are very sensitive to changes in spectral radiation; why is this acute sensitivity not a hindrance when we view the same objects under different conditions of illumination? After all, when a scene is photographed in tungsten light with daylight film, the developed picture certainly appears substantially more yellow than one's memory of the original scene. So why doesn't the page of this book *look* yellowish under the same illumination?

The ability of the visual system to perceive the same color despite changing illumination is known as *color constancy*. The facts of color constancy have been known for many years, but descriptions of it are most often ascribed to Edwin Land, the inventor of the Polaroid camera. In a series of compelling demonstrations[45], Land superimposed three separate transparencies of scenes which had first been photographed through short-, medium- and long-wavelength filters. He demonstrated that the colors of the objects in the scene remained the same despite gross changes in the light output of the three projectors: indeed, one of the projectors could be turned off and the full range of colors remained! In later demonstrations, Land illuminated a display of differently sized and differently colored rectangles with narrow-band short-, medium- and long-wavelength light. Because the display resembled the geometric paintings of Piet Mondrian, these displays are frequently referred to as 'Mondrians'. In these demonstrations, Land showed that the colors perceived did not depend on the relative intensities of the illuminating lights. This appears to flatly contradict color matching experiments, which are the basis of color science.

In fact, what Land's demonstrations show is that a theory of color vision that cannot account for perceived color in complex scenes is incomplete. Especially over the last five years, attempts have been made to develop such a model of color appearance based on the first two stages of color vision outlined above[46]. Land himself has derived algorithms for performing color constancy[47]. If the wavelength composition coming to the eye from every point in a scene is known, it is possible to compute a set of three numbers for each point in the scene that uniquely identify the color at that point: Land calls these numbers 'designators'. However, this computation is not a trivial one, and indeed there is little neurophysiological support for this model[48].

The main impetus of the recent work on color constancy is partly to account for Land's demonstrations; and partly to account for physiological evidence, from monkeys and from Man, showing regions of the brain that respond to the perceived color of an image and not its wavelength distribution[49]. The fact that an entirely successful model has not yet been developed does not invalidate the first two stages of color vision, but merely indicates the size of the problem.

2.4.2 Hue, Brightness and Saturation

It is also at these third stage mechanisms that the subjective qualities of hue, brightness and saturation are extracted. 'Color' is a generic term that we frequently use loosely, when in fact any color comprises three psychological properties.

Hue is the term that we most often use when we describe a color: it refers the quality of redness, greeness, blueness, *etc.*, that a color has. Grass, for example, has the hue of green. However, hue sensations are not discrete: they shade imperceptibly into one another, and this is why hues are frequently arranged in a circle in color space representations (see Chapter 3).

Brightness refers simply to how light or dark a color appears: this is not simply a function of how much light it emits or reflects, but also the brightness of adjacent colors (see Plate 3 and Section 2.4.1). Brightness is generally restricted to a description of emissive sources; when variations in the intensity of surface colors are considered, the corresponding term is lightness. Neither of these terms should be confused with luminance, since luminance is an objective measure that does not change with visual adaptation, or the spatial and temporal configuration of a computer display. But because these various configurations are infinite, it simplifies matters a great deal to assume a fixed set of conditions in which luminance and brightness are perfectly correlated. This assumption is made in subsequent chapters; to a first approximation this assumption is valid[50].

Saturation refers to how much white is in a color: pale colors, such as pastels, contain lots of white and appear desaturated; vivid colors contain little white and appear saturated. In common usage, changes in saturation are given the terms pale, deep, weak, strong or vivid.

There is no doubt that people prefer to use these three terms to describe colors; evidence for this comes from the popularity of those color spaces based around these three subjective terms (see Chapter 3). However, it is not yet clear how these three psychological correlates are constructed from the earlier stages of color vision.

2.4.3 Integrating features

The description of color vision outlined above has been concerned with explaining how we detect colors, and how we discriminate one patch of color from another. Of course, in the real world the visual system is concerned with detecting and discriminating objects; these objects have a number of features of which color is but one. For example, the red sports car about to overtake you on the left has a number of perceptual features that are integrated effortlessly: it is in a particular spatial location (to your left), it has a particular speed (faster than you), it has a particular size and orientation, and it has a particular color (red). All these characteristics are integrated by the visual and cognitive systems to produce a coherent moving object, and not a set of unrelated features.

The visual system achieves this integration by directing attention to the object: attention groups and segregates the world. The precise theoretical framework that has been used to account for these observations is outside the scope of this book[51]. Put simply, the visual system is seen to comprise a set of distinct modules whose job is to detect special features of the world (for example, color or orientation). Initially, the visual system forms a feature map in each module (for example, segregating green areas and red areas of the image in the color module in order to distinguish the red bus passing behind a tree).

The study of attention is especially relevant in the design of the user interface because it can identify features that group from features that segregate. For example, grouping might be used in a form-filling interface, identifying those areas of the form that must be filled in by the user. Segregation might be used to alert the user to a change of status on the display. This idea is further developed in Chapter 4.

3   Color deficiency

3.1   Types and incidence of color deficiency

About 8% of men and 0.4% of women are congenitally red-green color deficient[52]. These statistics include a rag-bag of color vision deficits, including (ironically) individuals with quite good color vision: in these cases their color vision is abnormal simply because it is different from the norm. Other individuals have very poor color discrimination. These latter individuals are dichromats: whereas the normal trichromat can match any light with three primaries, the dichromat needs only two. Dichromats account for about 20% of the color defectives. The remainder, so-called 'anomalous' trichromats, may have very good or very bad color vision depending on the degree of the anomaly. These individuals still require three primaries to make a color match, but the proportions of the three primaries in the match are significantly different from normal.

There are three simple models of congenital red/green dichromacy (that is, protanopes and deuteranopes). Either (a) dichromats simply 'lose' either the L or M cone pigment and it is not replaced: this can be referred to as the loss hypothesis; or (b) dichromats 'lose' either the L or M cone pigment and the 'empty' cones are filled up with the visual pigment that remains: this can be referred to as the *loss-with-replacement* hypothesis; or (c) the L and M cone signals are fused between the first and second stages of color processing and hence produce the illusion of a single visual pigment: this can be referred to as the *fusion* hypothesis.

The weight of evidence favors (b), the loss-with-replacement hypothesis[53]. If the L cones are lost the individual is termed a protanope; analogously, a deuteranope loses the M cones (see Table 2.1). Because the 'empty' cones are filled up with the pigment that remains, some changes to the second-stage of color processing detailed in Figure 2.9 might be expected. In particular, as well as the L-M channel being ineffective (because L=M in red/green dichromats), the luminance channel should be noticeably less red sensitive in protanopes and noticeably less green sensitive in deuteranopes. Although protanopes are noticeably less red sensitive, deuteranopes appear virtually normal: this is because the L cones, which deuteranopes retain, provide twice the input to the luminance channel as the M cones, which deuteranopes lack (see Section 2.3.2). In designing color deficiency tests (see below) this needs to be taken into account: two patches of color that are identical in luminance for a normal trichromat will have a large luminance difference for a dichromat, especially a protanope. Luminance normalization can be achieved for dichromats by using a different standard luminosity function[54].

It is still not entirely clear what happens in anomalous trichromats. Certainly the problem lies with their cone pigments, but it is not clear what happens to them. For example, it is possible that so called protanomalous subjects have 'retained' some of their M pigment, and similarly deuteranomalous subjects have 'retained' some of their L pigment. The quantity of the pigment they manage to salvage signifies the degree of their anomaly. This theory sees the deficiency as turning down the gain of one of the cone channels. Alternatively, the spectral sensitivity of one of the pigments may change: for example, the L pigment of protanomalous subjects may be shifted in the green direction. This theory states that the spectral sensitivity curve of the anomalous pigment is shifted bodily along the wavelength axis. The degree of anomaly is proportional to the extent of the shift; hence this model sees dichromats as the limiting case of anomaly, since the spectral sensitivity of one pigment has been shifted until it is exactly the same as the other.

Are there analogous deficiencies of the blue cones? A very much smaller percentage of men and women (less than 0.007%) are dichromatic in this way: they are termed tritanopes. It is not clear if the 'tritanomalous' subjects exist[55]. However, the tritan defect, like total color blindness, is so rare that for practical purposes it can be ignored. However, age is also known to affect color vision, mainly because of the yellowing of the lens of the eye. This causes a reduction in short-wave sensitivity, because the light reaching the S cones is preferentially absorbed by the lens. Just as Nero used the spectral properties of his favorite emerald to diminish the impact of red blood when viewing his lions eating Christians, the yellow lens of the human eye preferentially absorbs light that looks blue to us. This is sometimes used as a fanciful explanation of why elderly ladies are often seen with a blue rinse, since this color looks a distinguished shade of gray to them.

Table 2.1 summarizes the types of congenital color deficiency, their probable cause and the common color confusions.

Congenital defects are defects of the photoreceptors, the first stage mechanisms; are there analogous defects of the opponent, second stage mechanisms? Indeed, there is mounting evidence that various neurological diseases can cause damage to these pathways, although the evidence is not quite as neat as in the case of congenital defects. This is for three reasons. First, it may affect only one eye, or part of the visual field of one eye. Second, there is often an additional visual complaint in persons with acquired color deficiency (such as reduced visual acuity). And third, the color defect itself may get worse (or better) with time. The 'blue/yellow' channel was once thought to be especially vulnerable in acquired defects: and persons with this type of acquired color deficiency resemble congenital tritanopes. But it now appears that only a minority of neurological diseases are selective in which second-stage mechanism they attack[56]. As a consequence, the type of loss seen in acquired color deficiencies is varied and specific losses are rarely found.

3.2   Color deficiency and color displays

What is the relevance of this for users of color displays? Suppose for a moment that a clinician is attempting to read the output of a brain-scanner. The output is presented on a computer display in the form of a topographical map. 'Hot' areas of the brain are coded red and 'cold' areas are coded blue. Temperatures in between these values are spaced on a spectral scale in between blue and red. If the clinician were asked to identify the 'hot' areas of the brain (these might represent tumors or edema) it would be a trivial task. Now assume that the clinician is color deficient: how would the display look now? Unless some care was taken by the software designer to ensure that there were large luminance differences between the reds and greens and yellows, they might all look the same to him. Hence, identifying the 'hot' areas would be an impossible task; and if the color deficiency had gone undetected through medical school (as often it does) he might misdiagnose the patient's results.

Table 2.1: Classification of congenital color deficiency

Type of defect	Incidence (per cent)	Primaries in color matching task	Co-punctal point	Typical confusions	White matches	Probable cause
Achromatopsia	0.003	1	Not applicable	All colors look shades of grey	Many colours	Lacks two (or all) types of cone
Protanopia	1	2	$x_p = 0.7465$ $y_p = 0.2535$	Bluish-green & brown; green, olive, tan & red-orange; yellow-green, yellow & orange; blue & red-purple; blue-purple, violet & purple	Blue-green (494 nm)	L cones missing, probably replaced by M cones
Deuteranopia	1	2	$x_d = 1.4000$ $y_d = -0.4000$	Dull green & pink; olive & brown; yellow-green & red-orange; greenish-blue, dull blue & purple	Blue-green (499 nm)	M cones missing, probably replaced by L cones
Tritanopia	0.004	2	$x_t = 0.1748$ $y_t = 0.0000$	Green & greenish-blue; oranges & red-purples	Yellow-Orange (570 nm)	S cones missing
Protanomaly	1	3	Not applicable	Mild anomalous may appear normal. Severe anomalous tend towards protanopia	Not applicable	Spectral sensitivity of L cones shifted towards shorter wavelengths
Deuteranomaly	5-6	3	Not applicable	Mild anomalous may appear normal. Severe anomalous tend towards deuteranopia	Not applicable	Spectral sensitivity of M cones shifted towards longer wavelengths

Software designers can overcome this problem in a number of ways. Probably the easiest solution is to provide a set of selectable colors for the user that they can associate with the discrete temperature levels. Then users would be able to pick a set of colors for coding that they could quite easily discriminate from one another. One problem with this is that users may select a set of colors that are not ergonomically optimal for other reasons (see Chapter 4). A second problem is that a user with normal color vision may have already learnt the previous color code, and hence that user may find it difficult to interpret the results shown to him by his color deficient colleague if he is asked to consult.

Alternatively, the designer could insure that the set of colors chosen for the application represent a gray scale in the luminance domain. So dark blue might represent 'cold' spots and bright red 'hot' spots. To achieve this properly, each discrete step in luminance should be a constant multiple of the previous step (for example, a doubling) because the eye is a logarithmic detector in the luminance domain. Now the color defective will be able to use the luminance differences between the discrete levels to aid discrimination. One problem with this is that the red and blue display primaries (at least on cathode ray tubes) are often of comparably low luminance and it may be difficult to combine a spectral scale with a luminance scale.

A third alternative would be to test the color vision of users by including a color vision test at the beginning of the program (see Section 3.3). This could be used unproductively (that is, to exclude users) or productively. Productive use might be to classify the type of color deficiency and then select a set of colors that would be optimal for that user. For example, assume that a system has been designed that uses color coding in such a way that one or more of the three classes of dichromat would make discrimination errors. By including a color vision test at the beginning of the program, it would be possible to classify the user's deficiency. Then a separate coding system could be called upon that is optimal for that class of defective. This coding system would need to be based on the SML color space described in the next chapter. If the coding system was particularly clever, it might use exactly the same hues for each level of coding and simply change the luminances of each hue for the different users (remember that the luminosity function will be different for the different classes of dichromats; see Section 3.1). The more numerous band of normal users could then read the display in any mode using the coding system they already know.

3.3   Testing for color deficiency

The principle behind color vision tests is quite simple. Subjects are asked to discriminate two or more colors that are carefully chosen so that they excite one class of cone. For example, colors T_1 and T_2 are chosen so that they may be discriminated by S cones only. This means that T_1 and T_2 cause equal ratios of activity in the M- and L-cones. Hence, a subject unable to discriminate between T_1 and T_2 is assumed to have a deficiency with the S-cones. A similar logic is followed to detect protan and deutan subjects (see Chapter 3, Section 3.6.2).

There are numerous color deficiency tests available. They may be broadly classified into plate tests, arrangement tests and color matching tests. Of the plate tests, one of the best and quickest screening tests for congenital red/green color deficiency (protanopia and deuteranopia) is the Ishihara Test for Color Blindness[57]. In this test, the subject's task is to identify a number, or trace a path on a colored plate. The plates are cleverly designed so that the underlying hue variation, discriminable by trichromats, merges into the random lightness variation for dichromats. An analogous plate test that can identify tritanopia is the Farnsworth F2 plate[58]. Other types of plate test include the American Optical Company Hardy, Rand and Rittler (AO HRR) plates and the City University Color Vision Test.

Plate tests are suitable as screening tests but, despite the claims of the manufacturers, they are frequently unable to discriminate the type and extent of the color defect. For example, the number of errors a subject makes on the Ishihara test bears no relation to the extent of his or her color deficiency[59]. When a more sophisticated analysis is required, an arrangement test may be used. The best example of such an arrangement test is the Farnsworth-Munsell 100-hue test (abbreviated to FM 100-hue). This test uses a selection of 85 Munsell hues in four separate trays[60]. The hues are chosen so that they form a color circle in CIE color space (see Chapter 3 for a description of the Munsell and CIE color systems). The subject's task is to place the hues in each tray in their order according to color. The task is a difficult one, and normal subjects frequently make errors, although these are randomly distributed from tray to tray. On the other hand, subjects with congenital color deficiency make errors at specific and predictable parts of the hue circle. The data analysis procedure is laborious by hand, although there are a number of computer packages available that automate the testing procedure[61]. The FM 100-hue test has been proven to be a reliable and valid test of color vision, and has proven to be especially valuable in the assessment of acquired color deficiency. A shorter version of the FM 100-hue test is available, known as the Panel D-15 test because it uses only 15 colored chips in a single tray. This test is good at distinguishing the congenital defects, protanopia, deuteranopia and tritanopia.

In practice, plate tests are good at making the distinction between normal and defective subjects; and arrangement tests are good at classifying the defect into the broad categories of protanopia, deuteranopia and tritanopia. But neither type of test can reliably distinguish anomalous trichromacy from dichromacy. For this type of test an anomaloscope is required. An anomaloscope is a color matching device that uses lights rather than pigments. A subject is presented with a split field, one half of which is fixed in color; the task is to match this color with a mixture of lights in the other half field.

For example, to distinguish between the various classes of 'red/green' color defective (that is, protanopia and deuteranopia), one common test is to ask subjects to match a yellow with a mixture of red and green. For a normal observer, the red and green primaries will be mixed in equal proportion and there will be a very precise setting where the two half-fields look identical. Hence there are two dependent measures: the match point (that is, the exact red/green mixture) and the matching range. In contrast, dichromats will accept *all* possible red/green mixtures as a match to the yellow: they have no unique match point and the matching range is complete. Protanopes are distinguished from deuteranopes because the red primary appears very dark to them: hence a change needs to be made to the anomaloscope luminances. With anomalous trichromats, the matching range is not complete, but it is slightly larger or much larger than for normal subjects: the extent of the matching range indicates the extent of the defect. Deuteranomalous subjects are easily distinguished from protanomalous subjects because the match point of the deutan is shifted towards the green primary, and the match point of the protan is shifted towards the red primary.

There is an important warning that needs to be heeded before embarking upon color vision testing with plates and arrangement tests. Because the colors used in the tests are designed to lie in particular positions in color space, it is vital that the illuminating light is of the correct spectral power distribution. Section 2.4.1 made it clear that the perceived color of objects depends on the illuminating light. If incorrect illumination is used (for example, presenting the Ishihara test under tungsten illumination), the spectral position of the colors will be altered and misdiagnosis will result[62]. The correct ambient illumination for color vision testing is CIE illuminant C or CIE illuminant D_{65}; the level of the illumination should be between about 300 and 600 lux (see Chapter 5).

A more general warning about color vision testing in general is that the testing and data analysis should be supervised by an expert: this applies especially to anomaloscopes, but also to the FM 100-hue test. This is because the more sophisticated tests frequently produce results that are ambiguous, or that do not reflect one of the canonical forms of color deficiency shown in Table 2.1. This is not because the classification system is wrong, but because the results may be affected by a host of other factors, such as age, intelligence, medication, malingering, and even tinted spectacles! In particular, test results from subjects with acquired color deficiencies are notoriously difficult to analyse and should be referred to a professional. Sophisticated instruments like the anomaloscope require experience with color deficiency and a knowledge of psychophysical methods.

The existence of high-quality, computer-controled, color graphics displays makes them good candidates for the next generation of color deficiency tests. Such displays will allow accurate specification of the stimulus in space, time and color, and allow complete automation of the test procedure. There are as yet no commercially available tests that are computer based, although a number of provisional tests have been published[63]. This will certainly be an area of change in the 1990s.

4 Color vision: key points

• *Acute color judgements are best in the fovea. Restrict important color judgements to this area.*

• *Although the three cone types are loosely referred to as 'red', 'green' and 'blue' sensitive, their actual sensitivities are broad and overlapping. This means, for example, that M-cones may be more sensitive to the blue primary on a color display. Beware of associating the display primaries with the three classes of retinal cone.*

• *Because of the poor spatial and temporal resolution of chromatically opponent channels, try to include luminance differences between chromatic stimuli when it is important to make judgements in space (for example, between superimposed 'windows' on a display) or time (for example, between a moving mouse cursor and the background). This can be most easily achieved by drawing a thin black or white border around the object to provide the necessary luminance difference.*

• *Luminance is only approximately equal to brightness. If it is important to use equally bright colors in an application, do the selection by eye.*

• *Perceived color changes with the spectral content and the level of the ambient illumination. Design the display in the illumination that it is to be used.*

• *Design your display for the anticipated user population, considering both congenital color deficiency and acquired color deficiency (due, for example, to age).*

5   Further Reading

Boynton, R. M. (1979) *Human Color Vision*. New York: Holt, Rhinehart and Winston.

A comprehensive review by one of the world's leading color scientists.

Gouras, P. (1984) Color Vision. In N. N. Osbourne and G. J. Chader (Eds) *Progress in Retinal Research*, **3**: 227-261.

A review of color vision from a physiological perspective.

J. Optical Society of America **A 7** (1990) number 10, pages 1937-2051.

A special issue on applying visual psychophysics to display design. Includes seven articles specifically on color.

Lennie, P. (1988) Mechanisms of color vision. *CRC Critical Reviews in Neurobiology*, **3**: 333-400.

A recent review of color vision that considers possible cortical implementations of color constancy.

Mollon, J. D. (1988) "Tho' she kneel'd in that place where they grew..." The uses and origins of primate colour vision. *J. Experimental Biology*, **146**: 21-38.

A review of the evolution of color vision.

Pokorny, J., Smith, V. C., Verriest, G. and Pinckers, A. J. L. G. (1979) *Congenital and Acquired Color Vision Defects*. New York: Grune and Stratton.

A comprehensive review of color deficiency.

Rushton, W. A. H. (1972) Review lecture: Pigments and signals in color vision. *J. Physiology*, **220**: 1-31P.

The second half of this review, on signals, is now somewhat dated, but the first half, on pigments, remains an excellent introduction to the area.

6   Notes and References

1 See for example Travis, D. S. (1990) Applying visual psychophysics to user interface design. *Behaviour and Information Technology*, **9**: 425-438.

2 At light levels where rod and cones are operating together, color vision is not very good and is of no practical significance in display design. See Stabell, B. and Stabell, U. (1976) Rod and cone contributions to peripheral color vision. *Vision Research*, **16**: 1099-1104; Stabell, B. and Stabell, U. (1976) Effect of rod activity on color threshold. *Vision Research*, **16**: 1099-1104

3 Naka, K. I. and Rushton, W. A. H. (1966) S-potentials from colour units in the retina of fish (*Cyprinidae*). *J. Physiology*, **185**: 536-555.

4 Dartnall, H. J. A., Bowmaker, J. K. and Mollon, J. D. (1983) Human visual pigments: microspectrophotometric results from the eyes of seven persons. *Proceedings of the Royal Society of London Series* B **220**: 115-130.

5 Wyszecki, G. and Stiles, W. S. (1982) *Color Science*, 2nd edition (Wiley: New York) p 92.

6 Perry, V. H., and Cowey, A. (1985) The ganglion cell and cone distributions in the monkey's retina: implications for cortical magnification factors. *Vision Research*, **25**: 1795-1810; Packer, O., Hendrickson, A. E. and Carcio, C. A. S. (1989) Photoreceptor topography of the retina of the adult Pigtail Macaque. *J. Comparative Neurology*, **288**: 165-183.

7 Baylor, D. A., Nunn, B. J. and Schnapf, J. L.(1987) Spectral sensitivity of cones of the monkey *Macaca fascicularis*. *J. Physiology*, **390**: 145-160.

8 Dartnall, H. J. A., Bowmaker, J. K. and Mollon, J. D. (1983) Human visual pigments: microspectrophotometric results from the eyes of seven persons. *Proceedings of the Royal Society of London Series* B **220**: 115-130.

9 Schnapf, J. L. and Baylor, D. A. (1987) How photoreceptor cells respond to light. *Scientific American*, **256** (4): 32-39.

10 Baylor, D. A., Nunn, B. J. and Schnapf, J. L.(1987) Spectral sensitivity of cones of the monkey *Macaca fascicularis*. *J. Physiology*, **390**: 145-160..

11 König, A. and Dieterici, C. (1884) Uber die Empfindlichkeit des normalen Auges für Wellenlängenunterschiede des Lichtes. *Ann. Phys.*, **22**: 579-589.

12 See, for example, Stiles, W. S. (1939) The directional sensitivity of the retina and the spectral sensitivities of the rods and cones. *Proceedings of the Royal Society of London Series* B **127**: 64-105. Reprinted in Stiles, W. S. (1978) *Mechanisms of Colour Vision*. London: Academic Press.

13 Stiles, W. S. (1939) The directional sensitivity of the retina and the spectral sensitivities of the rods and cones. *Proceedings of the Royal Society of London Series* B **127**: 64-105.

14 See, for example, Stockman, A. and Mollon, J. D. (1986) The spectral sensitivities of the middle- and long-wavelength cones: an extension of the two-colour threshold technique of W. S. Stiles. *Perception*, **15**: 729-754. This description of Stiles' technique has been necessarily brief. For a more complete description, see Enoch, J. (1972) The two color threshold technique of Stiles and derived component color mechanisms. In D. Jameson and L. M. Hurvich (eds.) *Handbook of Sensory Physiology*, volume VII/4 *Visual Psychophysics*. Berlin: Springer, pp 537-567.

15 See for example, Baylor, D. A., Nunn, B. J. and Schnapf, J. L.(1987) Spectral sensitivity of cones of the monkey *Macaca fascicularis*. *J. Physiology*, **390**: 145-160, where a comparison is made between suction electrode data and Estèvez fundamentals; and Bowmaker, J. K., Dartnall, H. J. A., Lythgoe, J. N. and Mollon, J. D. (1978) The visual pigments of rods and cones in the rhesus monkey, *Macaca mulatta*. *J. Physiology*, **274**: 329-348, where a comparison is made between microspectrophotometric data and Stiles Π_4 and Π_5.

16 The full references are: Judd, D. B. (1951) Secretary's Report. "Colorimetry and artificial daylight". In *Proceedings of the 12th Session of the CIE*, Stockholm, vol. 1, Technical committee No 7. And: Stiles, W. S. and Burch, J. M. (1959) NPL colour matching investigation: final report (1958). *Optica Acta*, **6**: 1-26.

17 Smith, V. C., Pokorny, J. and Zaidi, Q. (1983) How do sets of color-matching functions differ? In J. D. Mollon and L. T. Sharpe (eds.) *Colour Vision: Physiology and Psychophysics*. London: Academic Press.

18 Colors that match perceptually but not physically are known as metamers; if they match physically too they are known as isomers.

19 Brindley, G. S. (1960) Two more visual theorems. *Quarterly J. Experimental Psychology*, **12**: 110-112.

20 Estevez, O. (1979) On the fundamental data base of normal and dichromatic colour vision. Ph.D thesis, University of Amsterdam, The Netherlands, Amsterdam: Krips Repro.

21 Boynton, R. M. (1986) A system of photometry and colorimetry based on cone excitation. *Color Research and Application*, 11: 244-252.

22 For a review see Lang, H. (1983) Trichromatic theories before Young. *Color Research and Application*, 8: 221-231.

23 See Mollon, J. D. (1982) Colour vision and colour blindness. In H. B. Barlow and J. D. Mollon (eds.) *The Senses*, pages 165-191. CUP: Cambridge.

24 Vimal, R. L. P., Pokorny, J., Smith, V. C. and Shevell, S. K. (1989) Foveal cone thresholds. *Vision Research*, 29: 61-78; Cicerone, C. M. and Nerger, J. L. (1989) The relative numbers of long-wavelength-sensitive to middle-wavelength-sensitive cones in the human fovea centralis. *Vision Research*, 29: 115-128.

25 For example, Williams, D. R., MacLeod, D. I. A. and Hayhoe, M. (1981) Punctate sensitivity of the blue-sensitive mechanism. *Vision Research*, 21: 1357-1375.

26 For a review see Mollon, J. D. (1982) A taxonomy of tritanopias. In G. Verriest (ed.) *Documenta Ophthalmologica Proceedings Series*, 33: 87-101.

27 For example, Williams, D. R., MacLeod, D. I. A. and Hayhoe, M. (1981) Foveal tritanopia. *Vision Research*, 21: 1341-1356.

28 Ahnelt, P. K., Kolb, H. and Pflug, R. (1987) Identification of a sub-type of cone photoreceptor, likely to be blue sensitive, in the human retina. *J. Comparative Neurology*, 255: 18-34.

29 Brindley, G. S. (1954) The summation areas of human colour-receptive mechanisms at increment threshold. *J. Physiology*, 124: 400-408.

30 See Mollon, J. D. (1982) A taxonomy of tritanopias. In G. Verriest (ed.) *Documenta Ophthalmologica Proceedings Series*, 33: 87-101.

31 These poor color combinations may be identified from the CIE diagram (see Chapter 3) as they lie along straight lines that converge on the point ($x = 0.1747$, $y = 0.0060$). This is the 'tritanopic confusion point' (Walraven, P. L. (1974) A closer look at the tritanopic convergence point. *Vision Research*, 14: 1339-1343): blue cones are necessary to discriminate colors that lie on straight lines that converge on this point. They may be more simply determined if plotted in SML cone space (see Chapter 3).

32 Rushton, W. A. H. (1979) King Charles II and the blind spot. *Vision Research*, 19: 225.

33 See, for example, Hurvich, L. M. and Jameson, D. (1957) An opponent-process theory of colour vision. *Psychological Review*, 64: 384-404; for a partisan review of one particular model of color opponency, see Hurvich, L. M. (1981) *Color Vision*. Sinaver: Mass.

34 For a review of this work, see DeValois, R. L. and DeValois, K. (1975) Neural coding of color. In E. C. Carterette and M. P. Friedman (eds.) *Handbook of Perception*, 5: 117-166. New York: Academic Press.

35 Derrington, A. M, Krauskopf, J. and Lennie, P. (1984) Chromatic mechanisms in lateral geniculate nucleus of macaque. *J. Physiology*, 357: 241-265.

36 Krauskopf, J., Williams, D. R. and Heeley, D. W. (1982) Cardinal directions of colour space. *Vision Research*, 22: 1123-1131.

37 See especially Figure 6 of Derrington, A. M, Krauskopf, J. and Lennie, P. (1984) Chromatic mechanisms in lateral geniculate nucleus of macaque. *J. Physiology*, 357: 241-265. The data for the 'blue/yellow' opponent cells in this study are less easy to interpret since they are contaminated by the effects of chromatic aberation.

38 See especially the chromatic cancellation technique of Jameson, D. and Hurvich, L. M. (1955) Some quantitative aspects of an opponent-colors theory: I. Chromatic responses and spectral saturation. *J. Optical Society of America*, 45: 546-552.

39 For example see Stromeyer, C. F. and Lee, J. (1988) Adaptational effects of short wave cone signals on red-green chromatic detection. *Vision Research*, 28: 931-940; and (iii) for the S - (L&M) channel, the weighting of L&M versus S is not known, for example see Boynton, R. M. (1979) *Human Color Vision*. New York: Holt, Rhinehart and Winston, p 248, note 2.

40 Mollon, J. D. (1989) "Tho' she kneel'd in that place where they grew..." The uses and origins of primate colour vision. *J. Experimental Biology*, 146: 21-38. Travis, D. S., Bowmaker, J. K. and Mollon, J. D. (1988) Polymorphism of visual pigments in a Callitrichid monkey. *Vision Research*, 28: 481-490.

41 For most purposes, 'luminosity' (a physical measure) and 'brightness' (a subjective measure) can be considered to be identical concepts, but the two are not truly identical. Brightness depends on other objects in the scene.

42 It has been pointed out that part of the reason for this correspondence is that the methods used to obtain V_λ may discriminate against a contribution from blue cones.

43 Cavanagh, P. (1987) Reconstructing the third dimension: interactions between color, texture, motion, binocular disparity, and shape. *Computer Vision, Graphics, and Image Processing*, **37**: 171-195; Ingling, C. R. and Grigsby, S. C. (1990) Perceptual correlates of magnocellular and parvocellular channels: seeing form and depth in afterimages. *Vision Research*, **30**: 823-828; Livingstone, M. S. and Hubel, D. H. (1987) Psychophysical evidence for separate channels for the perception of form, color, movement, and depth. *J. Neuroscience*, **7**: 3416-3468; Lu, C. and Fender, D. H. (1972) The interaction of color and luminance in stereoscopic vision. *Investigative Ophthalmology*, **11**: 482-490; Troscianko, T., and Fahle, M. (1988) Why do isoluminant stimuli appear slower? *J. Optical Society of America* **A5**: 871-880.

44 Ingling, C. R. and Martinez-Uriegas, E. (1983) The spatiochromatic signal of the r-g channel. In J. D. Mollon and L. T. Sharpe (eds.) *Colour Vision: Physiology and Psychophysics* (pp 433-444). London: Academic Press; Lennie, P. (1988) Mechanisms of color vision. *CRC Critical Reviews in Neurobiology*, **3**: 333-400.

45 For some flavour of these see Land, E. H. (1974) The Retinex theory of color vision. *Proceedings of the Royal Institute of Great Britain*, **47**: 23-58.

46 See for example D'Zmura, M. and Lennie, P. (1986) Mechanisms of color constancy. *J. Optical Society of America A* **3**: 1662-1672; Maloney, L. T. and Wandell, B. A. (1986) Color constancy: a method for recovering surface spectral reflectance. *J. Optical Society of America A* **3**: 29-33.

47 See for example Land, E. H. (1983) Recent advances in retinex theory and some implications for cortical computations: Color vision and the natural image. *Proceedings of the National Academy of Science USA*: **80**, 5163-5169.

48 For example, see Livingstone, M. S. and Hubel, D. H. (1984) Anatomy and physiology of a color system in the primate visual cortex. *The J. Neuroscience*, **4**: 309-356.

49 Zeki, S. (1980) The representation of colours in the cerebral cortex. *Nature*, **284**: 412-418; Lueck, C. J. *et al* (1989) The colour centre in the cerebral cortex of man. *Nature*, **340**: 386-389.

50 For a comprehensive treatment on the relationship between brightness and luminance, and for examples of when the relationship fails, see Cornsweet, T. N. (1970) *Visual Perception*. New York: Academic Press.

51 For reviews see Triesman, A. (1986) Features and objects in visual processing. *Scientific American*, **254**: 114-124; Triesman, A. (1988) Features and objects: the fourteenth Bartlett memorial lecture. *Quarterly J. Experimental Psychology*, **40A**: 201-237.

52 For an excellent review see Pokorny, J., Smith, V. C., Verriest, G. and Pinckers, A. J. L. G. (1979) *Congenital and Acquired Colour Vision Defects*. New York: Grune and Stratton. The reason for the higher incidence of color deficiency in men is that the defective genes are carried on the X chromosome; for an-up-to date review of the genetics of color vision see Nathans, J. (1989) The genes for color vision. *Scientific American*, February.

53 See Pokorny, J., Smith, V. C., Verriest, G. and Pinckers, A. J. L. G. (1979) *Congenital and Acquired Colour Vision Defects*. New York: Grune and Stratton, for a review; compelling psychophysical evidence that dichromats have the same number of functioning cones as normal trichromats is provided by Cicerone, C. M. and Nerger, J. L. (1989) The density of cones in the fovea centralis of the human dichromat. *Vision Research*, **29**: 1587-1595.

54 Wyszecki, G. and Stiles, W. S. (1982) *Color Science*, 2nd edition (Wiley: New York) page 92.

55 Pokorny, J., Smith, V. and Went, L. N. (1981) Color matching in autosomal tritan defect. *J. Optical Society of America*, **71**: 1327-1334.

56 Yeh, T., Smith, V. C., and Pokorny, J. (1989) The effect of background luminance on cone sensitivity functions. *Investigative Ophthalmology and Visual Science*, **30**: 2077-2086; Travis, D. S. and Thompson, P. (1989) Spatiotemporal contrast sensitivity and colour vision in multiple sclerosis. *Brain*, **112**: 283-303.

57 Most of the plate and arrangement types of color deficiency test described here can be obtained from large ophthalmic suppliers.

58 This is not available commercially but can be obtained free of charge from the New London Submarine Base, Groton, Connecticut, USA.

59 Cole, B. L. (1963) Misuse of the Ishihara Test for Colour Blindness. *British J. Physiological Optics*, **20**: 113-118.

60 There were originally 100 hues, but some were omitted as they were found to be perceptually too close together to be discriminated by those with normal color vision.

61 For example, Benzschawel, T. (1985) Computerized analysis of the Farnsworth-Munsell 100-hue test. *American J. Optometry and Physiological Optics*, **62**: 254-264; Lugo, M. and Tiedeman, J. S. (1986)

Computerized scoring and graphing of the Farnsworth-Munsell 100-hue color vision test. *American J. Ophthalmology*, **101**: 469-474.

62 See Pokorny, J., Smith, V. C., Verriest, G. and Pinckers, A. J. L. G. (1979) *Congenital and Acquired Colour Vision Defects*. New York: Grune and Stratton, pages 101-106 for support for this statement, and for more detailed information on lighting for color deficiency testing. See also Long, G. M. and Tuck, J. P. (1986) Color vision screening and viewing conditions: the problem of misdiagnosis. *Nursing Research*, **35**: 52-55.

63 For example, see Sellers, K. L., Chioran, G. M., Dain, S. J., Benes, S. C., Lubow, M., Rammohan, K. and King-Smith, P. E. (1986) Red-green mixture thresholds in congenital and acquired color defects. *Vision Research*, **26**: 1083-1097; Anstis, S., Cavanagh, P., Maurer, D., Lewis, T., MacLeod, D. I. A. and Mather, G. (1986) Computer-generated screening test for colorblindness. *Color Research and Application*, **11**: S63-S66; Arden, G. B., Gündüz, K. and Perry, S. (1988) Colour vision testing with a computer graphics system. *Clinical Vision Sciences*, **2**: 303-320; Mollon, J. D. and Reffin, J. P. (1989) A computer-controlled colour vision test that combines the principles of Chibret and of Stilling. *J. Physiology*, **414**: 5P.

3

SPECIFYING COLORS ON COLOR DISPLAYS

1   Overview

This Chapter describes methods of color specification. Any color in the world can be defined by just three numbers. These three numbers form a three-dimensional 'color space' within which colors may be specified, allowing accurate exchange of color information. Computer displays use the electronic RGB color space, in which a color is defined by the relative proportions of the red, green and blue display primaries required to produce it. This type of color space has two major disadvantages: first, because different displays have different display primaries, accurate color specification is not possible; and second, it is psychologically non-intuitive because people do not think of a color in terms of the relative proportions of red, green and blue light. Alternative color spaces are available that allow color to be accurately specified and that are more psychologically intuitive. This chapter describes eight alternative color spaces and provides the information required to transform to them from RGB color specifications.

2   Introduction: the need for color specification

Although the number of applications that use color are many and varied, it is generally the case that color is used on visual displays for one of four reasons. First, it may be used for aesthetic purposes, where the precise colors used are unimportant. What matters for these applications is simply that the final display looks appealing. To achieve this, the rules of color harmony should be followed. Second, color may be used for formatting purposes: that is, to segregate or group different types of visual information. Third, color may be used for coding: that is, symbolically, to signify meaning. Guidelines for achieving color harmony and for using color for formatting and coding are given in Chapter 4. Finally, color may be used on displays to represent color *qua* color, that is for realism. This includes applications such as computer-aided design, where products are 'built' and may be shown to customers as an example of the finished version; or for example in the printing industry, where precise color specification and color judgements must be made. This chapter is primarily concerned with such 'realistic' applications. It provides the necessary information to accurately specify the colors on color displays.

If you were asked: "how many colors are there in the world?", what would you say? About a hundred? A thousand? Ten thousand? Stop reading for a moment and take a look around. How many colors can you see? How many can you name? The chances are that you won't be able to name more than about eleven; psychologists have shown[1] that people are quite happy to classify virtually all colors by using the basic color names: white, gray, black, red, green, yellow, blue, pink, brown, orange and purple. But we can certainly distinguish many more colors than this. In a brave attempt to list the elementary sensations of the human mind, one of the great ancestors of experimental psychology, E. B. Titchener, decided there were about 35,000 elementary color sensations[2].

This demonstrates the inadequacy of relying on a simple naming system to classify colors precisely. Take for example the yellow color that Kodak use as part of their corporate identity. Since Kodak are in the business of color reproduction, it is quite important to them that this color remains constant: so that when I see a Kodak film in a chemists in London I recognise it as exactly the same brand as the Kodak film I might see in a drugstore in New York. But if Kodak attempted to standardize this color by simply telling printers in London and New York that they wanted yellow packaging, the odds that the two packages looked the same in color would be long indeed. In fact, Kodak have a patented color, Kodak yellow, that printers must match. In practice, Kodak provide printers with three colored swatches, one that is a perfect match to Kodak yellow, and two others that bracket the color and provide the printer with tolerance limits. If the printed color does not match any of the three, Kodak will reject it.

As an example closer to home, when I run out of paint when decorating I want to be able to return to the store and get paint of exactly the same color. If I just ask for 'green' paint, the chances of me obtaining exactly the same color paint are remote, to say the least. Part of the problem of course is that human language is just not rich enough to describe the vast array of colors that we see. This is why paint manufacturers need to think up such a wealth of color names that often bear no psychological relevance to the colors used. Could you guess the color of *Flambeau*, for example? Is *Whitby Brown* named after the color of the beach? Or the sea?

> "...it has been the custom for a long time to invent color names, particularly for clothing, and such names have changed with the styles of the time. In the sixteenth century, for instance, French women wore colors called *rat color, widow's joy, envenomed monkey* and *chimney sweep*. The eighteenth century produced *rash tears, Paris mud, stifled sigh* in France and *red-hot bullets* and *smoke of the Camp of St. Roche* in England. Only yesterday (1930) they could be matched with *folly, lucky stone, elephant's breath* and in 1946 with *sun love, town blond* and *cocoblush* or *Virginia turf, radar blue* and *avenue gray*."[3]

In fact, if we agree that color names are inadequate for describing color sensation then we need some method of describing colors in a consistent and reproducible way: so that a paint manufacturer can produce two batches of green paint of exactly the same color; or so that when I specify a color to you, you are able to exactly reproduce that color on your terminal screen.

A practical example of the usefulness of color specification when applied to system design is the choice of color palette provided for the user. For example, a paint package may provide a palette of colors for the user, or a network management system may provide a system for user-selectable colors. Assume that the user has selected a red and a green from the palette, and now wishes to interpolate, or shade, between the two colors. Should the central color in the mixture be yellow (as with additive mixture) or should it be gray (as with subtractive mixture)? And if there were going to be a dozen colors between the red and the green, what precise values should each color take? By using a numerical color space, precise values can be computed; the precise choice of color space will determine which interpolation model is used.

Because our color vision is based on quantal absorptions in three classes of cone (Chapter 2), it should come as little surprise that color space is three dimensional. As a consequence, all color spaces use three dimensions to represent color. How color spaces differ is in their labeling of the three axes. Some color spaces plot the physical proportions of the lights used to realize the color; others use axes loosely (or directly) related to the psychological variables hue, saturation and brightness (see Chapter 2, Section 2.4.2); and others plot directly the excitation of the three classes of cone. Each approach has its own merits and demerits. In practice, there is no ideal color space: your choice will depend on what color manipulations you wish to perform.

This review of color spaces is selective. Rather than review the many color spaces in circulation, examples of the genre are considered. For example, there are two main color order systems in use: the Munsell Book of Color and the Optical Society of America Uniform Color Scale. Because of their similarity, only one (the Munsell system) is considered here. Because of its status as an international standard, CIE color space is referred to throughout this chapter; it is described in detail in Section 3.5.

3   Methods of color specification

What makes a good color space? In choosing a color space for your own purposes, some of the following features may or may not be of importance to you. They are listed here so that you may compare the 'ideal' space with those reviewed. The importance of any item in this list will depend on your application, and so the ordering of an item in the list should not be taken as a measure of its importance. With this qualification, an ideal color space for electronic displays will have the following features:

• *Perceptually uniform.* Equal steps in the color space should be equally discriminable: a step of ten units should be ten times more salient than a single step.

• *Easy to navigate.* Users should find the space intuitive to move around in. This feature is crucial in painting applications where users may wish to select, or even mix, a very particular color.

• *Closely related to the physiology of the visual system.* This may be necessary for research purposes or for designing applications to assess color vision.

• *Accurate color specification* should be possible. This may be required in order to generate hard-copy from a display, or to ensure that all displays running the same application produce exactly the same colors (portability).

• The color space should be *easily implementable* on an electronic display.

Because all of the color spaces described in this chapter are simply linear transformations of each other, it occasionally simplifies notation to present the definition of the color space in terms of a matrix. Each matrix is a set of three simultaneous equations and may be solved by conventional methods (see Appendix 1)[4]. In order to help make the transformations as simple as possible, Appendix 2 contains functions, written in the 'C' programming language, that implement most of the transformations described here.

One assumption underlying the descriptions of the color spaces that follow is that lights behave linearly: that is, the luminance produced by mixing two lights together is simply the algebraic sum of the two individual luminances. This assumption is generally true for lights, but it will not be true for the voltages applied to the display primaries. This is because the function relating display luminance and voltage is non-linear for virtually all commercially available monitors, and hence doubling the voltage will not double the luminance. Hence, all computed RGB values should first be corrected before sending these values to the digital-to-analog converters. This procedure is fully described in Chapter 5.

3.1   Electronic color spaces

3.1.1 RGB color space

In order for a color to be shown on a computer screen, it is necessary for that color to be expressed as a mixture of the three display primaries (see Chapter 1). This is achieved by sending three numbers to the digital-to-analog converters (dacs) that in turn send a voltage to each of the three electron guns. These three numbers are the core of the RGB space. The RGB color space should hence be considered as a three dimensional space with the origin at zero. Colors that plot at the origin would of course appear black. A gray scale would be represented by a vector from the origin along which R, G and B values are equal. The maximum value that each dac value can attain is defined by the number of bits per pixel, and these values are conventionally normalized (usually to 1). Hence the values for each axis may lie between zero and 1 and the entire color space is contained within a cube (see Figure 3.1).

The RGB color space is based on the common observation that most colors can be created by suitably mixing together three 'primary' lights. The main advantage of the space is that it is very easy to specify display colors (see next section). However, equal geometric steps in this space are not equally discriminable. For example, a step of ten units on the green axis may be more salient than ten units along the blue axis[5]. Secondly, novices used to subtractive color mixture often find it difficult to navigate within this color space. For example, users are more used to thinking of mixing magenta and yellow pigments to obtain an orange or yellow and not the red and green lights that are required to obtain a yellow on an electronic display. Hence, features such as luminance and saturation are not simple to visualize in this space. Thirdly, since different monitors use different sets of primaries, color space co-ordinates are not colorimetrically specified. For example, unique yellow (a yellow that is neither reddish nor greenish) may have the co-ordinates (1.0, 1.0, 0.0) on one monitor and (0.8, 1.0, 0.0) on a second.

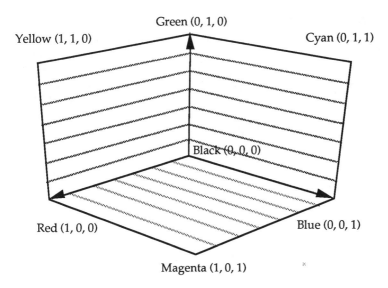

Figure 3.1: RGB color space. Whites, not shown in this figure, would be represented on a vector from the origin to the point (1, 1, 1).

Table 3.1: Typical RGB specifications

Red dac	Green dac	Blue dac	RGB
255	0	0	(1.00, 0.00, 0.00)
128	128	128	(0.502, 0.502, 0.502)
50	100	200	(0.196, 0.392, 0.784)

Specifying colors in the RGB system is simplicity itself. All you need to do is state the fraction of each primary relative to its maximum value.

As an example, take an 8 bits per pixel graphics monitor that can hence take values between 0 and 255 for each primary. Typical RGB specifications are given in Table 3.1.

3.1.2   YIQ color space

The YIQ color space is the color space used by television engineers and has its basis in the NTSC television transmission system. This system is used by those computers that drive domestic television sets. The color space evolved from the necessity to broadcast color transmission signals that were compatible with monochrome signals. The video signal, V, has three components: a luminance or Y signal that carries the information needed by monochrome television sets; and a pair of chromatic signals, an in phase or I signal and a quadrature or Q signal.

In the NTSC system the color signals I and Q are transmitted as modulations of a subcarrier frequency interleaved with the luminance Y signal. The full details of television transmission need not concern us here, but briefly the reason for this arrangement is that television is bandwidth limited, and this technique effectively fits all the necessary information into around 4 MHz. The technique is enterprising from the perspective of visual perception because it makes use of the fact that our color vision is used mainly for low frequency objects. In the NTSC system, fine detail is transmitted in the luminance signal; color is shown for medium and large objects only. Television transmission is a fine example of how a knowledge of human limitations can be put to efficient use in designing information technology.

The main feature of the YIQ color space is that it neatly fits man and machine, at least in terms of bandwidth. Additionally, since any display using YIQ color space is necessarily tied to a specific set of display phosphors, accurate color specification is possible. However, the amount of bandwidth allocated to the chromatic signal is inadequate when relatively fine color detail needs to be displayed (for example, text). Secondly, in television transmission, crosstalk may occur between the luminance signal and the chromatic signal that is interleaved with it; this results in bogus colors being displayed. One example is the shimmering colored patterns created on television by finely striped suits or shirts (indeed, television presenters usually avoid such fabrics). Moreover, the space is neither perceptually uniform nor simple to navigate within.

The matrix conversion from YIQ to RGB for the NTSC set of primaries is:

$$\begin{bmatrix} Y \\ I \\ Q \end{bmatrix} = \begin{bmatrix} 0.300 & 0.590 & 0.110 \\ 0.600 & -0.280 & -0.320 \\ 0.210 & -0.520 & 0.310 \end{bmatrix} \begin{bmatrix} R \\ G \\ B \end{bmatrix}$$

And the inverse of this matrix is:

$$\begin{bmatrix} R \\ G \\ B \end{bmatrix} = \begin{bmatrix} 1.000 & 0.948 & 0.624 \\ 1.000 & -0.276 & -0.640 \\ 1.000 & -1.106 & 1.730 \end{bmatrix} \begin{bmatrix} Y \\ I \\ Q \end{bmatrix}$$

The NTSC set of primaries are defined as:

Primary	CIE x	CIE y
Red	0.67	0.33
Green	0.21	0.71
Blue	0.14	0.08

3.2   Perceptual color spaces

3.2.1 HSV color space

The three axes of the HSV color space stand for hue, saturation and value and the purpose of the color space is to provide users with a more intuitive means of mixing colors than the RGB color space[6]. For example, if you wanted to produce a pink on your color display, an intuitive means of achieving this would be to select a red and then add some white to it, since most people would agree that pink is a desaturated version, or a tint, of red. But if colors were being manipulated in RGB color space, it is not at first obvious where you would get the white from since the three independent controls are over the red, green and blue display primaries. In the HSV color space, there is a separate control for saturation.

Although at first sight this color space sounds radically different to the RGB color cube, it is simply a deformed version of the cube (see Figure 3.2 and Plate 4). For example, take the vector representing grays and whites in the RGB color cube. This vector goes from RGB (0, 0, 0) (black) to RGB (1, 1, 1) (white). This represents the central value (or luminance) axis in HSV; it is formed by tilting the RGB color cube onto its black corner. Now, if you looked along this vector from the black end, you would see a plane hexagon with the hues laid out in sequence; this represents the hue plane in HSV (see Figure 3.2). Because the plane is approximately circular, colors are specified by their hue angle between 0 degrees and 360 degrees; for example, 120 degrees for blue and 240 degrees for green. Finally, the saturation dimension is specified by moving in from the hue plane towards the central, value axis. Intuitive terms used to describe color, such as tint, shade and tone, are

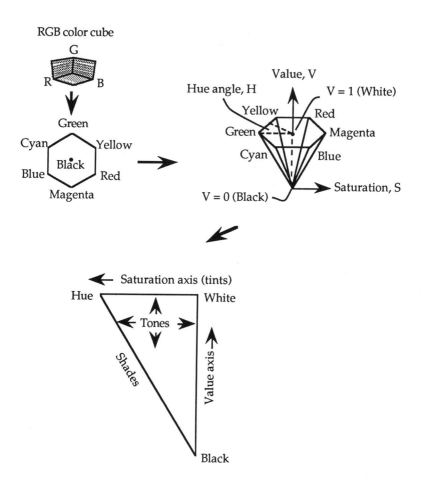

Figure 3.2: HSV color space can be thought of as simply a different way of looking at RGB color space. If RGB space is viewed from its black corner, looking towards the white point (that is, along the black-white vector), the hues are laid out on a hexagon. This hexagon represents the hue plane. Saturation is changed by movement away from the black-white vector; movement along the black-white vector changes a color's value. Changing saturation can be thought of as changing tint; all possible tones plot inside a triangle formed by these axes.

easily represented in this space. Figure 3.2 demonstrates this conversion pictorially.

HSV color space has not been developed through experimentation; rather it is based on the fact that colors can be characterized by the psychological features of hue, saturation and brightness. There are a number of alternatives to the HSV color space that essentially characterize color in a similar way; because of their similarity they will not be reviewed here[7].

The main advantage of HSV color space is that users find navigation intuitive within this color space. For example, an application may first show a user the fully saturated hue plane from which a color should be selected; saturation and value can then be specified by first displaying the selected hue and next altering saturation and value by, for example, reading back the x and y co-ordinates of a mouse cursor.

There are three main disadvantages with HSV color space. First, equal geometric steps in this space are not equally discriminable. A change of 10% on either the value or the saturation axis will be more noticeable on some parts of the axis than on other parts; and hue appears to change more rapidly in some parts of the hue circle than in other parts. Second, since different monitors use different sets of primaries, color space co-ordinates are not portable. Third, and most seriously, saturation and hue are confounded with luminance. Take, for example, the hexagonal arrangement of hues in HSV space (Figure 3.2). Although these hues are spaced on a plane of constant value, they will still differ in luminance. This is most easily seen by considering the case when value and saturation are at maximum. At this point, the green hue will be produced by maximum modulation of the green primary, and the blue hue will be produced by maximum modulation of the blue primary. Now, for a crt display the difference in luminance between the green and blue hues could be as much as a factor of five. Hence, these two hues will also differ in luminance. Because the visual system is very sensitive to changes in luminance (see Chapter 2), this limits the usefulness of HSV color space when accurate color usage is required.

To convert RGB values to HSV take the following steps:

1. Given R, G and B values (between 0 and 1), first find the maximum (MAX) and minimum (MIN) values.
2. To compute value (V) and saturation (S):

$$V = MAX$$
$$S = (MAX - MIN) / MAX$$

3. To compute the hue (H):

If S = 0, (from step b) the color is gray and so the hue is undefined. Otherwise, compute how much of the second most important color there is relative to the most dominant color:

$$R1 = (MAX - R) / (MAX - MIN)$$
$$G1 = (MAX - G) / (MAX - MIN)$$
$$B1 = (MAX - B) / (MAX - MIN)$$

Now,

if R = MAX and if G = MIN, then H = 5 + B1
else if R = MAX and if G ≠ MIN, H = 1 - G1
else if G = MAX and if B = MIN, then H = R1 + 1
else if G = MAX and if B ≠ MIN, H = 3 - B1
else if R = MAX then H = 3 + G1
else H = 5 - R1

Finally, convert H to degrees by multiplying by 60.
Note: S and V will lie between 0 and 1; H will lie between 0 and 360.

To convert HSV values to RGB take the following steps:

1. Convert H from degrees to hexagon section (HEX):

$$HEX = H / 60$$

2. Calculate MAIN_COLOR, SUB_COLOR and the three variables VAR1, VAR2 and VAR3 from the expressions:

$$MAIN\_COLOR = INT(HEX)$$
$$SUB\_COLOR = HEX - MAIN\_COLOR$$
$$VAR1 = (1 - S) \times V$$
$$VAR2 = (1 - (S \times SUB\_COLOR)) \times V$$
$$VAR3 = (1 - (S \times (1 - SUB\_COLOR) \times V$$

3. Then,

if MAIN_COLOR is 0, then R= V, G = VAR3 and B = VAR1
if MAIN_COLOR is 1, then R= VAR2, G = V and B = VAR1
if MAIN_COLOR is 2, then R= VAR1, G = V and B = VAR3
if MAIN_COLOR is 3, then R= VAR1, G = VAR2 and B = V
if MAIN_COLOR is 4, then R= VAR3, G = VAR1 and B = V
if MAIN_COLOR is 5, then R= V, G = VAR1 and B = VAR2

3.2.2 NCS color space

Recently, the Swedish Standards Institution have recommended the use of a system for specifying colors known as the Natural Color System (NCS)[8]. The three co-ordinates of the NCS color space are hue (designated Φ), blackness (designated s), and chromaticness (designated c). The system is based on the apparent uniqueness (see Chapter 2) of the color pairs red (R) and green (G), blue (B) and yellow (Y), and black (S, after the German, schwarz) and white (W). These six colors represent the reference points of the system. The idea is that each color pair represents a continuum: so for example, yellow is a mixture of red and green, and if we add more red we get a reddish yellow, and if we add more green we get a greenish yellow. The crucial point is that we cannot see a reddish green (or a bluish yellow). Each continuum is divided into 100 parts and colors are specified by their location within this framework. As with the Munsell system (see Section 3.4.1), a color atlas is available, although this is intended merely to illustrate the color space and not necessarily to be used as a tool.

The experimental basis of the color space is the statement of psychological opponency described in Chapter 2 (Section 2.3.1). We now know that this is a flawed analysis of the second-stage of color processing, although it may still account for higher-order color perceptions. The reported advantages are that it is easy to use, and colors are evenly spaced within NCS[9]. However, there is little difference between the NCS space and Munsell color space, and in fact simple transformations between the two exist[10]. It is therefore likely that NCS space is no more than a different sampling and description of the same color space as Munsell. The NCS color space has stimulated a great deal of research, and the ultimate test will be if the system is adopted by the color community in preference to competing color spaces.

To reproduce the NCS color space on an electronic display, follow the next three steps.

1. Construct a database relating NCS co-ordinates to CIE 1931 (x, y) and Y co-ordinates[11]. Write a program that will give you the CIE co-ordinates when the NCS co-ordinates are entered.

2. Write a program to convert between CIE 1931 (x, y) color space and RGB color space (see Section 3.5.1).

3. Now combine the two programs so that you can type in the NCS co-ordinates, hue (Φ), blackness (s) and chromaticness (c) and generate the appropriate color on your display.

3.3　Linguistic color spaces

Linguistic color spaces are appealing because we are all used to specifying colors in terms of their linguistic appearance[12]. It is decidedly easier to specify a color as blue, or bluish-green, or pale bluish-green, than it is to quantify the color in terms of three numbers that are meaningful only in a graphical system of color representation that may be difficult to understand.

3.3.1　CNS color space

The Color Naming System (CNS)[13] is a simplified version of the color naming system proposed by the Inter-Society Color Council and the National Bureau of Standards (ISCC-NBS). In the ISCC-NBS system, English words are used to classify colors along the dimensions of hue, saturation and lightness. In the original system, pages of equal hue in the Musell color space (see Section 3.4.1) were divided into ranges and assigned color names (see the lower right of Figure 3.4). The principle behind the system was that colors could be defined over six 'levels'. Levels 4-6 are numeric systems (for example, Munsell color space and CIE 1931 (x, y) color space; see Sections 3.4.1 and 3.5.1); these are used when very accurate color specification is required. The remaining three levels use progressively more sophisticated linguistic tags. So for example, 'yellow' is a level 1 description; 'greenish yellow' is a level 2 description; and 'brilliant greenish yellow' is a level 3 description. Level 3 descriptions are characterized by adding modifiers (simple adjectives) to level 2 hue descriptions. In total, 267 color names can be generated by this scheme; the advantage of the system is that each color name is associated with a particular Munsell swatch and hence can be colorimetrically specified with great accuracy.

The difficulty with the system is that the level 3 modifiers are not spaced systematically over each Munsell page. So for example, on one page of bluish-green colors, the 'vivid' modifier refers to all Munsell chromas above 11; on another page of pinks, the modifier refers to Munsell chromas above 11 and Munsell values above 6.5 (see Section 3.4.1 for a description of Munsell notation).

This level of description has been simplified in the CNS. The terms for hue may be achromatic (seven names) or chromatic (six names; see Figure 3.3). Modifiers to the generic chromatic names are provided by five terms for lightness and four terms for saturation. As with the original ISCC-NBS system, combining color names specifies a color that lies between the two generic hues: in the NCS, these hues are assumed to be separated by quartile intervals and hence an intermediate color may lie exactly between or one-quarter closer to a generic hue (see Figure 3.3b). This generates 31 chromatic hue names. Since these can be

Plate 1 Magnified examples of some different types of pixel arrangements. A delta arrangement (left) and the arrangement produced by a trinitron (right).

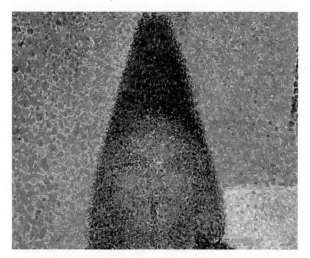

Plate 2 Georges Pierre Seurat, 'Invitation to the Sideshow/La Parade,' (detail) Metropolitan Museum of Art, bequest of Stephen C. Clark, 1960.

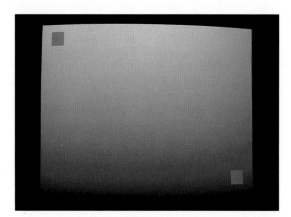

Plate 3 This plate demonstrates brightness contrast. The two gray squares in this picture have the same luminance but they differ in perceived brightness. The difference in perceived brightness is caused by the differing surround luminance.

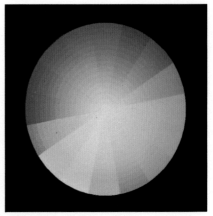

Plate 4 This plate shows the hue circle in HSV color space (left); and a plane of equal value, where colors differ in their relative H and S values (right).

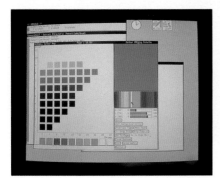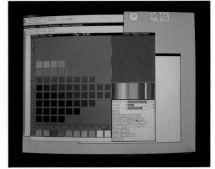

Plate 5 An implementation of Munsell color space on a Sun workstation. In this implementation, the required Munsell page is selected from the rainbow index on the middle right-hand panel. Selected chips can be placed in a 'drip tray' at the bottom and stored on disk for later use. A color mixing palette is provided if the required color cannot be found on the Munsell system: colors are produced by moving the H, S and V sliders. The chromaticity co-ordinates of the mixed color can be provided by selecting the 'CIE' button. Because perceived color depends acutely on the surrounding colors, the background on which the chips are viewed can be varied from the standard white.

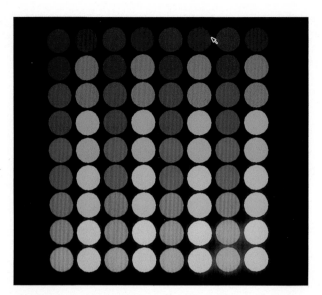

Plate 6 In this plate, each row has a constant luminance and each column has a constant hue. The question is: will the visual system group the columns (that is, the hues) or the rows (the luminances)?

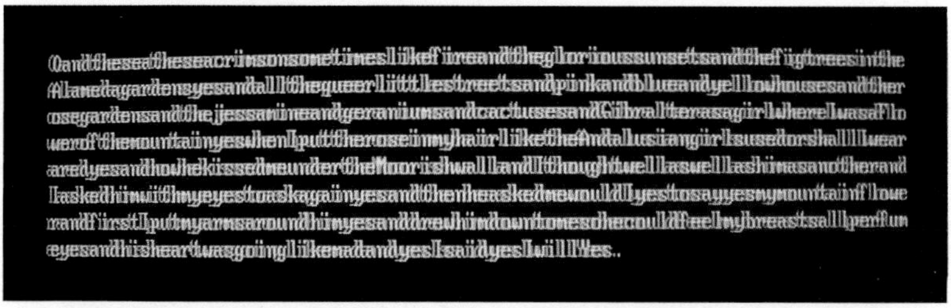

Oandtheseatheseacrimsonsometimeslikefireandtheglorioussunsetsandthefigtreesinthe
Alamedagardensyesandallthequeerlittlestreetsandpinkandblueandyellowhousesandther
osegardensandthejessamineandgeraniumsandcactusesandGibralterasagirlwhereIwasaFlo
werofthemountainyeswhenIputtheroseinmyhairliketheAndalusiangirlsusedorshallIwear
aredyesandhowhekissedmeundertheMoorishwallandIthoughtwellaswellashimasanotherand
IaskedhimwithmyeyestoaskagainyesandthenheaskedmewouldIyestosayyesmymountainflowe
randfirstIputmyarmsaroundhimyesanddrewhimdowntomesohecouldfeelmybreastsallperfun
eyesandhisheartwasgoinglikemadandyesIsaidyesIwillYes..

Plate 7 Passages of text that are not delineated by white space are very hard to read.

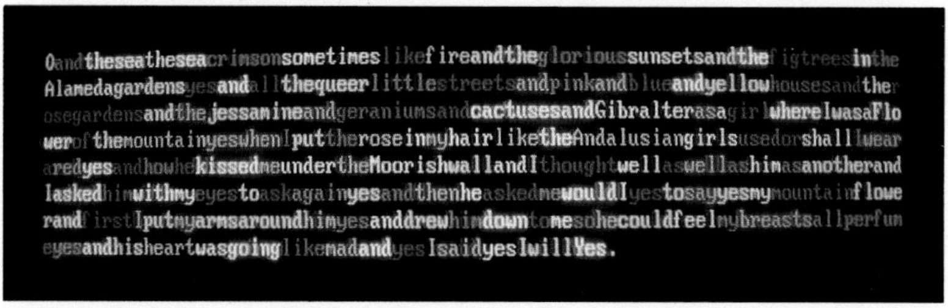

Oandtheseatheseacrimsonsometimeslikefireandtheglorioussunsetsandthefigtreesinthe
Alamedagardensyesandallthequeerlittlestreetsandpinkandblueandyellowhousesandther
osegardensandthejessamineandgeraniumsandcactusesandGibralterasagirlwhereIwasaFlo
werofthemountainyeswhenIputtheroseinmyhairliketheAndalusiangirlsusedorshallIwear
aredyesandhowhekissedmeundertheMoorishwallandIthoughtwellaswellashimasanotherand
IaskedhimwithmyeyestoaskagainyesandthenheaskedmewouldIyestosayyesmymountainflowe
randfirstIputmyarmsaroundhimyesanddrewhimdowntomesohecouldfeelmybreastsallperfun
eyesandhisheartwasgoinglikemadandyesIsaidyesIwillYes.

Plate 8 Whereas using color to delineate words makes reading effortless. This is because the visual system is able to use the different colors of each word to signify the word boundaries.

Plate 9 Color can be used to make an object 'pop out' from the surrounding objects. In this plate, finding the book on Project Management is a slow process; identifying the orange book is almost instant.

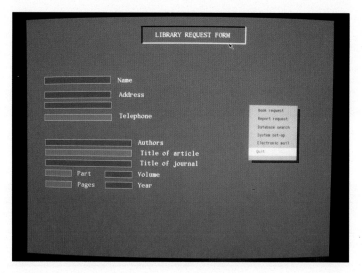

Plate 10 This interface to a library request system uses a green background to signify compulsory input and a blue background to signify optional input.

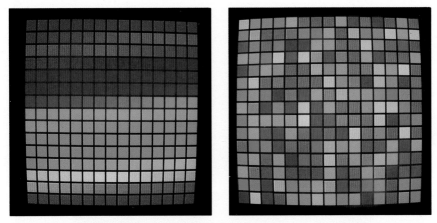

Plate 11 One principle of color harmony is that harmony=order. This plate shows two arrangements of the same colors; one arrangement is ordered by hue in HSV space; the other is arranged randomly. Subjects do, in fact, describe the ordered sequence as more pleasing than the random sequence.

Plate 12 This plate demonstrates color contrast. Although the gray border is exactly the same color at all points, it looks cyanish when superimposed on the pink square and pinkish when superimposed upon the cyan square.

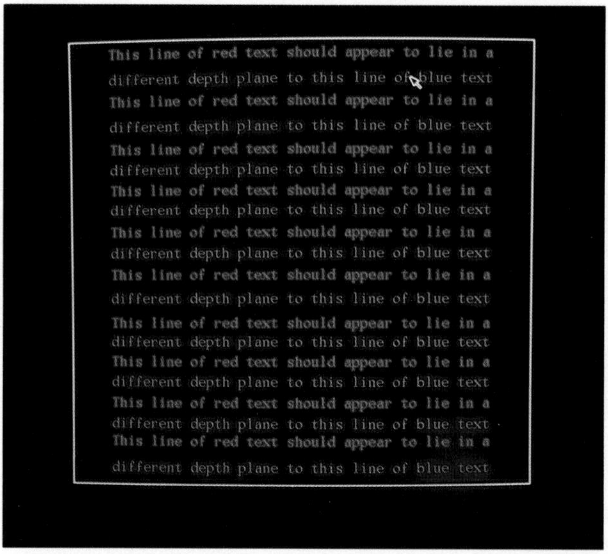

Plate 13 This plate demonstrates chromostereopsis. When viewed under direct illumination, the red and blue words appear to lie in different depth planes (the effect can be enhanced by placing pinholes in front of the eyes, while maintaining stereoscopic viewing).

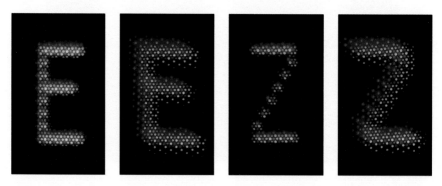

Plate 14 This plate shows examples of well-converged and badly converged color tubes.

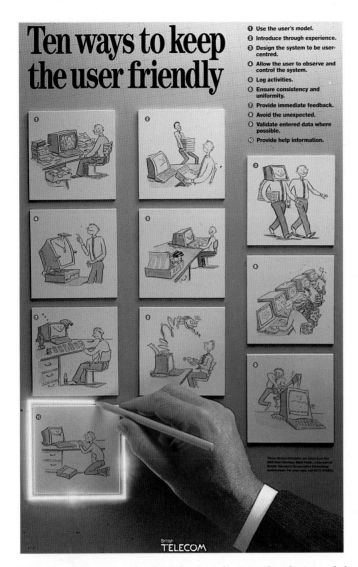

Plate 15 Ten general principles to adopt in the design of the user interface. © British Telecom 1990, reprinted with permission.

modified by five lightness terms and four saturation terms, a grand total of 620 (31 x 5 x 4) chromatic color names are possible, with seven additional achromatic color names. An example of a complete specification might be 'light gray' for an achromatic color or 'dark, strong, purplish-blue' for a chromatic color.

As well as the considerable work that went into devising the ISCC-NBS system[14], the experimental basis of this color space has recently been enhanced. It has been shown[15] to be a more valuable color space than either RGB or HSV when color naming is required. However, although the color space has a theoretical gamut of 627 colors, only 480 of these can be found in the Munsell Book of Color; and since brown and orange are used synonymously, there are really only 340 distinct colors in the Munsell book that are found in the CNS[16]. This number is far below the number of achievable colors on quite unsophisticated color displays, and hence there will be certain colors that cannot be named. This seriously limits the potential of CNS as a comprehensive color space. However, one potential application of CNS is as a 'ballpark' color space: users could type in the approximate color they wanted using CNS, and then cause small changes to this color using a secondary system (for example, HSV). However, the most significant hindrance to the uptake of CNS on electronic displays is that the appropriate algorithms are not yet available to convert to and from RGB space[17]. However, this problem is easily soluble: all that is required is to specify the 340 Munsell chips that correspond to the CNS color names and relate the two by simple table look-up. Then, the Munsell values can themselves be reproduced on the display (Section 3.4.1 describes how to do this).

The CNS color space may be realised on an electronic display by the following procedure.

1. If the hue is achromatic, it should be described by one of the following names (see Figure 3.3a):
Achromatic hue names: black, very dark gray, dark gray, gray, light gray, very light gray and white.
Go to step 4.
2. If the hue is not achromatic, identify the hue of the color on the hue circle (see Figure 3.3b).

If the color falls in the middle of two unique color names (for example, blue and purple) the color name is a composite (for example, blue-purple). If it falls one-quarter closer to one color (for example, blue) than the other, use the *-ish* suffix (for example, purplish-blue). The hues should be chosen from the following list (see Figure 3.3b):
Chromatic hue names: blue, purple, red, orange, brown, yellow and green. Note: brown is considered to be synonymous with orange.

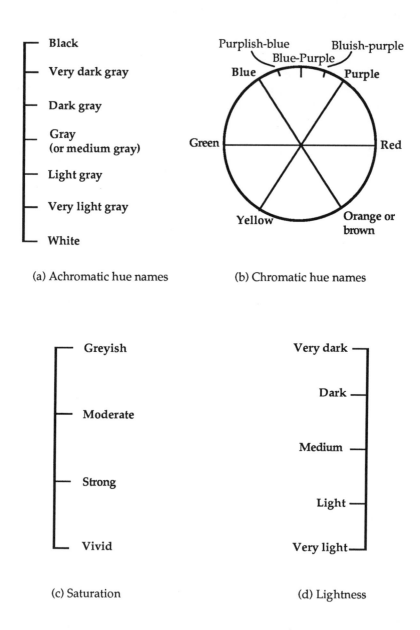

(a) Achromatic hue names

(b) Chromatic hue names

(c) Saturation

(d) Lightness

Figure 3.3: The available color names in the Color Naming System.

3. If the lightness is medium and the saturation is vivid, no modifiers are required since these are assumed by default. Otherwise choose a lightness from the list (see Figure 3.3 parts c and d):
Lightness modifiers: very dark, dark, medium, light and very light.
Saturation modifiers: grayish, moderate, strong and vivid.
4. Exit.

3.4 Color order systems

There have classically been two color order systems in general use: the Munsell system, and the Optical Society of America Uniform Color Scales. Because they are qualitatively the same, only the Munsell system is considered here[18].

3.4.1 Munsell color space

The Munsell color space is commonly used in the design industry for specifying colors. It is very much a perceptual color space, with its three axes representing hue, value (lightness) and chroma (saturation). The system is most conventionally used by referring to the Munsell Book of Color[19] which contains printed samples, at just-discriminable steps, of the colors in the color space.

The hue of a color is first broadly defined by a letter code: purple (P), blue (B), green (G), yellow (Y) and red (R), with intermediate hues specified by the double-letter codes PB, BG, GY, YR, and RP (see Figure 3.4). The hue is then more specifically defined by ascribing it a number on a ten-point scale. The value (or lightness) of a color is a number between 0/ (very dark) and 10/ (very light). Chroma (saturation) is a number between /0 (gray) and /14 (highly saturated), with these numbers representing the difference betweeen that color and a neutral gray of the same value. In practice, this is achieved by skimming through the Munsell Book of Color and picking the swatch that most closely matches the sample. So for example, a saturated lime green would have the Munsell hue, value, chroma notation 5GY 7/12. Achromatic (or 'neutral') colors have notations such as N 1/0 (for black) and N 9/0 (for white; in practice, the /0 chroma symbol is conventionally omitted). Figure 3.4 shows some of the color names from the ISCC-NBS system (for the Munsell pages 3G-9G) that corresponds to Munsell specifications.

The Munsell system has been in use for many years now[20], and indeed some of the color vision tests described in Chapter 2 use colors selected from the Munsell book of color. The main advantages of the color space are that it is easy to use, and fairly simple to navigate within (although a number of users confuse value and chroma[21]). The main disadvantage is that, because it uses pigment samples whose color is

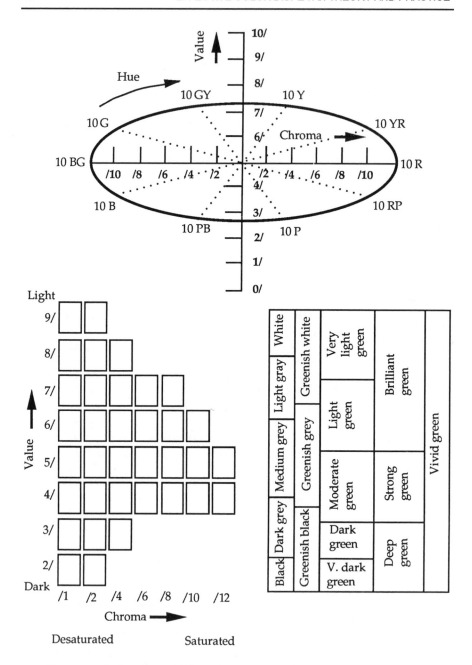

Figure 3.4: A slice through Munsell color space. The top half of the figure represents a schematic version of the overall color space; the lower half represents a slice taken at constant hue.

intimately tied to reflected light, the samples must be viewed under controlled illumination (for example, one of the CIE standard illuminants). Incorrect illumination will lead to incorrect color matching. Fortunately, in a modification of the Munsell system, known as the Munsell renotation system[22], the CIE 1931 (x, y) co-ordinates of each Munsell sample was specified; this means the exact color of the samples may be reproduced on an electronic display, under the assumption that they are viewed under CIE illuminant 'C'.

The Munsell color space may be reproduced on an electronic display using the following procedure.

1. Using the data from the Munsell renotation system (see Appendix 3), construct a look-up table so that each Munsell hue, value and chroma sample corresponds to particular CIE 1931 (x, y) co-ordinates, and a 'luminance factor', Y. Y is defined as

$$Y = \frac{\text{Reflected light}}{\text{Incident light}}$$

and can be taken as analogous to CIE Y (see Section 3.5). Because it is the ratio of relected to incident light, the precise values of Y in Appendix 3 may be scaled up or down by a constant to alter the perceived brightness of the assumed illuminant. Of course, all Y values in the Appendix should be multipled by the same constant.

2. Next, write a program to convert between CIE 1931 (x, y) color space and RGB color space (see next section).

3. Now combine the two programs so that you can type in the Munsell hue, value and chroma of a sample and generate the RGB values required to reproduce this sample.

4. It might be interesting to reproduce the Munsell Book of Color on your display by presenting 'pages' of constant hue, or constant chroma or constant value. An example of the Munsell Book of Color implemented in this way on a Sun workstation can be seen in Plate 5.

3.5 The CIE system

3.5.1 *The CIE XYZ space*

The most widespread method of color specification that uses instrumental methods is the Commission Internationale de l'Eclairage (CIE) *XYZ* system. There are a number of colorimeters that conveniently allow you to measure the CIE co-ordinates of display phosphors, and most display manufacturers will supply the CIE co-ordinates of their monitors on request.

The CIE system is based upon a set of color matching functions like those described in Chapter 2 (see Figures 2.7 and 2.8). Color matching functions define any color by three values, known as *tristimulus values* (for example, the XYZ triplet in Figure 2.8). These three numbers describe a three-dimensional color space. However, it lacks the (deceptive) geometric simplicity of other three-dimensional color spaces, such as HSV, and so it is both difficult to draw and interpret. Even Stephen Hawking, the brilliant theoretical physicist, claims to have problems in visualizing three-dimensional spaces[23].

Consequently, colors in CIE XYZ space are conventionally specified by their projection on a two-dimensional plane. Co-ordinates in this plane are known as *chromaticity co-ordinates*, and the diagram itself is known as a chromaticity diagram. The chromaticity co-ordinates are denoted by the symbols x, y and z and they are related to the tristimulus values by the following simple algebraic expressions:

$$x = \frac{X}{X+Y+Z}$$

$$y = \frac{Y}{X+Y+Z}$$

$$z = \frac{Z}{X+Y+Z}$$

You may remember from Chapter 2 that the XYZ set of tristimulus values are a transformation of the original set of color matching functions. The transformation was thought necessary because some tristimulus values were negative (due to the fact that one of the primary lights sometimes had to be mixed with the standard light). The data were therefore transformed by selecting a set of unreal or 'imaginary' primaries. These imaginary primaries (so-called because they cannot be physically produced) were chosen so that (i) all co-ordinates of truly physically realizable colors are positive; (ii) the z co-ordinate would be zero for most of the longer wavelengths (*i.e.* $x + y = 1$); and (iii) points that plot on the ordinate, including the red and blue imaginary primaries, (where $y = 0$) carry zero luminance (this line is hence termed the alychne which means 'without light').

Essentially, the space is a (slightly distorted) color triangle, the apices of which represent the colors red, green and blue (see Figure 3.5). All the colors that we are able to see can be plotted in this space, with white close to the center. Highly saturated colors plot at the sides of the triangle: the locus of these colors is known as the *spectral locus* since this is where the spectral colors plot. As a color becomes more desaturated (that is, whiter), it is plotted closer to the center of the triangle.

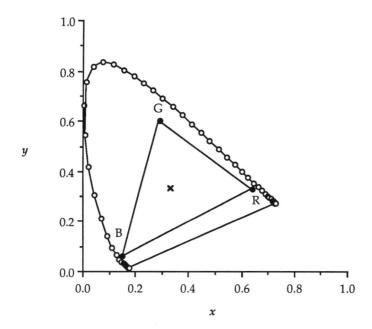

Figure 3.5: CIE (x,y) color space with the location of spectral colors at 5 nm intervals and the positions of the UK PAL System 1 television phosphors. All possible mixtures of the three display phosphors fall on or within the lines of this triangle. Hence, there are a number of colors that cannot be produced with these television phosphors, but display manufacturers have not yet gone to the expense of producing a fourth primary (in the blue-green part of the spectrum) to pull the triangle into a rectangle and hence increase the color gamut. This is probably because most colors in the real world are not highly saturated, and so their omission is rarely noticed. The cross near the center of the diagram plots the position of an equal energy white.

Figure 3.5 shows the CIE diagram with the location of spectral colors at 10 nm intervals and the co-ordinates of the UK PAL System 1 television phosphors[24] denoted by R, G and B. All possible mixtures of the three display phosphors fall on or within the lines of the RGB triangle. Hence, there are many colors that cannot be produced with these phosphors (because most colors in the real world are not highly saturated, this deficiency is rarely noticed). The cross near the center of the diagram plots the position of an 'equal energy' white. There are lots of different whites; an equal energy one is simply one that has equal energy throughout the visible spectrum. The y-axis can be thought of as representing how much green is in a color and the x-axis how much red. Hence blues plot near the origin, since they have little red or green in them.

The usefulness of the CIE representation is that it allows color specification in a universal language. The system is now so ingrained that it should be used whenever you are required to specify color precisely. Unfortunately, many research reports on the use of color in electronic displays are uninterpretable because the colors used are not specified in a reproducible way. And although CIE (x, y) space was not specifically designed to include perceptual qualities such as saturation, these can still be clearly represented in the diagram (see Section 3.5.3).

However, although the space is fine for specifying color, it does not represent what is happening in color vision especially well; in fact it obfuscates relationships in color vision that may be better represented by other color metrices. Moreover, there is a temptation to place points equally within the particular color space that is used: so for example, if you had to choose half-a-dozen colors to use on your display you might be tempted (very reasonably) to position them proportionally in this space. But unfortunately, equal geometric steps in CIE (x, y) space do not correspond to equal perceptual steps: we are much more sensitive to steps near the blue corner of the diagram, and much less sensitive to steps near the green corner, than to steps near the red corner[25]. Second, since the color space is ultimately based on lights (either physical or imaginary) and not on what we know about the mechanisms of color vision, it can be somewhat confusing. One commentator[26] has written:

> "The CIE triangle is brilliantly ingenious as an aid to the calculation of chromaticities which can be upheld in a court of law where colour specification is in dispute. But the triangle is monstrous as an indication of what is going on in the mechanism of vision. It displays all colours as a mixture of three primary lights, none of which have an existence that can be easily imagined. One of the three primaries is bright: it is a pure green from which is subtracted a lot of red which it does not contain. The other two primaries are quite dark; they have strong colour but zero luminance. These do not seem to me ingredients that lead to clarity in our conception of colour mechanisms and I am astonished that some physiologists and many psychologists employ them to instruct the young and bewilder the old."

Before specifying display colors in CIE (x, y) space it is necessary to compute the tristimulus matrix of your display.

There are two methods of computing the tristimulus matrix. Both methods require the chromaticity co-ordinates of the three phosphors in CIE (x, y) space. In addition, method 1 requires the chromaticity co-ordinates of the white that the three phosphors produce when turned on at their maximum. Method 2, which is somewhat simpler, requires the relative luminances of the three phosphors.

Method 1
Use this method if you do not know the relative luminances of the three phosphors.
1. Obtain the CIE (1931) x, y chromaticity co-ordinates of each primary from the manufacturer or if you have your own colorimeter measure them yourself. You can then compute z for each primary from the relationship:

$$x + y + z = 1$$

Write down the matrix:

$$\left[C \right] = \begin{bmatrix} x_r & x_g & x_b \\ y_r & y_g & y_b \\ z_r & z_g & z_b \end{bmatrix}$$

An example of such a matrix for a typical display is:

$$\left[C \right] = \begin{bmatrix} 0.601 & 0.298 & 0.143 \\ 0.363 & 0.598 & 0.070 \\ 0.036 & 0.104 & 0.787 \end{bmatrix}$$

Now compute the inverse of C, C^{-1}. From the example above:

$$\left[C^{-1} \right] = \begin{bmatrix} 2.3591 & -1.1183 & -0.3292 \\ -1.4417 & 2.3820 & 0.0501 \\ 0.0826 & -0.2636 & 1.2791 \end{bmatrix}$$

2. Obtain the CIE chromaticity co-ordinates (x_w, y_w, z_w) of the white formed by driving each primary to its maximum. For the monitor above these values were (0.289, 0.321, 0.390).
3. Compute the tristimulus values of the white, X_W, Y_W and Z_W, from the following:

$$X_W = \frac{x_w}{y_w}$$

for example, $X_W = 0.9003$;

$$Y_W = 1.0000$$

$$Z_W = \frac{z_W}{y_W}$$

for example, $Z_W = 1.2150$.

Y_W is set to 1 since all that is generally required is the relative luminances.

Now compute:

$$\begin{bmatrix} V_1 \\ V_2 \\ V_3 \end{bmatrix} = \begin{bmatrix} C^{-1} \end{bmatrix} \begin{bmatrix} X_W \\ Y_W \\ Z_W \end{bmatrix}$$

In our example:

$$\begin{bmatrix} V_1 \\ V_2 \\ V_3 \end{bmatrix} = \begin{bmatrix} 0.6056 \\ 1.1449 \\ 1.3648 \end{bmatrix}$$

4. Finally, compute the nine-element tristimulus matrix, **T**, by computing:

$$\begin{bmatrix} T \end{bmatrix} = \begin{bmatrix} C \end{bmatrix} \begin{bmatrix} V_1 & 0 & 0 \\ 0 & V_2 & 0 \\ 0 & 0 & V_3 \end{bmatrix}$$

In our example:

$$\begin{bmatrix} T \end{bmatrix} = \begin{bmatrix} 0.601 & 0.298 & 0.143 \\ 0.363 & 0.598 & 0.070 \\ 0.036 & 0.104 & 0.787 \end{bmatrix} \begin{bmatrix} 0.6056 & 0 & 0 \\ 0 & 1.1449 & 0 \\ 0 & 0 & 1.3648 \end{bmatrix}$$

$$= \begin{bmatrix} 0.3640 & 0.3412 & 0.1952 \\ 0.2198 & 0.6846 & 0.0955 \\ 0.0218 & 0.1191 & 1.0741 \end{bmatrix}$$

Most of the color space manipulations that follow are based on either this matrix or on its inverse, T^{-1}. In our example,

$$\begin{bmatrix} T^{-1} \end{bmatrix} = \begin{bmatrix} 3.8953 & -1.8466 & -0.5435 \\ -1.2593 & 2.0806 & 0.0438 \\ 0.0605 & -0.1932 & 0.9372 \end{bmatrix}$$

Method 2
Use this method if you know the relative luminances of the three phosphors.
1. Follow Step 1 of Method 1.
2. For each phosphor, write down the relative luminances of the three phosphors. For example, if the luminance of the red phosphor is 21.98 cd/m^2, the green phosphor is 68.46 cd/m^2 and the blue phosphor is 9.56 cd/m^2, then:

$$Y_r = 0.2198, Y_g = 0.6846 \text{ and } Y_b = 0.0956$$

Note that these are relative values and add up to one: this normalization procedure is achieved by dividing each individual luminance by the sum of the three luminances. These are the Y tristimulus values.
3. Compute the X and Z tristimulus values from the Y tristimulus value and the chromaticity co-ordinates for each primary:

$$X_r = Y_r \frac{x_r}{y_r}$$

for example, $X_r = 0.2198 \times \dfrac{0.601}{0.363} = 0.3639$;

$$Z_r = Y_r \frac{z_r}{y_r}$$

for example, $Z_r = 0.2198 \times \dfrac{0.036}{0.363} = 0.0220$;

and similarly for the green and blue primaries. By this method:

$$\begin{bmatrix} T \end{bmatrix} = \begin{bmatrix} 0.3639 & 0.3412 & 0.1953 \\ 0.2198 & 0.6846 & 0.0956 \\ 0.0220 & 0.1191 & 1.0748 \end{bmatrix}$$

The small differences between the tristimulus matrix computed here and the one computed in Step 4 Method 1 above are due solely to rounding errors.

Now, in order to convert to and from CIE (x, y) color space, perform the following steps.

1. To compute the tristimulus values, X, Y and Z, that correspond to a specific **RGB** vector:

$$\begin{bmatrix} X \\ Y \\ Z \end{bmatrix} = \begin{bmatrix} T \end{bmatrix} \begin{bmatrix} R \\ G \\ B \end{bmatrix}$$

where **T** is the tristimulus matrix computed above; then compute the chromaticity co-ordinates:

$$x = \frac{X}{X + Y + Z}$$

$$y = \frac{Y}{X + Y + Z}$$

$$z = \frac{Z}{X + Y + Z}$$

2. To compute the RGB values given chromaticity co-ordinates x and y and luminance Y^{27}, first calculate the tristimulus values:

$$X = x \begin{bmatrix} \frac{Y}{y} \end{bmatrix}$$

$$Y = Y$$

$$Z = (1 - x - y) \begin{bmatrix} \frac{Y}{y} \end{bmatrix}$$

Then:

$$\begin{bmatrix} R \\ G \\ B \end{bmatrix} = \begin{bmatrix} T^{-1} \end{bmatrix} \begin{bmatrix} X \\ Y \\ Z \end{bmatrix}$$

where T^{-1} is the inverse of the tristimulus matrix computed above.

3.5.2 The CIELUV space

A significant problem with the CIE 1931 (x, y) diagram is that equal geometric steps are not equal perceptual steps. This is a problem because it makes it difficult to space colors so that they are equally discriminable; and related to this, it makes the computation of the magnitude of color difference between two color samples non-trivial.

In 1960, the CIE proposed a uniform color space (UCS) which went some way to achieving perceptual linearity; and in 1971[28] this was modified and extended to three dimensions. Two separate color spaces were proposed: one for representing lights, and another for representing colorant mixtures (as required, for example, in the dyestuff and textile industries). The latter color space is known as the CIE L*a*b* (or CIELAB) space and because its application is not intended in electronic displays, it will not be considered here. The former color space, which may be applied to electronic displays, is known as the CIE L*u*v* (or CIELUV) space. The main difference between the two spaces is that straight lines in CIE 1931 (x, y) space remain straight lines in CIELUV space, but not in the CIELAB space. This feature was considered important when colored lights are mixed additively, for example in color television.

The experimental database for this color space is the color matching functions (or the modifications of these) used to define the CIE 1931 (x, y) space. The two main advantages of the CIELUV color space is that it is approximately perceptually uniform, and computing the color difference between two color samples is straightforward (see below). However, it has imperfections: like the CIE 1931 (x, y) color space, it assumes very particular conditions of viewing (a 2° isolated field) that may not apply to your application. The CIE themselves admit that "Further research on uniform color spaces and color-difference formulae is required"[29]. However, where an approximately uniform color space is required, the CIELUV color space is the best available option. This space could be used, for example, to select a set of optimal colors for display presentation[30] by maximising the color difference between each color in the pallette. Evaluating the size of the color difference required may require some provisional data-gathering but specifying color differences is a useful procedure because it offers a quantitative metric by which to say how different two colors are, or how different two colors need to be. For example, a system viewed under bright sunlight in an aircraft cockpit will require larger color differences than the same system used under the tungsten light of an office.

To compute the L*, u* and v* values that correspond to a specific RGB vector carry out the following:

1. Either measure the u', v', and Y co-ordinates directly with a colorimeter; or compute them from the CIE x, y and Y co-ordinates by calculating the tristimulus values:

$$X = x\left[\frac{Y}{y}\right]$$

$$Y = Y$$

$$Z = (1 - x - y)\left[\frac{Y}{y}\right]$$

and then computing:

$$u' = \frac{4X}{X + 15Y + 3Z}$$

$$v' = \frac{9Y}{X + 15Y + 3Z}$$

Using the same methods, compute u'_n and v'_n and Y_n (the co-ordinates of the monitor's white point).

2. If $\left[\frac{Y}{Y_n}\right] > 0.008856$,

$$L^* = 116\left[\frac{Y}{Y_n}\right]^{1/3} - 16$$

$$u^* = 13L^* (u' - u'_n)$$

$$v^* = 13L^* (v' - v'_n)$$

If $\left[\frac{Y}{Y_n}\right] < 0.008856$,

$$L^*_m = 903.3\left[\frac{Y}{Y_n}\right]$$

and the computations for u* and v* remain the same.

The *color difference* between two colors may now be computed in the following way.

1. Define the two colours in CIE LUV space.
2. Compute the difference between the two samples in their L*, u* and v* co-ordinates. Denote these values as ΔL*, Δu* and Δv*.

3. Then the color difference, ΔE^*_{uv}, is given by:

$$\Delta E^*_{uv} = \sqrt[2]{(\Delta L^*)^2 + (\Delta u^*)^2 + (\Delta v^*)^2}$$

3.5.3 Perceptual dimensions and CIE space

At first sight, the CIE color spaces seem non-intuitive. Just as users find it difficult to mix a color based on the proportions of red, green and blue primaries in the RGB color space, surely they would find it difficult to mix colors based on the relative proportions of x, y and Y, or L*, u* and v*? Yet just as HSV color space is simply another way of looking at RGB color space, these same perceptual dimensions map onto other color spaces[31]. For example, in CIE (x, y) color space (Figure 3.5), the 'hue circle' is simply the horseshoe locus of spectral colors. Luminance increases out of the page. Saturation is a measure of the distance of a hue from the white point. Although the following example uses CIE color space, the same procedure may be used for any color space.

In order to map hue, saturation and value onto CIE (x, y) color space it is necessary to first choose a white point in the space (for example, $x = 0.333$, $y = 0.333$, see Figure 3.5). This will be the central axis of the perceptual color space: hence, increasing Y (the luminance) is now analogous to the central value axis of HSV. This luminance axis extends into and out of the page through the point marked with a cross: the representation in Figure 3.5 is simply one slice through the space. The hue axis is the outer boundary of hues that are linked by the three phosphors of the display: hence, this locus is in fact triangular (see Figure 3.5) and not circular as in HSV. Saturation is represented by excursions from the white point (marked by a cross in Figure 3.5) to the hue boundary. Because the luminance values of each of the primaries will almost certainly differ, the shape of the color space when studied in three-dimensions will lack the (deceptive) three-dimensional geometry of HSV color space. This more accurate representation shows, for example, that greater luminance can be achieved with the green primary than with the red and blue primaries, at least for crts. This important information is lost in the HSV representation.

The main advantage of this type of representation is that the three axes, luminance, saturation and hue, are truly independent. This makes it simple to specify a hue or saturation scale across which luminance is held constant, a procedure not possible in HSV but which may be important in color coding applications (see Chapter 4). This representation combines the important features of color specification with the important features of color perception: it makes the space both precise and intuitive. It is a simple transformation that can be applied to both of the CIE color spaces described in this section and to the color space described in the next section.

If CIELUV color space is used, then the correlates of lightness, chroma and hue have already been computed.

1. In CIELUV color space, the correlate of lightness is given by the quantity L*.

2. To compute the chroma, C, calculate

$$C = \sqrt[2]{\left[(u^*)^2 + (v^*)^2 \right]}$$

3. To compute the saturation, S, calculate:

$$S = \frac{C}{L^*}$$

3.6   Color spaces for research

3.6.1   SML color space

Since what ultimately constrains color vision is the activity of the three classes of cone, a useful theoretical color space would be one that represented these activities directly. One way to achieve this is to describe a three-dimensional space where the three axes represent the excitation of each cone class. Figure 3.6 shows such a color space. The vertical axis represents the activity in the S cones; the remaining two axes represent the activity in the M and L cones.

Consider for a moment lights that lie along the vector cd in this color space. Because this line lies in the plane of S and L cones, the output from M cones is zero. Moreover, because the line is orthogonal to the L axis, colors that plot along this line will have exactly the same effects on L cones. Consequently, colors that plot on this vector can be discriminated only by S cones, since this is the only value that changes as the vector is traversed. The vector could be moved so that its base sits within the ML plane; but so long as the vector is still parallel with the S axis, colors that plot along the vector will have a constant effect on M and L cones, and again only the output from S cones will vary. Hence there are an infinite number of vectors in SML space along which only S cone output will vary, and similar statements can be made about the M and L cone axes.

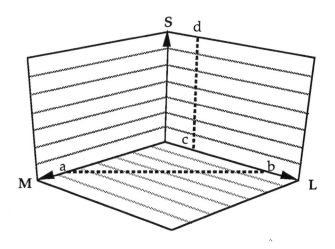

Figure 3.6: SML color space. The S, M and L axes represent the modulations of the three classes of cone. Black is represented at the origin, where S=M=L=0. The line ab represents a vector along which the ratio of M and L cones is constant; the line cd represents a vector along which only the output of S cones varies.

Now consider the vector ab. Along this vector the output from S cones is constant at zero. What changes as the vector is traversed is the ratio M:L. You might remember from Chapter 2 that this ratio appears to be an important one for color vision since it appears to be the ratio computed by one of the color difference channels.

It is now straightforward to design an instant color deficiency test. Colors that lie along vectors parallel to any of the cone axes (for example, the line cd) may only be discriminated by that class of cone; this type of color modulation would hence allow us to detect subjects with congenital color blindness who lack one of the three classes of cone. Colors that lie on vectors where the ratio M:L is changing (for example, the line ab) would be invisible to the acquired color defective who lacked this color difference channel. It is left as an exercise for the reader to work out where vectors would plot that would stimulate only the S-(L&M) color difference channel, and the L&M luminance channel.

The experimental basis for this color space is the considerable work on color matching described above and in Chapter 2. This work has led to a set of cone fundamentals derived by V. Smith and J. Pokorny. The main advantage of the space is that it is easy to visualize the effects of colors on the three classes of cone and to specify colors accurately. The disadvantages are that the space is not perceptually uniform and hue, saturation and luminance are not explicitly represented in the space (although see Section 3.5.3).

Colors may be specified in cone space by the following procedure.

1. Compute the matrix V obtained by multiplying the matrix T computed in Section 3.5.1 by the Smith-Pokorny fundamentals:

$$\left[V\right] = \left[T\right]\begin{bmatrix} 0.00000 & 0.00000 & 0.01608 \\ -0.15514 & 0.45684 & 0.03286 \\ 0.15514 & 0.54312 & -0.03286 \end{bmatrix}$$

For example, for the display tristimulus matrix given in Section 3.5.1.

$$\left[V\right] = \begin{bmatrix} 0.3640 & 0.3412 & 0.1952 \\ 0.2198 & 0.6846 & 0.0955 \\ 0.0218 & 0.1191 & 1.0741 \end{bmatrix}\begin{bmatrix} 0.00000 & 0.00000 & 0.01608 \\ -0.15514 & 0.45684 & 0.03286 \\ 0.15514 & 0.54312 & -0.03286 \end{bmatrix}$$

Hence for this display:

$$\left[V\right] = \begin{bmatrix} 0.0004 & 0.0019 & 0.0173 \\ 0.0447 & 0.2637 & 0.0487 \\ 0.1752 & 0.4208 & 0.0469 \end{bmatrix}$$

2. Then, to obtain S, M and L given R, G and B:

$$\begin{bmatrix} S \\ M \\ L \end{bmatrix} = \left[V\right]\begin{bmatrix} R \\ G \\ B \end{bmatrix}$$

3. And to obtain R, G and B given S, M and L:

$$\begin{bmatrix} R \\ G \\ B \end{bmatrix} = \left[V^{-1}\right]\begin{bmatrix} S \\ M \\ L \end{bmatrix}$$

3.6.2 Specifying chromaticity co-ordinates in SML space

A very useful feature of the CIE diagram is that it represents three variables in a two-dimensional plot by using chromaticity co-ordinates. Similarly, it would be an advantage to take a two-dimensional plane in SML color space and specify a color in terms of its chromaticity co-ordinates.

We can do this in a number of ways. One way is analogous to the CIE system: we can define a two-dimensional plane where:

$$S + M + L = 1$$

(see Figure 3.7) and hence define the chromaticity co-ordinates as:

$$s = \frac{S}{S + M + L} \quad m = \frac{M}{S + M + L} \quad \text{and } l = \frac{L}{S + M + L}$$

Because s, m and l sum to unity, we need only plot two of the variables, since the third is implicit. Figure 3.7 shows the spectrum locus of m plotted against l, and the co-ordinates of a typical graphics monitor.

We could achieve a similar feat by choosing a plane where the sum of the responses of two of the cones is equal[32], for example the plane where the output of the M and the L cones sum to unity (see Figure 3.8). This is useful because our detection of luminance is considered to depend only on the the sum of activity in the L and M cones (see Chapter 2) and hence the plane is an *equiluminant* one: luminance is constant throughout the diagram. Therefore, at each point in this space, if the response of the L cones is known, it is possible to compute the response of the M cones since L + M = 1. The other axis represents the response of the S cones, also divided by the sum of the M and L cone responses.

Hence, the chromaticity co-ordinates (s, m and l) may also be defined as:

$$s = \frac{S}{M + L}$$

$$m = \frac{M}{M + L}$$

$$l = \frac{L}{M + L}$$

This two-dimensional representation is shown in Figure 3.8. The open symbols represent the spectrum locus with spectral colors plotted every 10 nm; the filled symbols shows the display primaries of a typical graphics monitor.

The origin (where $l = 0$, $s = 0$) represents unique activation of the M cones. If we could produce such a light it would plot at this point. We cannot produce such a light, because there is no point in the visible spectrum where the M cones are uniquely sensitive: this can be seen from the spectral sensitivities plotted in Chapter 2. No matter which spectral light we choose to stimulate the M cones, either the S or the L cones will also be stimulated.

The point $l = 1$, $s = 0$ represents unique activation of the L cones: we can almost achieve this with a long-wave spectral light.

Since the x-axis of the graph represents the ratio of activity in the L and M receptors it can be plotted as extending from zero to unity (representing increasing L cone activity) or *vice versa* (representing decreasing M cone activity). Because this axis is a null axis for S cones (that is, their output is constant) it is sometimes termed the Constant S axis. We cannot represent the point of unique S cone excitation in this figure: by definition, because at all points in the space L + M = 1. However, we can represent *changes* in the excitation of S cones: this is precisely what is shown on the y-axis. Because the ratio of M to L is constant along the y-axis, this axis is sometimes termed the Constant M&L axis.

Hence, the main advantage of this space for thinking about color vision is that it makes certain relationships quite obvious. For example, consider the color vision of a protanope, the color deficient individual who lacks the normal L cones of color vision. Such an individual will find impossible any color discriminations that rely on the L cones that he lacks: and such discriminations are represented in this diagram by lines which emanate from the L corner (where $s = 0$, $l = 0$) since all points along any individual line cause the same ratio of activity in both the M and S receptors. Similarly, a deuteranope who lacks the normal M cones of color vision will confuse colors that lie on lines emanating from the M corner (where $s = 0$, $m = 0$). This is because the ratio of L to S cone activity is identical on any one such line. Finally, the tritanope (the very rare individual who lacks the normal S cones of color vision) will confuse all colors that lie on the same vertical line in the diagram, since the ratio of L to M cone activity along such a line will be constant.

Appendix 4 provides, at 10 nm spectral wavelengths, the color matching functions, the S, M and L cone modulations, and both types of chromaticity co-ordinate. These data may be used for color modeling purposes and to construct cone chromaticity diagrams of the types shown in Figures 3.7 and 3.8.

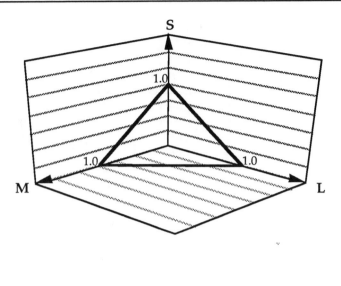

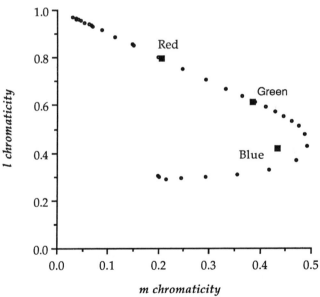

Figure 3.7: SML color space. In the upper figure, the triangle in bold represents the plane in cone space where S+M+L=1.0. Plotted in the lower part of the figure is the m chromaticty against the l chromaticity. The small symbols represent the spectral colors; the larger symbols represent the display primaries of a graphics crt.

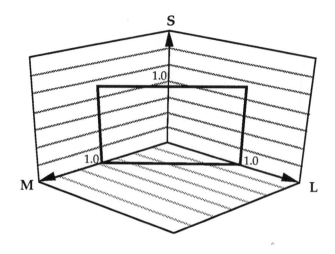

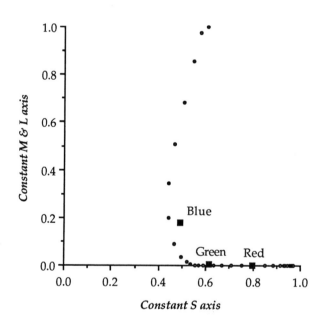

Figure 3.8: As Figure 3.7, except now a different plane in cone space has been selected to specify chromaticity co-ordinates.

4   Specifying color: key points

• *The ultimate decision on which color space to use will depend on precisely what it is that you require to do. There is no one color space that fulfills all criteria.*
• *Where perceptual uniformity is important, select NCS, CNS, Munsell, or CIELUV.*
• *Where ease of navigation is important, select HLS, NCS, CNS or Munsell.*
• *Where accurate color specification is important, select any color space except RGB and HLS. All of the other color spaces can be transformed to CIE.*
• *Where ease of implementation is important, select RGB or HLS.*
• *Where it is important for the color space to be physiologically meaningful (for example in the design of color deficiency tests) use SML.*

5   Further reading

Cornsweet, T. N. (1970) *Visual Perception.* New York: Academic Press.

Excellent introduction to cone space.

Hunt, R. W. G. (1989) *Measuring Colour.* Chichester: Ellis Horwood.

A standard reference text, especially useful if your interest in color extends to areas where the rules of additive color mixture no longer hold, such as color printing.

Meyer, G. W. and Greenberg, D. P. (1988) Color-defective vision and computer graphics displays. *IEEE Computer Graphics and Applications,* September, 28-40.

A scholarly review by leaders in the field of computer graphics. Additionally describes the implementation of a color deficiency test on a color display.

Rushton, W. A. H. (1972) Review lecture: Pigments and signals in colour vision. *J. Physiology,* **220**: 1-31P.

Further arguments for using a cone space.

Smith, A. R. (1978) Color gamut transform pairs. SIGGRAPH '79 Proceedings, published as *Computer Graphics,* **12**: 12-19.

Description of the HSV model.

Tonnquist, G. and Heng, L. (1989) Application of color video displays to color research, *Displays*, **10**: 171-180.

Description of the NCS model and its applications to electronic displays.

Displays, (1989) **10**, Number 3.

Special issue on color. See especially the introductory comments to this issue by V David Hopkin.

6   Notes and References

1 Berlin, B. and Kay, P. (1969) *Basic Color Terms*. Berkeley: University of California Press. Boynton, R. M., Fargo, L., Olson, C. X. and Smallman, H. S. (1989) Category effects in color memory. *Color Research and Application*, **14**: 229-234.

2 Cited in Brown, R. and Herrnstein, R. J. (1975) *Psychology*. London: Methuen, page 5.

3 Boring, E. G., Langfeld, H. S. and Weld, H. P. (1948) *Foundations of Psychology*. New York: John Wiley and Sons.

4 See for example Bronson, R. (1969) *Matrix Methods: An Introduction*. London: Academic Press.

5 For example, Derefeldt, G. and Hedin, C. (1989) Visualization of VDU colours by means of CIELUV colour space. *Displays*, **10**: 134-146, have shown that colors equally spaced in RGB color space are non-uniformly distributed in the CIELUV perceptually uniform color space.

6 Smith, A. R. (1978) Color gamut transform pairs. SIGGRAPH '79 Proceedings, published as *Computer Graphics*, **12**: 12-19.

7 See for example the hue, lightness, saturation (HLS) colour space described by Metrick, L. (1979) Status report of the graphics standards committee, *Computer Graphics*, **13**(3); and the hue, value and chroma (HVC) color space described by Taylor, J. M., Murch, G. M. and McManus, P. A. (1989) TekHVC: a uniform perceptual color system for display users. *Proceedings of the Society for Information Display*, **30**: 15-21.

8 For a review see Hard, A. and Sivak, L. (1981) NCS - Natural Color System: A Swedish standard for color notation. *Color Research and Application*, **6**: 129-137.

9 Derefeldt, G., Hedin, C. E. and Sahlin, C. (1987) Transformation of NCS data into CIELUV colour space. *Displays*, **8**: 183-192; Derefeldt. G.,

Hedin, C. E., and Sahlin, C. (1990) NCS colour space for VDU colours. *Displays*, **11**: 8-27.

10 Judd, D. B. and Nickerson, D. (1975) Relation between Munsell and Swedish Natural Color System scales. *J. Optical Society of America*, **65**: 85-90.

11 These values may be found in Swedish Standard SS 01 91 03 *CIE tristimulus values and chromaticity co-ordinates for colour samples in SS01 91 02 (SIS)* Swedish Standards Institution, Sweden, 1982.

12 For a scholarly and entertaining review see Chapanis, A. (1965) Color names for color space. *American Scientist*, **53**: 327-346.

13 Berk, T., Brownstone, L. and Kaufman, A. (1982) A new color naming system for computer graphics. *IEEE Computer Graphics and Applications*, **2**:, 37-44. See also Tominaga, S. (1987) A computer method for specifying colors by means of color naming. In G. Salvendy (ed.) *Cognitive Engineering in the Design of Human-Computer Interaction and Expert Systems*, Elsevier: Amsterdam, pp 131-138.

14 US Department of Commerce, National Bureau of Standards (1976), *Color: Universal Language and Dictionary of Names*, NBS Special Publication 400, US Government Printing Office, Washington DC, SD Catalog Number C13.10:440.

15 Berk, T., Brownstone, L. and Kaufman, A. (1982) A new color naming system for computer graphics. *IEEE Computer Graphics and Applications*, **2**:, 37-44.

16 Berk, T., Brownstone, L. and Kaufman, A. (1982) A new color naming system for computer graphics. *IEEE Computer Graphics and Applications*, **2**:, 37-44 (page 41).

17 One algorithm exists for converting CNS color space to HLS color space, although this is not based on psychophysical evidence. See Farhoosh, H. and Schrack, G. (1986) CNS-HLS mapping using fuzzy sets. *IEEE Computer Graphics and Applications*, **6**, 28-35.

18 For a description of OSA system see Hunt, R. W. G. (1989) *Measuring Colour*. Chichester: Ellis Horwood. As with the Munsell system, there is no simple algorithm to transform between OSA color specifications and CIE color space. However, the necessary data to produce a look-up table of the type presented for the Munsell system in Appendix 3.3 can be found in Wyszecki, G. and Stiles, W. S. (1982) *Color Science*. Wiley: New York, 2nd edition, pp 866-877.

19 Munsell, A. H. (1976) *Munsell Book of Color.* Munsell Color, Macbeth: New York.

20 See Nickerson, D. (1976) History of the Munsell Color System, Company, and Foundation. *Color Research and Application,* 1: 7-10, 69-77, 121-130.

21 Pokorny, J., Smith, V. C., Verriest, G. and Pinckers, A. J. L. G. (1979) *Congenital and Acquired Colour Vision Defects.* New York: Grune and Stratton, p36.

22 Newhall, S. M., Nickerson, D. and Judd, D. B. (1943) Final report of the OSA subcommittee on spacing of the Munsell colors. *J. Optical Society of America,* 33: 385.

23 Hawking, S. W. (1988) *A Brief History of Time.* New York: Bantum Books. p 24.

24 From Table 6.1 of Pearson, D. E. (1975) *Transmission and Display of Pictorial Information.* London: Pentech Press.

25 MacAdam, D. L. (1942) Visual sensitivities to color differences in daylight. *J. Optical Society of America,* 32: 247-274.

26 Rushton, W. A. H. (1972) Review lecture: Pigments and signals in colour vision. *Journal of Physiology,* 220: p17P.

27 Note that the luminance reading, Y, should be relative to the luminance used to compute T in Section 3.5.1.1 (*i.e.* Y_w). Y_w is the maximum possible luminance and is usually set equal to one.

28 CIE, Recommendations on Uniform Color Spaces, Color-Difference Equations, Psychometric Color Terms, Supplement No. 2 of CIE Publication No 15 (E-1.3.1) 1971, Bureau Central de la CIE, Paris, 1978.

29 CIE, Recommendations on Uniform Color Spaces, Color-Difference Equations, Psychometric Color Terms, Supplement No. 2 of CIE Publication No 15 (E-1.3.1) 1971, Bureau Central de la CIE, Paris, 1978 (page 10).

30 For example, see Merrifield, R. M. (1987) Visual parameters for color crts. In H. J. Durrett (ed.) *Color and the Computer,* pp 63-81. New York: Academic Press; De Corte, W. (1986) Optimal colors, phosphor and illuminant characteristics for CRT displays: the algorithmic approach. *Human Factors,* 28: 39-47.

31 See for example Taylor, J. M., Murch, G. M. and McManus, P. A. (1989) TekHVC: a uniform perceptual color system for display users. *Proceedings of the Society for Information Display,* 30: 15-21.

32 MacLeod, D. I. A. and Boynton, R. M. (1979) Chromaticity diagram showing cone excitation by stimuli of equal luminance. *J. Optical Society of America*, **69**: 1183-1186.

4

CODING, FORMATTING AND DESIGN

1   Overview

This chapter is concerned with the use of color to code, format and design visual displays. Its aim is to identify rules and guidelines for appropriate color use. The chapter first notes some general considerations, such as for what color is and is not suitable. Next the use of color is considered in three areas of system design: formatting, coding and aesthetics.

When correctly used, the benefits of color are unrivalled. It can be used to format displays by grouping and highlighting different information, such as items on a form. It can be used to color code, by identifying categories and by showing trends and relationships in information. It can be used for aesthetic purposes: users prefer color screens to monochrome screens, and the use of color can encourage system uptake. However, when incorrectly used, color has the potential to make a system unusable.

2   Introduction

There is no doubt that users prefer color screens to monochrome screens, despite the fact that performance differences cannot always be measured[1]. Even if this were the only benefit of color, it has been suggested that the use of color should be encouraged since this in turn should encourage the use of computers. In Chapter 3 it was stated that color is used on visual displays for one of four reasons. These are:

- Realism
- Formatting
- Coding
- Aesthetics

The previous chapter dealt with the first of these, realism. The aim of this chapter is to provide principles and guidelines to enable designers to use color to code and format displays (Sections 3 and 4), and to provide a set of simple rules for color aesthetics (Section 5). The rest of this section provides some preliminary remarks on the use of color on visual displays[2].

2.1   Advantages and disadvantages of using color

Color is not the only method of coding objects. We could also code by shape (take for example the wide range of monochrome icons on WIMP computer interfaces), or position (as occurs, for example, on a keyboard), or orientation (for example, an altitude indicator), or frequency (for example, the blink rate of a cursor could signify different operating modes). System designers frequently choose color merely because it is a simple method to use, but it may not always be the most appropriate. Before choosing to use color coding, ensure that other methods are not preferable. Indeed, as graphical displays become more sophisticated we may begin to find that other perceptual dimensions are used for coding purposes: such as texture or depth.

Why use color? The decision to use color rather than another method of coding should be based on a full analysis of the user's task (methods for carrying out such an analysis are provided in Chapter 5). Color may then be used if it is necessary to:
- Designate or emphasize a specific target in a crowded display.
- Segment or distinguish an area of the display.
- Provide warning signals or signify low probability events.
- Group and 'chunk' information.
- Imply certain physical states.
- Provide an aesthetically pleasing display.

It is important to remember that using color can be disadvantageous in some applications. In particular, color may:
- Distract when irrelevant and result in information overload.
- Depend on viewing and stimulus conditions.
- Be ineffective for the color deficient.
- Result in information overload.
- Unintentionally conflict with cultural conventions.
- Cause unintended visual effects.

If color space is going to be used to convey features of information space, which color space should be used? Chapter 3 should be of some help in making that decision. Because we are concerned with coding psychological dimensions, it would seem most appropriate to color code by using the perceptual dimensions of hue, saturation and brightness. At first inspection, the HSV space and its derivatives would appear the best candidates since these color spaces claim to represent these dimensions explicitly. However, it was pointed out in Chapter 3 that this color space actually confounds hue and saturation with luminance, and for precise work it is unsuitable. Fortunately, the same perceptual dimensions can be easily mapped onto the CIE and cone spaces (see Chapter 3, Section 3.5.3), and for accurate work it is these that should be used. For casual work however, HSV space will suffice. The rest of this chapter deals with color coding using the variables hue, saturation and luminance[3] without tying them to any particular color space.

2.2   Hue, saturation or brightness?

Color varies along three dimensions: hue, saturation and brightness (see Chapter 2 Section 2.4.2). Which dimension of color is most effective for formatting a display? An answer to this depends on a number of factors. Usually, the information on the screen represents different categories that bear no relationship to each other. So for example, an accountancy spreadsheet may have two columns containing debits and credits. These two categories are unrelated, and so are best coded by large differences in hue, for example red for debits and green for credits. Hue is suited to formatting this type of information because we readily segregate hues into categories, almost certainly because we can associate these categories with linguistic tags[4]. This is not the case with saturation nor with luminance.

However, consider the example of a menu driven interface that has a number of choices that become unavailable when a particular option is selected. So for example, the 'cut' option in a word processing package may be unavailable until text is selected. In this type of instance, luminance is a very effective cue for formatting the display. Available options may be colored a light green, with unavailable options colored a much darker green. This helps convey the idea to the user that an option has been 'turned off'. Saturation might also be used here to imply that an option had 'faded away'. However, if instead hue had been used in this example, the switch in color would be inappropriate to the change in status. For example, a menu option that switched in color from light green to yellow would convey to the user a change of function, implying that the option was still available but now did something different. More formal assignments of color to menu-based computer interfaces might be considered in order to improve navigation through the system[5].

2.3   Which colors and how many?

Which set of colors should be used for color coding? As a general guideline, large differences in hue should be used to code qualitative information to emphasize its categorical nature; and small differences in hue, or alternatively saturation and luminance, should be used for quantitative information to emphasize its ordered nature (see Section 4).

Table 4.1: Set of six colors of maximum contrast. These can be converted to RGB specifications using the algorithms in Chapter 3.

Color name	X	Y	Z
Reddish-purple	48.41	25.69	63.81
Blue	14.13	8.7	85.87
Yellowish-gray	62.53	58.57	14.87
Yellowish-green	36.15	69.65	14.42
Red	43.31	21.65	7.22
Bluish-gray	66.23	78.64	101.70

Frequently, hue, saturation and luminance differences may be used to obtain a set of colors that contrast maximally with each other. It makes good sense to use colors that differ in chromaticity and luminance since this will mean that color deficient individuals stand a good chance of using the color code as well as color normals. The procedure for achieving a set of maximally contrasting colors can be realized quite simply by selecting values according to some constraint, for example colors that are maximally separated from each other in a three-dimensional color space[6]. If the color space is perceptually linear, it is a fair assumption that the colors should contrast maximally with each other. Algorithms for carrying out such a selection in CIE L*u*v* color space have been published[7], and these algorithms should transfer to any three-dimensional color space that is perceptually uniform. One set of six colors derived in this way is shown in Table 4.1. One problem with algorithms such as these is that they may not choose colors that serve as good linguistic examplars of the group; so for example in Table 4.1 there is neither a unique yellow nor a unique green.

How many different colors can be used in a coding task? Despite the fact that we can discriminate many thousands of different colors, the number that we can identify absolutely is pitiably small: probably around eleven. However, this depends on practice: it has been shown that (with five months' practice) up to 50 colors may be recalled with perfect accuracy. Unfortunately, this skill declines rapidly if the user has no exposure to the task[8]. Clearly, in the design of a usable system, the aim is for as few colors as possible to meet the needs of the task. This is partly to avoid screen clutter and partly to ensure discriminability between the colors. The 'chunking' rules described below (Section 3.1) are usually taken to suggest that the capacity of short-term memory for color is about seven items; and it is commonly recommended that, if it is important for users to make associations with the colors used, then this number should not be exceeded.

In order that the set of colors used may be easily distinguished from each other they should fall into separate linguistic categories. This sets an upper limit of eleven colors: white, gray, black, red, green, yellow, blue, pink, brown, orange and purple. However, these so-called "eleven colors that are never confused"[9] have the potential to make a display appear garish and unattractive, and experience suggests that it is wise to restrict the maximum number of colors to fewer than this.

2.4   Two general principles

2.4.1 Design for monochrome first

One frequent mistake when using color on displays is to use color as a 'first resort' for display formatting. For example, a table of numbers or a poorly designed form will be simply colored in to give a veneer of structure. In fact, color should be used redundantly in formatting: that is, the structure of the display should be evident to a user even if the display were used in monochrome. The purpose of using color is to emphasize certain relationships, or distinguish certain areas, and not to give a global structure.

In many instances, color coding is redundant because there are other cues available to distinguish the objects. For example, telephone kiosks in the UK are color coded according to whether they are phonecard only (green) or coin only (yellow). Gas stations group their fuel pumps by hue: green for unleaded, black for leaded and blue for diesel. This is despite the fact that these objects differ in other ways: both phone kiosks and fuel pumps are distinguished by written signs. Yet the hue coding is intrinsically useful: from a distance, the driver can locate the correct fuel pump without commiting himself to a particular aisle. Indeed, redundant color coding appears to improve performance in search tasks[10].

The message that redundant color coding is useful in the real world should be adopted by designers of color displays. Wherever color coding is used, aim to make it a secondary cue. This can be most effectively summarized by a simple guideline: *design for monochrome first*. (Of course, this is especially the case if the display may be used by color defective individuals). For example, in a graphical representation of a local area network, the icon representing a personal computer should be easily distinguishable from the icon representing a fileserver. In the subsequent color-coded version, the icon representing personal computers might be colored yellow, and the icon representing a fileserver might be colored green. The color coding would allow the system administrator to distinguish the different types of computer system at-a-glance, but appreciation of the color coding is not required to use the interface. Instead, color is used almost as a transparent aid. Similarly, a monochrome form-filling interface could be first separated into related areas by using carriage returns and tab stops[11]. The titles of each field and the structure of the form should instruct the user which fields require compulsory input and which fields are optional. In the color-coded version, optional input fields could be distinguished from compulsory input fields by using two different colors of text, or different colors of highlighted background. Again, this would guide the user's behavior to the appropriate response.

2.4.2 Use the user's model

One of the rules for color coding mentioned below is that the color coding should be meaningful. This means that the coding should be relevant to the user. In the sense used here, relevance means that the coding is of use to the user and can be understood. How can this understanding be facilitated?

Before the user sits down in front of the system, he will have a set of preconceived ideas of what the system is trying to achieve. This is commonly referred to as the user's 'mental model' of the system[12]. This mental model will comprise a set of beliefs developed from experience with paper-based or similar electronic systems: so for example, an accountant will be used to seeing negative balances marked in red. A well designed system will make use of these preconceptions because, by exploiting the model, usability is enhanced. Chapter 5 provides methods for carrying out an analysis of the user's task; use these methods to identify any color code to which the user has previously been exposed.

In order to exploit the user's model it is necessary to find out what the user's model is, for example through interviews and questionnaires (these are described in Chapter 5). But with color, the designer has an immediate insight into at least part of the user's model because we all have a set of cultural associations with color. We are all aware of particular associations that we have with color since the English language is full of them. For example, a person may be 'feeling blue', or be 'green with envy', or have a 'yellow streak', or be so angry that he 'sees red'. It is commonly thought that color may affect a part of ourselves normally closed to consciousness: a recent example of this is a novel treatment for violent prisoners in West Yorkshire (they are placed in a shocking-pink cell)[13]. Most of these associations are learnt through experience, and some are strong enough to elicit physiological responses. For example, the color red can induce photoconvulsive EEG responses in people with a history of epilepsy, and actually prevent these responses when presented in conjunction with blue. (It has been suggested that persons prone to epilepsy wear spectacles that filter long-wavelength light). In normal individuals, blood pressure, respiration and heart rate may be influenced by color[14]. There is even some evidence that the clothing color of interviewees may have a significant influence on hiring decisions made by businessmen[15].

Table 4.2 lists a set of symbolic associations with color that apply in Western culture. There are a number of qualifications that must be associated with this table. First, compared to our considerable knowledge of the psychology and physiology of the mechanisms of color vision, our knowledge of this area of color is truly paltry. There is very little published data that may be considered; indeed, much of our knowledge in this area is anecdotal. Second, it needs emphasis that the associations of certain concepts, feelings or emotions with certain colors are culturally determined. (This table is based on the responses of American college students[16]). One intriguing example from Communist China exemplifies this point well. Since the revolution was symbolized by the color red, some members of the Red Guard complained about the use of this color to mean 'stop' in traffic lights. They argued that the traditional ordering of traffic lights should be reversed: that is, green should stand for 'stop' and red should stand for 'go' since the color red was seen as symbolising progress. More recently, it has been shown that in North America most individuals associate the concept 'cold' with the color blue; but in China the salient color here is white[17]. Third, even within a culture there is 'interference' between concepts: in the West, red may signify 'take immediate action' but it can also signify 'stop'; additionally, red may stand for 'hot' or 'danger' or 'on' (as in power). Fourth, some of these tabulated associations are stronger than others: so for example, green for go and red for stop are almost universal in Western culture, whereas blue for off is associated by only around one in three individuals. And finally, this table need not be followed slavishly: so long as the coding is used consistently, users can learn other associations with color[18].

Table 4.2: List of symbolic associations with color that apply to Western culture. Note that these associations may not apply to other cultures.

Concept	Color	Percentage association
stop	red	100
go	green	99
cold	blue	96
hot	red	95
danger	red	90
caution	yellow	81
safe	green	61
on	red	50
off	blue	32

A second way of exploiting the user's model is to use naturalistic color coding where possible. So, for example, on a head up display the sky should be coded blue and the earth brown. If it was necessary to code the documents on a desktop according to their age, older documents could be coded yellow and newer documents white, hence emphasising the natural concept that paper yellows with age[19].

3   Formatting

Depending on the required effect, screens can be formatted using two related but distinct principles: one exploits the tendency of the visual system to segregate and group objects of the same hue; the other exploits the tendency of the visual system to quickly locate an object of a novel hue in a crowded display.

3.1   Principle 1: Use color to group

Objects of similar hue tend to align themselves together. An example of this is shown in Plate 6. Many examples of nominal color information in the real world can be found in nature: for example differences in color can be used to group different species of plant, or to distinguish the sex of a monkey. It is useful in formatting displays for two reasons: first, it can help to group different but related information into meaningful units; and second, it can help to segregate areas of the display.

A classic example of the use of color to segregate information is the London Underground map, where different lines are demarcated according to color. The color coding is so effective that visitors to London frequently leave the city remembering the fact that they stayed near the 'red line' rather than the Central Line. Exactly the same feature is used on conventional maps: on road maps, for example, motorways are frequently coded blue and A-roads red. This enables the navigator to quickly decide upon a particular route. Medicines are frequently color coded; this provides a fairly simple way for the pharmacist to make an initial crude distinction between different drugs. Large catalogues frequently group different pages into sections by hue coding their outer edge. Maps of large buildings or shopping centers may use hue to help customers find particular locations: for example, within a shopping complex, department stores might be coded blue and chemists might be symbolized by a green cross[20].

Using color for grouping is particularly effective when different layers of an object must be shown at the same time: that is, when a three-dimensional object is being represented in two dimensions. For example, color can be used to distinguish the front and rear layers of a printed circuit board: the front layer of tracks might be coded red and the rear layer might be coded green. Designers are then able to 'see through' the board and segregate the two layers. Of course, there are a host of other issues here, such as: what should the color be where two separate areas overlap? Should one color hide the other, or should the overlapping area represent an additive or subtractive combination of the two colors?[21] Hue is also a useful aid for distinguishing separate systems that may overlap physically in space. Medical textbooks use color to distinguish physiological systems from each other: the nervous system may be coded blue and the blood capillaries may be coded red. For example, a CAD workstation may hue code the different systems of a car within a three-dimensional drawing: perhaps showing the steering system in red, the electrical system in green and the transmission in brown.

Psychologists have known for some time[22] that our ability to recall items from memory is improved if we are able to group information into meaningful units or 'chunks'. For example, spend 30 seconds memorizing the following string of characters, and then try to recall as many letters as possible in their correct serial position:

syalpsidrolocevitceffe

It is likely that you could recall only around seven letters. Yet, if I reversed the order of the letters and formed them into a more meaningful string[23] you would find it a trivial task. The limit on short-term memory is set by meaningful bits of information: hence, a random string of five letters comprises five bits of information, while a five-letter word comprises only one bit. This chunking process can be greatly facilitated by using color to group, structure and assign meaning to sets of symbols.

One example in display design might be to color code the outline structure of a computer program. For example, programming languages such as 'C' and Pascal convey information by their spatial structure: progressive levels of programming (for example, loops) are symbolized by indentation. It turns out that this concept can be just as effectively conveyed by using a color code[24]. A second example comes from reading. Words are conventionally separated by white space. This makes it simple for the visual system to delineate the beginning and end of words and hence 'chunk' strings of letters together. Passages of text that are not delineated by white space are very hard to read (see Plate 7). Yet it has been shown that color can be just as effective at delineating words as white space[25]. This is demonstrated in Plate 8. This finding is especially useful in situations where display size is small or where all of the available line capacity of a screen is required.

A grouping method might also be used in the design of a previously introduced HyperCard stack: the buttons on the home card could be color coded and the cards to which these buttons lead could echo the coding (for example, by discretely coding the border of the card with the same hue). This would help users locate themselves within the stack of information.

3.2   Principle 2: Use color for emphasis

When an object is sufficiently different in color from the surrounding objects it instantly segregates, or 'pops out', of the background. This effect is not unique to the color domain. It has been shown that a number of perceptual features segregate effortlessly from each other. One example is orientation. If an oblique line is presented among a set of vertical lines, it readily 'pops out' of the background. This particular effect can be exploited in the design of control panels (see Figure 4.1). Rather than search for the target item (in this case an oblique oriented indicator) by serially inspecting each object in turn, perceptual segregation allows us to search for the object by a parallel process.

The theoretical framework used to account for these observations was briefly considered in Chapter 2 (Section 2.4.3). Put simply, the visual system is seen to comprise a set of distinct modules whose job is to detect special features of the world (for example color or orientation). Initially, the visual system forms a feature map in each module (for example, segregating green areas and red areas of the image in the color module). This level of analysis is pre-attentive: within a feature map, figure/ground separations are effortless: their performance signature is 'pop out'. Deeper levels of analysis, where feature maps are joined together to specify an object, require attention. These objects do not 'pop out': they require serial analysis of a scene.

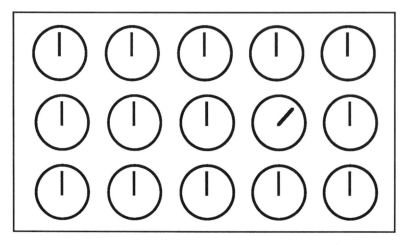

Figure 4.1: When an oblique line is presented among a set of vertical lines it immediately 'pops out' of the display. This feature of perceptual organization can be used in the design of computer interfaces and control panels. The normal setting for the cluster of dials represented here is vertical; when a dial shows an aberrant reading this is represented by an oblique setting. Color is an equally effective cue.

In terms of color, one frequently cited example is demonstrated in the picture of a library shelf shown in Plate 9. If asked to select the book on Project Management from the selection of books shown, you would need to carry out a serial search through the bookcase before you found the correct one. But if you were told the spine of the book was yellow, then it would be a trivial task[26]. An example of segregation applied to screen design would be a form where all the fields requiring compulsory input have a green background, and those fields with optional input have a blue background (see Plate 10). Because the green and blue areas are readily distinguished from each other, it is a simple matter for the operator to locate those areas which require some input. Color could be used on a graph to distinguish between different data sets. This type of coding is especially useful when three or more line graphs must be shown on one graph at the same time: color helps make the distinction effortless.

When formatting a display, color is useful in emphasizing screen or column headings. Frequently this type of formatting may be redundant: for example, the heading may already be distinguished by capital letters. Nevertheless, using color for emphasis in this way provides additional help for the user in segmenting the screen. Color is also a great help in identifying a specific target: for example, a stockbroker's system may help to identify a rising share price in green. And color can be used to link at the same time. So for example, selecting the name of the share in the previous example could highlight a selection of companies whose business is based in the same area. The dealer can then quickly identify those companies whose shares may be influenced by the rise.

However, be warned that this type of emphasis can become distracting and hence lose its power when overused. Try to restrict emphasis to one or two key items on the display.

4 Coding

4.1 The six principles of color coding

There are six simple rules for color coding. These rules apply to all instances where color is used to code information. For specific types of information there will be additional specific guidelines (see below) but these six principles should be adhered to by all systems. Adherence does not guarantee that a system will be usable, but it does make usablity more probable.

The colors used in a coding task should be:

• *Discriminable*: the chosen colors should be discriminable from each other by the predicted group of users. This may include those with congenital color deficiencies as well as those with acquired color deficiencies, such as the elderly. This can usually be achieved by aiming for a large luminance contrast between the foreground and background: for example, light green on a dark blue background (see Section 6.5). For certain applications (where absolute identification of the color is important) it is advisable to use colors that are good examples of their group. So for example, use a true yellow rather than a yellow that is slightly green or orange.

• *Detectable*: the chosen colors should be detectable by the predicted group of users under the ambient illumination that the display will be used.

• *Perceptually equal steps*: the discrimination steps between the chosen colors should appear approximately the same. If a set of five colors is chosen, and two of those colors are very similar, those colors will be associated. The user will think they are linked or related in some way.

• *Meaningful*: the code should have some relevance to the user. For example, in a telephone directory, business numbers might be coded green and personal numbers might be coded blue. This coding would be relevant if the user (a) wanted to distinguish between these two categories; and (b) understood the code that was being used. However, if the user did not understand the code, or if he wished to find all of the telephone listings for one city, the existing color code would at best be irrelevant and at worse a hindrance.

• *Consistent*: if the 'Help' option is coded green on one screen, it should be coded green on all screens. Moreover, this color should be 'reserved' once it has been claimed for an option. So in this example, help should always be signified by green and green should always signify help.

• *Aesthetically pleasing*: use as few colors as possible and ensure that the chosen colors do not clash or vibrate (see Section 5).

These six rules provide general principles. The remaining parts of this section consider additional principles that should be useful when coding specific types of information.

A central issue in the use of color in display design is: how should information be color coded? This question is surprisingly complex, but can be simplified by considering the number of color dimensions available for the task and the different types of information that we may wish to code. First, color has three dimensions: hue, saturation and brightness (see Chapter 2, Section 2.4.2, and Chapter 3). Second, there are broadly two types of information: quantitative and qualitative. Qualitative information is distinguished by its quality or nature: this type of information separates into categorical groups (for example, names of countries, on/off, species of plant). Formatting a display into groups can be considered a form of qualitative coding. In contrast, quantitative information is distinguished by its quantity or amount and can be ordered in numerical series (for example, population of countries).

These various type of information can be considered to comprise an information space, just as hue, saturation and luminance comprise a color space. Hence, the question is not simply 'How should information be color coded?' The question is 'How does information space map onto color space?'. For the purposes of information coding, information can be considered to fall into three discrete sections: categories or names; quantitative scales; and ordered categories or names.

4.2   Coding categories or names

Qualitative color coding can be used to perceptually classify objects according to type, condition or group. This type of information is generally classed as *nominal*. Examples of nominal information include folders on a desktop, television channels or different airlines flying into Kennedy airport. As a specific example, a link in a network management system may be in one of two states: working or faulty. This could be coded simply by coloring the working link as a green circle and the faulty link as a red cross (the use of a redundant spatial code will improve search times and make the display usable by those with color deficiency).

The example given here for coding uses hue and not saturation or luminance. As a general rule of thumb, categories or names are better coded by large differences in hue; this is for two reasons. First, because hues are arranged in a circle in color space, there is no beginning or end. Hence, it is not possible to assign relative values to widely separated hues because hue is not a continuum. Both saturation and luminance, on the other hand, can be thought of as continua: luminance varies from light to dark, and saturation varies from white to a vivid hue. Because they are continua, saturation and luminance imply relative values. If either of these scales were assigned to categories or names, they would imply a relative scaling that might be inappropriate. Similarly, small steps in hue should not be used to code categories or names because these too imply a relationship: hence the sequence greenish-yellow, yellow, yellowish-orange, implies a relationship between the three states. This misrepresents the information, which by definition has no relationship between the categories.

4.3   Coding quantitative scales

In the previous examples of color coding, no value has been assigned to the colors used: the purpose of the color coding is simply to group or segregate objects in the scene. In the real world, color is used to denote physical properties of objects: for example, to distinguish between ripe and unripe fruit and vegetables, or to judge the health of a person by the color of their skin[27]. We judge the freshness of meat by its color and reject meat that appears greenish. Interestingly, fresh red meat frequently appears greenish under tungsten illumination: this is why supermarkets light their meat counters with a particular type of fluorescent lighting that improves the perceived color of the product.

With quantitative information, measures are spaced continously along a variable. It differs from qualitative information in that the distances between any two numbers on the scale are of known size. Temperature is a classic example. One conventional mapping between temperature and color is to code the cooler end of the scale blue and the hotter end of the scale red, with the full rainbow of colors in between.

This type of color coding is frequently seen in infra-red images that have been coded to identify temperature gradients.

However, the designer should be careful when using hue to code this type of information, because the underlying hue variation may actually destroy the relationship between the levels. This will be especially apparent when the information is quantized into a small number of steps (say half-a-dozen) and then these steps are mapped onto the full rainbow sequence of colors. This is a problem because there is no logical sequence for ordering colors that differ by very large steps in color space: for example, what is the 'correct' sequence for the colors blue, pink, brown, green, yellow and red? It is erroneous to assume that we have some hard-wired intuitions for a spectral sequence (i.e. red, orange, yellow, green, blue, indigo, violet). If this were true, school children would not find it necessary to learn mnemonics such as "Richard Of York Gains Battles In Vain". Such mnemonics are not required to rank colors in saturation or brightness, or when *small* steps in hue are considered: for example, subjects with normal color vision are quite good at arranging the colored chips in the FM 100-hue test (see Chapter 2) into an ordered color sequence, even though the chips differ only in hue from each other.

In summary, if hue is chosen to represent interval information, ensure that the steps between hues are small and logically related. So for example, choose the six colors green, green-yellow, yellow, yellow-orange, orange-red, red.

Saturation may also be used to code quantitative information. For example, the size of a bolt might be represented on a control system. If the size is within (say) ± 0.1 mm, this could be symbolized by a white icon. If an inspection shows that the size of the bolts is beginning to exceed this value, the icon could turn progressively redder along a saturation scale from white. If the size of the bolts begins to fall below the tolerance limit, the icon could turn progressively greener along a saturation scale from white. As a second example, the temperature of the human body should stay around 37° C and variations of only a few degrees above or below this can be fatal. An icon representing a patient's temperature might signify 37° C by white; as the temperature drops below this level the color could change to more saturated blue, and as it varied above this level it could change to more saturated red. By assessing the saturation of the icon, the medical assistant can immediately assess the patient's condition at a glance, without needing to spend time reading a graph. In both of these examples, the wise designer will use color redundantly: for example, the icon in the first example could shrink or expand its size relative to a reference outline.

Note that when very accurate judgements are required in the previous application, the assistant will need to read a more conventional temperature scale. This problem applies not only to color, but to any method of representing data, other than a numerical scale or a table of values. The use of color to code this type of information should be considered analogous to the use of graphs as visual aids. The usefulness of graphical representation of data is to perceive trends and structure, and not for judging absolute values. In contrast, a table of numbers is ideal for judging absolute values but poor at identifying trends. Hence, color should be used for coding quantitative information when a user needs to identify changes from some norm, or needs to identify a pattern or structure within the data.

4.4   Coding ordered categories or names

It is frequently the case that the categories to be coded are related to each other, but not in any quantitative way. For example, clothes sizes are usually divided into the categories small, medium, large and extra-large. There is no overlap between the categories, so that if you fall midway between a medium and a large you must either choose a pullover that is slightly too small for you or one that is slightly too big. Clothing stores sometimes use color to code just this type of information by placing color stickers on the clothes hangers, packaging and labels. In many countries, money is color coded: for example, in the UK five pound notes are blue/green and ten pound notes are brown. This may be why many European visitors to the United States make errors with the currency: US dollars with different face values do not differ in color.

A further example of color coding this type of information is provided by a novel word processing system that identifies previous edits of the document by a hue code[28]. When an article is written in pen or pencil, it is simple to distinguish the areas that have undergone revision from those that are still quite 'raw'. Conventional word processing loses this information: one passage of text looks as honed as another passage. By color coding the more recent material and by making these colors 'fade' over time, it is simple to distinguish the new passages from those that have undergone revision (a revised passage may contain various colors that correspond to the dates of various revisions). When documents are multi-authored, comments can be inserted in color (presumably red) to distinguish them from the main body of the text.

Unless it is vital to maintain the rank order of the information, ordered categories should be hue coded using large hue differences. Frequently, the precise order of ordered categories is unimportant (as in the clothing example given above) and so this should rarely cause difficulty.

4.5   Coding many dimensions

All of the previous examples have used color to code a single dimension. But it is plausible that, in combination with some other attribute, color can be used to code many dimensions. This is particularly useful when it is necessary to code more than about half-a-dozen states because when more than this number of colors are used the display may appear garish and confusing.

For example, an air traffic control system may need to code aircraft into their origin (internal flights *versus* international flights) and the name of the airline (British Airways, Cathay Pacific, PanAm, SwissAir and Aeroflot). If color alone were used for this purpose, ten different colors would be required (five airlines times two origins). By combining color with some other attribute (for example, shape) the number of colors used can be reduced. So for example, internal flights might be symbolized by a square and international flights by a triangle; and the five airlines might be coded red, green, blue, yellow and cyan. Hence a yellow triangle might represent Cathay Pacific and a red square Aeroflot. The ten categories can hence be coded with only five colors. Of course, the number of colors can be reduced further by increasing the number of symbols.

5   Aesthetics

With only a handful of unsuitably chosen colors it is possible to make a display look garish and unattractive. This problem has been coined "color pollution" which helps emphasize the fact that it applies as much to the environment as it does to color displays. For example, in Tokyo in 1981 some new buses appeared on the streets painted in yellow and red. There was a great outcry against the color of these buses by citizens and the media, until the color of the buses was changed to green. The cause of this furore was not simply the precise yellow and red used for the buses, but the combination of these colors with the environment in which they were used. A spokeswoman for the Ministry of International Trade and Industry said[29]:

> "In the busy streets of Japan, which are overloaded with miscellaneous outdoor advertisements, red and yellow are common environmental colors. Tokyo citizens found the addition of red and yellow buses unbearable. This situation is different from the more refined and quiet environmental colors used in various Western cities".

One argument for using color on displays is to encourage user acceptance of a system. It would be a shame to be hoist by one's own petard by using color in a way that made the final display unappealing to users, despite being optimal from the point of view of the visual system. The aim of this section is to provide some ground rules on using color appropriately in this way. This is not simply of interest to the designer of the user-interface; it is likely that artists and graphic designers will be using computer displays progressively more in the near future. One prediction is that the graphic designer of the future will work with a color display as a workbench and a powerful, interactive computer system as a toolbox[30].

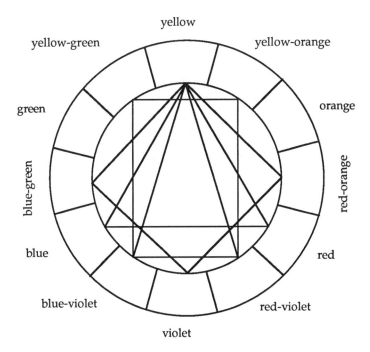

Figure 4.2: Methods for deriving harmonious colors. According to Itten, colors are harmonious if they are complementary: so in this diagram, for example, yellow and violet would be a harmonious pair of colors. Moreover, triads or tetrads of colors may be harmonious. So for example, the rotated square indicates that blue-green, yellow, red-orange and violet are harmonious. Simply rotating the square identifies a second sequence of harmonious colors.

As a preamble, it is important to stress that aesthetics is not an alternative to color coding or formatting, but it should complement color coding. A well designed display will not only help users perform the task, but also encourage them to use the system. After all, if a user has to sit down in front of a system for hours at a time, it is important that he or she enjoys looking at the screen.

Our everyday experience tells us that there are some colors that 'go' with each other, and other colors that clash. This is especially pertinent to the design of computer displays, because it is remarkably easy to use the default color palette of a system to create the most garish and unattractive screens. It would consequently be very useful if psychologists could pass on rules or guidelines for color aesthetics so that designers of displays could avoid the most obvious pitfalls.

Unfortunately, because of individual differences perhaps, this area has been severely neglected in psychology. Colors that 'go' for one person may clash for another. But certainly artists and designers follow a set of heuristics when designing displays: and indeed, textbooks of art frequently talk of 'color harmony', as if it is a body of definite facts. But these facts have not been tested empirically: they are derived through trial and error, and a little theory. This section considers these empirical rules.

The Swiss artist and teacher, Johannes Itten (born 1888), was the most formidable thinker in this area. Just after the First World War, Itten became a master at the famous Bauhaus school of art in Weimar, Germany and he spent much of his life passing on what he saw as the basic elements of color theory. At the Bauhaus he shared the position of master with such notable artists as Paul Klee and Vasily Kandinsky. In 1964, Itten published a major book[31], *The Art of Color*, in which he formulated his ideas on color theory. Itten's main thesis was that there are seven types of color contrast which together 'constitute the fundamental resource of color design' (see Section 6.2). Color harmony is a smaller part of Itten's work, but since it is the part in which we are most interested it will be dealt with at length here.

5.1   Principle 1: Use complementary colors

Itten writes: "Two or more colors are mutually harmonious if their mixture yields a neutral gray". In order to demonstrate these guidelines, Itten provides a 'color circle' that may be used to select harmonious colors. This color circle is represented in Figure 4.2. All complementary pairs, all triads whose colors form equilateral or isosceles triangles, and all tetrads forming squares or rectangles, are claimed to be harmonious. These color combinations are described as 'chords'; some of these chords have been sketched into Figure 4.2 (others can be calculated by simply rotating the triangle, square or rectangle within the color circle).

Given the rigor required for color specification spelt out at length in Chapter 3, this particular color circle may at first sight appear casual. In fact, Itten emphasizes that the colors must appear unique: the three primaries (red, yellow and blue) "must be defined with the greatest possible accuracy... [and] the three secondary colors have to be mixed very carefully". This is achieved by eye, viewing each color against a neutral gray background. Psychophysical experiments show observers are very accurate in their choice of unique hues. Given the number of hues is small, and that this is not meant as a method of color specification, this is not a serious criticism.

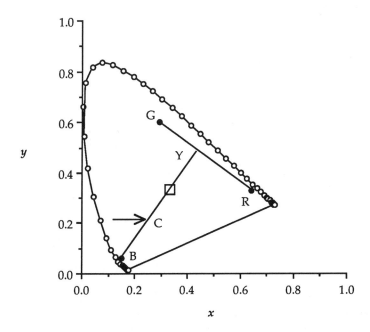

Figure 4.3: Using CIE color space to produce complementary colors. The filled symbols represent the location of the three display phosphors. The open square represents the white point. See text for further details.

Color on displays is produced by additive mixture (see Chapter 1), whereas the three primaries used in Itten's system are subtractive. Now, some color pairs that are complementary for subtractive mixture (where red and green when mixed will form gray) will not be complementary for additive mixture (where red and green will form yellow). As a consequence, the same principle generates different sets of harmonious colors. This appears not to concern graphic designers too much: apparently, each type of complementary relationship is uniquely harmonious[32].

It is very simple to generate pairs of harmonious colors by applying this principle to the CIE (x, y) diagram. To achieve this, carry out the following steps.

1. Choose any color in gamut in the CIE diagram (for example, the color Y in Figure 4.3).
2. Draw a straight line (BY in Figure 4.3) from this color through the white point (for example, $x = 0.333, y = 0.333$).
3. Read off the CIE co-ordinates of the point on the line BY that is equidistant from this point (the color C in Figure 4.3).
4. So long as these two colors have the same luminance, when they are mixed together they will form white ($x = 0.333, y = 0.333$).

5.2   Principle 2: Use a logical sequence

A second principle derived from Itten's work is that a selection of colors will be harmonious if they are arranged in some logical order. The 'logical order' is merely a sequence that can be derived from any of the color spaces described in Chapter 3. This results in an infinite number of harmonious combinations, yet provides a useful constraint on certain combinations to avoid. This is because harmonious colors can be considered to lie close to each other on a vector in color space. So for example, a scale of, say, a dozen colors in HSV color space could be constructed where hue (H) and luminance (V) are kept constant, and only saturation (S) varies. This scale will be harmonious. Similarly, luminance and hue could co-vary, keeping saturation constant, in order to produce a harmonious sequence. In contrast, a set of colors that were chosen randomly in color space will not be harmonious.

Merely paging through a color atlas where colors are laid out in a logical sequence, such as the Munsell Book of Color, will provide you with some feel for this principle. Such color atlases are extremely pleasing to the eye. Plate 11 demonstrates some harmonious and non-harmonious combinations derived in this way. It is not entirely clear if any and all vectors in color space will be harmonious. So for example, would a spiral vector be harmonious? Perhaps the crucial point is that the connection between the various samples can be easily discriminated; this implies that any vector will be harmonious so long as the perceptual steps are small enough.

6 Special problems with color

After you have designed the display, you may notice some odd problems. For example, a color may suddenly appear quite different when presented in conjunction with other colors. The way the visual system works means that there are a number of aberrations or illusions involved in the process of seeing color, and the aim of this section is to bring some of these effects to your attention. Each subsection begins with a particular 'symptom'; the idea is that, having designed a system, you notice these symptoms while prototyping. The following subsections may explain why the effect has happened and how to fix it.

6.1 Using color in the peripheral visual field

6.1.1 Symptoms

Colored objects change their color as the direction of gaze alters; in the extreme visual field they may lose their color altogether; a warning signal fails to attract attention if the user is not looking directly at the signal.

6.1.2 Cause

Originally, it was thought that the peripheral visual field was red/green color deficient, and this led to the development of maps of the retina[33] divided up into color zones. Such figures purport to show regions of visual space in which we are most sensitive to blues, yellows, reds and greens. Figures such as these are useful to designers of color displays because they can be used to support design decisions about which colors should be used where on the screen. For example, if we were relatively insensitive to reds and greens in the peripheral visual field, these might be comparatively poor colors to use if we wanted to present information to the user.

A serious problem with ergonomic guidelines of this sort is that luminance and hue are frequently confounded by the use of color names. There are numerous blues, greens, reds and yellows and unless these are equated for luminance and saturation, it is impossible to say very much about their discriminability from each other. Current guidelines imply that a bright green stimulus on a dark red background will be less perceptible in the periphery than a blue stimulus on an equally bright yellow background. However, this is unlikely given the fact that the luminance differences provided by the first stimulus are likely to be at least as salient as the purely chromatic differences provided by the second. Much of the ergonomic literature on color has not emphasized the fact that luminance differences are as potent an agent for discrimination and detection as are chromatic differences.

In fact, recent psychophysical and physiological evidence for these 'color zones' is lacking. For example, there is no asymmetry in the distribution of the three cone types across the retina[34]. Evidence merely suggests that the nasal retina has a higher *density* of cones and nerve cells than the temporal retina[35]. Psychophysical evidence shows that the drop in color sensitivity outside the fovea affects all hues equally, at least in the perifovea[36], and can be neutralized simply by using larger areas of color[37]. This could be predicted from the fact that progressively more peripheral retina is served by fewer ganglion cells than the central retina[38].

Therefore, with the exception of the fovea, which unarguably has superior color discrimination, and the very central foveal region, which is unarguably blue-blind or tritanopic, there is no firm evidence for regions of specific types of color discrimination within the retina. Our color vision is not so acute in the peripheral visual field, but this affects all hues equally.

6.1.3 *Solution*

If, despite having the same color co-ordinates, the perceived color of an object in the periphery is different to the perceived color of an object in central vision, increase the size of the object in the periphery.

Since the visual system is very sensitive to changes in contrast, luminance changes will be just as effective as chromatic changes in attracting a user's attention. So for warning signals in the peripheral visual field, use large values of luminance and/or chromatic contrast. No one hue will be better than another.

6.2   Color contrast effects

6.2.1 *Symptom*

The perceived color of an object alters as other colors are placed in the scene. Plate 12 demonstrates this effect (known as color contrast). This Plate shows a gray square superimposed upon a split field. The left half of the field is pink and the right half is cyan. Although the gray square is exactly the same color at all points, it looks cyan-ish when superimposed on the pink square and pinkish when superimposed upon the cyan square.

6.2.2 *Cause*

This can be quite simply interpreted from the model of color vision outlined in Chapter 2 as an antagonism between the color of the object and the color of the surround. It suggests the type of color opponency found in second-stage mechanisms.

This antagonism can be used by designers of displays to enhance perceived color. In the nineteenth century, for example, tapestries woven by Michel Chevreul appeared to contain various colors but in fact contained red and gray yarns only[39]; and the artist Constable used flecks of red in his paintings to enhance the perceived green of foliage[40].

6.2.3 Solution

If it is important to avoid "enhancing" color in this way then (1) use a gray or black background on which to view the object; and (2) ensure that different colors in the scene are not adjacent to each other. Contrast effects disappear when the two colors are physically separate from each other.

6.3 Chromatic abberation

6.3.1 Symptom

When saturated blue is used for fine detail or at edges, the image appears blurred.

6.3.2 Cause

The eye is a fascinating optical instrument, but like all optical instruments it suffers from certain physical limitations of which the designer of color displays should be aware. The most notable limitations are diffraction and spherical and chromatic aberration. Diffraction of light causes some blurring of the image, especially for small pupil sizes (that is, high light levels), but this should not be a problem to a user performing under moderate light levels, unless exceedingly fine optical resolution is required. Similarly, the spherical aberration of the lens of the eye causes only a minor degradation of the retinal image.

But the most important optical aberration that designers should note is the longitudinal chromatic aberration of the lens: short-wavelength (violet) light is brought to a focus slightly in front of the retina, and long-wavelength (red) light is brought to a focus slightly behind the retina (see Figure 4.4). The effect is two to three times worse for short- than for long-wavelength light[41]. This is a common problem with optical systems (for example, cameras) where it is overcome by cementing one positive and one negative lens together so that the effects are counterbalanced. Chromatic aberration can be clinically significant (over a dioptre[42], D, of defocus) and the human visual system reduces its effects by placing an inert yellow pigment, known as macular pigment, over the central foveal region. This pigment helps to absorb the short-wave light rays that are so badly blurred by the lens of the eye. However, this pigment does not eradicate the effects of chromatic aberration: it is just good enough in our everyday activities, because the eye is rarely presented with the kind of highly saturated, spectrally narrow-band, stimuli that make chromatic aberration so apparent. But phosphors on electronic displays are highly saturated and certain combinations are likely to reveal the limitations of the human optical system.

The worst combination from the point of view of chromatic aberration would be saturated blue and saturated red, especially with blue used to represent fine detail since blues are blurred to a greater extent. Moreover, because of chromatic aberration, the human lens changes its state of accommodation depending on the wavelength of the incident light. This has been known for quite some time: for example[43], a 700 nm (deep red) target requires 0.47D of over-accommodation; a 546 nm (greenish yellow) target 0.19D of under-accommodation; and a 405 nm (deep violet) target 1.59D of under-accommodation.

What about accommodation to the non-monochromatic colors generated on a color display? When accommodation is measuredwith a conventional display[44], the red primary alone requires 0.14D of over-accommodation, the green 0.14D of under-accommodation and the blue 0.30D of under-accommodation. The effects of chromatic aberration for broadband phosphors are hence predictably not as severe as for monochromatic lights, but the difference between the red and blue primaries (0.44D) is still significant.

6.3.3 Solution

Accommodation is close to normal when any two primaries are simultaneously switched on: hence desaturating the targets removes the problem. If 'eye strain' reflects the degree to which an observer must change accommodation, a display that uses highly saturated reds and blues should be avoided. However, it has been pointed out[45] that the eye has a depth of field of some 0.6 D under good conditions of illumination; this should fully compensate for these effects. Nonetheless, given the discussion below (section 6.5) of perceptual anomalies associated with short-wave stimuli, wise designers will avoid excessive use of blue for spatial detail: this should make the effects discussed here negligible.

6.4   Chromostereopsis

6.4.1 Symptom

Saturated red and blue when presented together appear to lie in different depth planes: the red may appear to literally 'stand out' of the display. A demonstration of this effect may be seen in Plate 13. If you look at this Plate under direct illumination, the red and blue words should appear to lie in different depth planes (the effect can be enhanced by placing pinholes in front of the eyes, while maintaining stereoscopic viewing; see Figure 4.5).

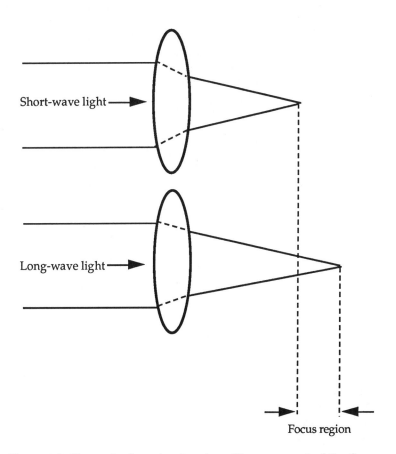

Figure 4.4: Chromatic aberration in a lens. The upper part of the figure shows where short-wave light is brought to a focus; the lower part of the figure shows where long-wave light is brought to a focus. A stimulus that contains both short- and long-wave light will never be perfectly focused by this lens. In a person with 6/6 vision, the retina will lie within the focus region such that short-wave light is focused well in front of the retina, and long-wave light slightly behind the retina.

6.4.2 *Cause*

This effect is known as *chromostereopsis* and was first reported on in the nineteenth century[46]. It results from the fact that the optical axis and the visual axis of the eye are not coincident[47]. This situation can be exaggerated by the use of pinholes and for ease of exposition, Figure 4.5 shows such an exaggerated case. The eye shown on the left half of the figure is an 'ideal' eye in that the optical and visual axes are coincident. However, it still suffers from chromatic aberration. Hence, blue rays are focused in front of the retina, and red rays behind the retina. The red and blue rays form 'blur circles' on the retina, but because these are perfectly superimposed in our ideal eye, our visual system (if we had a pair of eyes like this) would not be subject to chromostereopsis.

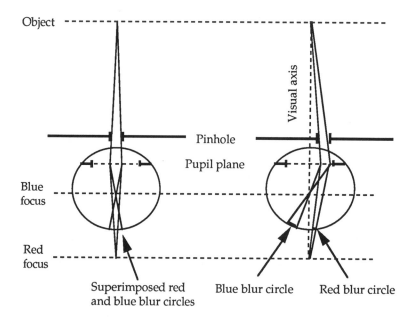

Figure 4.5: The main cause of chromosteropsis is that the optical and visual axes of real eyes are not coincident. This figure shows this by comparing an 'ideal' eye (left) with a 'real' eye (right). (For full explanation see text). After Allen, R. C., and Rubin, M. L. (1981) Chromostereopsis. *Survey of Ophthalmology*, **26**: 22-27.

The right hand diagram exaggerates the real situation. Now the visual and optical axes are misaligned. However, the points of focus for the blue and red rays remains the same as with our ideal eye, because the focal length of the lens of the eye stays the same[48] as we move off the visual axis. But the blur circles formed by the blue and red rays will obviously change, as shown in the figure. We now have two images, spatially displaced on the retina. Given a fellow eye, subject to the same misalignment, we now have the conditions required for stereopsis. Hence the illusion of depth.

However, this explanation is only valid for small pupil sizes. With large pupil sizes it is often found that the depth effect reverses: that is, if a subject sees red in front of blue with small pupils, he may see blue in front of red with larger pupils. One explanation of this[49] has been in terms of the fact that for cone vision, light entering the center of the pupil appears brighter than light entering off-center. This effect, known as the Stiles-Crawford effect after its discovers, is due to the fact that the cone cells are anatomically oriented towards the center of the pupil. Essentially, with large pupils, the Stiles-Crawford effect causes the retinal regions of maximal sensitivity to change with changing pupil size. This shifts the effective binocular retinal disparity, and may even cause the illusion to reverse.

6.4.3 *Solution*

Avoid simultaneous use of saturated red and saturated blue.

6.5   Luminance differences

6.5.1 *Symptom*

Despite large differences in hue, a particular combination of text and background color is hard to read (for example, blue on black or yellow on white). The outline of an object (for example, a window on a display) is hard to distinguish from the background. A moving object (for example, a mouse cursor) is difficult to locate or track.

6.5.2 *Cause*

A common question among display designers is: which pairs of colors should (or should not) be used in a text processing task?[50] This question is a surprisingly complex one, since (given a high quality graphics display with a potential of showing over sixteen million colors) there is an almost infinite number of possible combinations. Moreover, since the red, green and blue primaries may vary considerably from one display to another, so-called 'optimal' combinations may be monitor-specific. This accounts for the fact that many guidelines are contradictory on this issue, especially since most of the human factors guidelines have been developed from work on displays with comparatively small color palettes. For example, with the introduction of the IBM EGA card in the 1980s, a number of studies looked at various combinations of foreground text and background colors, rigorously comparing each of the 120 possible combinations[51]. However, since the chromaticities and especially the relative luminances of the three phosphors varies so much between displays, very little of this work can be generalized. This is because, on one display, the red and blue primaries may have very similar luminances, whereas on another display the luminances may differ by a factor of two. Consequently, the results of many studies apply only to the very display on which the guidelines were derived.

It is instructive to consider one frequent recommendation, that is to avoid yellow text on a white background. When the 'yellow' and 'white' are selected from the standard EGA set of colors, the resulting color combination is indeed extremely difficult to read. Is this because of some special feature of the two chosen hues? Consider how these two colors are produced with the EGA card. 'Yellow' is produced by maximally modulating the red and green primaries (R+G) whereas 'white' is produced by maximally modulating all three primaries (R+G+B). Now, the blue primary on a crt contains little luminance information, and consequently the 'yellow' and 'white' have very similar luminances since they differ only in the contribution of the blue primary. Hence, any problem in reading 'yellow' text on a 'white' background can be ascribed to the very similar luminances of the two colors[52] (see also Chapter 2). This can be simply demonstrated on any 8-bit frame buffer display that allows independent variation of foreground text and background colors. Try out the previously taboo combination of yellow on white and you will find that altering the luminance contrast alone, and leaving the hue unchanged, will render completely illegible text easily readable.

In practice, this makes it very easy to generate guidelines for the use of color for text displays. The central tenet is that luminance contrast is vital (Chapter 5 describes how to measure contrast). So the hue and saturation of the text foreground and background may be disregarded, with certain qualifications. (The main qualification is to avoid saturated blue and saturated red; see Sections 6.3 and 6.4). This means that so long as the luminance contrast is the same, green on blue will be as legible as yellow on white.

These effects may be caused by the fact that the object and the background have very similar luminances. Psychophysical evidence[53] suggests that the luminance channel is better equipped for many visual tasks than the chromatic channel (see Chapter 2). For example, the luminance channel outperforms the chromatic channels on tests of spatial vision (such as form perception and acuity) and motion perception. Hence, despite large differences in hue and/or saturation, performance deficits will be found if the luminances of the two colors are similar.

Performance deficits are especially noticeable when visual discrimination depends only on signals in S cones. But this does not mean that you should avoid the use of blue on your display (except for the use of saturated blue to represent fine detail; see above), since the M cones are very sensitive to light that appears blue to us. However, it does mean that you should avoid discriminations that depend *only* on S cones. These types of discrimination can be predicted from the SML color space described in Chapter 3. Large areas of color where discrimination is unimportant, such as the background color of a display, often appear very pleasing in blue.

However the use of different colors that are *discriminated* only by S cones should be avoided. There are a number of reasons for this. The first is that, because of the relative paucity of short-wave receptors in the very center of the fovea, the normal retina is blue-blind or 'tritanopic' over the central 25 minutes of visual angle[54]. Clearly, if two small stimuli are to be discriminated in an application based on color coding, they should be able to be discriminated by M and/or L cones.

Although there is currently some disagreement about whether short-wave cones do or do not contribute to our perception of luminance (see Chapter 2), because of their comparative rarity and insensitivity any input from short-wave cones to a luminance system must be slight indeed, and for most practical purposes can probably be ignored. Consequently, stimuli that differ only in their relative excitation of S cones will not differ in luminance. Because a luminance difference is needed to detect edges, such stimuli should not be placed adjacent to each other. For example, on a terminal screen with multiple windows, the windows should not differ from each other only in their amount of blue or their edges will appear fuzzy and indistinct. This could be easily remedied by drawing a black or white border around each window.

6.5.3 *Solution*

The color of an object and its background should differ in luminance; this is especially so for reading from color displays, for example[55]. For alphanumerics, aim for a luminance contrast of at least 3:1 between text characters and the background. For non-alphanumerics, this can be most easily achieved by drawing a black or white border around the object.

6.6   Disturbing visual after effects

6.6.1 Symptom

After staring at large areas of bright color, other colors appear less vivid. After reading green text on a black background, source documents appear pinkish.

6.6.2 Cause

At some time or another, we have all experienced an after-image. For example, one after-image to which we have all been exposed is that caused by a photographic flash. After-images are fixed on the retina, and this is why they appear to float about in space and change perceived size. After-images may be caused by bright, high contrast displays. Because they act like a veiling reflection, an after-image will cause an apparent desaturation of screen color. When the retina is exposed to a green light for some time, objects in the world may begin to take on a rosy glow when the light is extinguished.

Frequently, these after-images last for many hours, or even days. In this case, they are not after-images, but the result of a perceptual phenomenon known as a *color-contingent* after-effect. The classical demonstration of this is known as the McCullough effect[56], after its discoverer. An observer is adapted to a pattern of leftward-tilted green and black bars and rightward-tilted red and black bars. It is hence a pattern in which color is contingent on orientation. When the same pattern is viewed in black-and-white, leftward-tilted bars look pinkish and rightward-tilted bars look greenish. One explanation of the effect is that there are neurons in the visual system sensitive to both the color and the orientation of an object; when these neurons are adapted, either in the laboratory or in front of the green-phosphor visual display, they cannot make their normal contribution when viewing a monochrome pattern.

6.6.3 Solution

Take regular work pauses (see Chapter 5). Additionally, the McCullough effect can be most easily abolished by avoiding saturated, colored text on a black background.

7   Coding, formatting and design: key points

General
- *Design for monochrome first.*
- *Use the user's model of how color is used in the real world.*

Formatting
• *Choose a dark or dim background, such as deep blue on a crt, and bright foreground colors.*
• *Relate separate areas by using a common hue, for example a common background or text color.*
• *Highlight regions by using colors that contrast with the background in hue, saturation and luminance.*
• *Be careful not to highlight too many groups at once. Restrict highlighting to one or two key items.*
• *Where legibility is important (for example, for text/background combinations) choose a foreground color that contrasts at least 3:1 with the background.*
• *Try not to use more than about five different colors at any one time.*

Coding
• *Question whether color coding is the best way to represent the information. There are numerous methods of coding information: is color the best for this particular application?*
• *Follow the six principles: the chosen colors should be discriminable, detectable, perceptually equal, meaningful, consistent and aesthetically pleasing.*
• *Distinguish the information you wish to code as either categories or names, quantitative information or ordered categories or names.*
• *Categories or names: use large hue differences. This emphasizes its categorical nature.*
• *Ordered categories or names: use large hue differences unless it is important to maintain the rank order of the data. If the rank order must be preserved, follow the guidelines for coding quantitative information.*
• *Quantitative information: use small hue differences, or a saturation or luminance code. These scales emphasize the relationship between different levels of the information.*
• *Except for quantitative information, restrict the number of colors to around half-a-dozen. If it is necessary to code more states than this, consider multidimensional coding.*

Aesthetics
• *Color displays should be aesthetically pleasing as well as functional.*
• *For pleasing displays, follow the two principles of color harmony: complementary colors are harmonious; and harmony = order.*

Special Effects
• *Avoid saturated blue for fine detail.*
• *Avoid saturated red and blue in conjunction.*

• *Perceived color changes with the presence of other colors in the scene, due to color contrast. Where important color judgements are to be made, objects should be viewed against an achromatic background.*
• *Be aware of the short-and long-term effects of visual adaptation.*

8   Further reading

Christ, R. E. (1977) Review and analysis of color coding research for visual displays. *Human Factors*, **17**: 542-570.

The classic review of color coding, mainly concerned with visual search tasks.

Durrett, H. J. (1987) (Ed.) *Color and the Computer*. London: Academic Press.

The second half of this book contains a set of case studies concerned with color coding displays. Some of the papers are of patchy quality, but the paper by Reising and Aretz on computer graphics in military cockpits is particularly interesting.

Gallitz, W. O. (1985) *Handbook of Screen Format Design*. QED Information Services Inc: Mass.

An excellent source of general design information.

MacDonald, W. A. and Cole, B. L. (1988) Evaluating the role of colour in a flight information cockpit display. *Ergonomics*, **31**: 13-37.

A case study that identifies tasks for which color is suited and which emphasizes the need for a full analysis of the user's tasks.

Robertson, P. J. (1980) *A Guide to Using Colour on Alphanumeric Displays*. IBM Technical Report G 320-6296-0. IBM United Kingdom Laboratories Ltd.

Although this is now rather dated, it still provides a source of sensible advice for the designer of non-graphical color displays, especially form-filling type systems.

Smith, S. L. and Mosier, J. N. (1986) *Guidelines for designing User Interface Software* (Technical Report ESD-TR-86-278), Hanscom Air Force Base, MA: USAF Electronic System Division.

A set of general and specific guidelines for screen design, with some comments on color.

Walraven, J. (1985) The colours are not on the display: a survey of non-veridical perceptions that may turn up on a colour display. *Displays*, **6**: 35-42.

An entertaining review of special effects that you may (or may not) wish to produce.

9 Notes and References

1 Christ, R. E. (1975) Review and analysis of color coding research for visual displays. *Human Factors*, **17**: 542-570; Kellog, R. S., Kennedy, R. S. and Woodruff, R. R. (1983) Comparison of colour and black-and-white visual displays as indicated by bombing performance in the 2B35 TA-4J flight simulator. *Displays*, **4**: 106-107; Stokes, A., Wickens, C. and Kite, K. (1990) *Display Technology: Human Factors Concepts*. Chapter 7. Philadelphia: Society of Automative Engineers.

2 Other reviews can be found in: Cowan, W. (1988) Colour psychophysics and display technology: avoiding the wrong answers and finding the right questions. *SPIE Vol 901 Image Processing, Analysis, Measurement and Quality*, pp 186-193; Davidoff, J. (1987) The role of colour in visual displays. *International Review of Ergonomics*, **1**: 21-42; Kaufmann, R. and McFadden, S. M. (1989) The use of colour on electronic displays. *Proceedings of the Annual Conference of the Human Factors Association of Canada*, pp 21-30; Murch, G. M. (1986) Human factors of colour displays. In F. R. A. Hopgood, R. J. Hubbold and D. A. Duce (eds.) *Advances in Computer Graphics II*. Berlin: Springer-Verlag.

3 For simplicity, luminance is considered rather than brightness; see Chapter 2, Section 2.4.2.

4 Davidoff, J. B., Ostergaard, A. L. (1988) The role of colour in categorical judgements. *Quarterly J. Experimental Psychology*, **40A**: 533-544.

5 For examples of this see McDonald, J. E., Molander, M. E. and Noel, R. N. (1988) Color-coding categories in menus. *CHI '88 Proceedings, Association for Computing Machinery*, pp 101-106; Paul, R. J. and Helander, M. G. (1989) Effectiveness of a color metaphor in menu navigation. *Proceedings of the Annual Conference of the Human Factors Association of Canada*, pp 145-149.

6 There is a complication here because the feasible region (that is, the region containing all the colors that (a) can be generated on the display and (b) agree with the constraints) is of a quite complicated nature (W. De Corte, personal communication).

7 Carter, R. C. and Carter, E. C. (1982) High-contrast sets of colors. *Applied Optics*, **21**: 2936-2939; DeCorte W. (1990) Recent developments in the computation of ergonomically optimal contrast sets of CRT colours. *Displays*, **11**: 123-128.

8 Hanes, R. M. and Rhoades, M. V. (1959) Color identification as a function of extended practice. *J. Optical Society of America*, **49**: 1060-1064.

9 Boynton, R. M., Fargo, L., Olson, C. X. and Smallman, H. S. (1989) Category effects in color memory. *Color Research and Application*, **14**: 229-234; Smallman, H. S. and Boynton, R. M. (1990) Segregation of basic colors in an information display. *J. Optical Society of America*, **A7**: 1985-1994.

10 Simon, J. R. (1984) The effect of redundant cues on retrieval time. *Human Factors*, **26**: 315-321.

11 For an excellent review of this area see Gallitz, W. O. (1985) *Handbook of Screen Format Design*. QED Information Services Inc: Mass.

12 See, for example, Johnson-Laird, P. N. (1989) Mental models. In M. I. Posner (ed.) *Foundations of Cognitive Science*, pp 469-499, Cambridge, MA: MIP Press; and Wilson, J. R. and Rutherford, A. (1989) Mental models: theory and application in human factors. *Human Factors*, **31**: 617-634.

13 Hall, C. (1989) Pink cells to calm inmates who see red. *The Independent*, 14th April.

14 For an excellent review of this area see Kaiser, P. K. (1984) Physiological responses to color: a critical review. *Color Research and Application*, **9**: 29-36.

15 Damhorst, M. L. and Reed, J. A. P. (1986) Clothing color value and facial expression: effects on evaluations of female job applicants. *Social Behaviour and Personality*, **14**: 89-98.

16 Bergum, B. O. and Bergum, J. E. (1981) Population stereotypes: an attempt to measure and define. *Proceedings of the Human Factors Society*, 25th Annual Meeting, pp 622-665. Human Factors Society.

17 Courtney, A. J. (1986) Chinese population stereotypes: color associations. *Human Factors*, **28**: 97-99.

18 Smith, S. L. and Mosier, J. N. (1986) *Guidelines for designing User Interface Software* (Technical Report ESD-TR-86-278), Hanscom Air

Force Base, MA: USAF Electronic System Division. (NTIS No. AD A1777 198).

19 Salomon, G. (1990) in B. Laurel (ed.) *The Art of HCI Design*. Addison Wesley.

20 The related area of the use of color in cartography is not considered here. For a review see Olson, J. M. (1987) Color and the computer in cartography. In H. J. Durrett (ed.) *Color and the Computer*, pp 205-219. London: Academic Press.

21 For a discussion of this see De Weert, C. M. M. (1986) Superimposition of colour information. *Color Research and Application*, 11: S21-S26. For a comprehensive treatment of the role of colour coding in circuit board layout, see Beretta, G. B. (1988) *Selecting colours for representing VLSI layout*. Report number P88-00226, Xerox PARC, California; and Beretta, G. B. (1988) *A new approach to imaging IC layout and schematics*. Report number P87-00013, Xerox PARC, California.

22 Miller, G. A. (1956) The magical number seven plus or minus two: some limits on our capacity for processing information. *Psychological Review*, 63: 81-97.

23 The more meaningful string of characters is effectivecolordisplays

24 van Laar, D. L. (1989) Evaluating a colour coding programming support tool. In A. Sutcliffe and L. Macaulay (eds.) *People and Computers V*. CUP: Cambridge. pp 217-230.

25 Hopkin, V. D. (1986) Delimiting words in a display by colour instead of spacing. *J. Institution of Electronic and Radio Engineers*, 56: 117-122.

26 Boynton, R. M. and Dolensky, S. (1979) On knowing books by their colours. *Perceptual and Motor Skills*, 48: 479-488.

27 Hertzman, C., Walter, S. D., From, L. and Alison, A. (1987) Observer perception of skin color in a study of malignant melanoma. *American Journal of Epidemiology*, 126: 901-911.

28 Lippman, A. W., Bender, W., Solomon, G. and Saito, M. (1985) Colour word processing. *IEEE Computer Graphics and Applications*, 5: 41-46.

29 Kodama, A. (1990) The problems of environmental colour design in Japan. *Ergonomics*, 33: 763-774.

30 Stone, M. C. (1986) Color, graphic design, and computer systems. *Color Research and Application*, 11: S75.

31 Itten, J. (1961) *The Art of Color: The Subjective Experience and Objective Rationale of Color.* Trans, Ernst van Haagen, New York: Van Nostrand Reinhold. This is a substantial book (about 11 x 12 inches, with 155 pages). For an abridged version, see Itten, J. (1970) *The Elements of Color.* Trans, Ernst van Haagen, New York: Van Nostrand Reinhold.

32 Heddell, P. (1988) Color harmony: new applications of existing concepts. *Color Research and Application,* 13: 55-57; Marx, E. (1983) *Optical Color and Simultaneity.* New York: Van Nostrand Reinhold.

33 For example, Murch, G. M. (1984) Physiological principles for the effective use of color. *IEEE Computer Graphics and Applications,* November: 49-54; Boring, E. G., Langfeld, H. S. and Weld, H. P. (1948) *Foundations of Psychology.* New York: John Wiley and Sons.

34 For contrary psychophysical evidence see Wooton, B. R., Wald, G. (1973) Color-Vision mechanisms in the peripheral retinas of normal and dichromatic observers. *J. General Physiology,* 61: 125-145. For contrary anatomical evidence see Marc, R. E. and Sperling, H. G. (1977) Chromatic organization of primate cones. *Science,* 196: 454-456.

35 Perry, V. H., and Cowey, A. (1985) The ganglion cell and cone distributions in the monkey's retina: implications for cortical magnification factors. *Vision Research,* 25: 1795-1810.

36 Healey, A. and Travis, D. S. (1990) unpublished observations.

37 Noorlander, C., Koenderink, J. J., Ouden, R. J. and Edens, W. (1983) Sensitivity to spatiotemporal colour contrast in the peripheral visual field. *Vision Research,* 23: 1-11.

38 Precise equations for scaling the size of objects so that they are as easily detected in the periphery as they are in central vision have been developed. See Rovamo, J. and Virsu, V. (1979) An estimation and application of the human cortical magnification factor. *Experimental Brain Research,* 37: 495-510. For a review of this area see Pointer, J. S. (1986) The cortical magnification factor and photopic vision. *Biological Reviews,* 61: 97-119.

39 Sekuler, R. and Blake, R. (1985) *Perception* p 202. Alfred A. Knopf, New York.

40 MacDonald, L. W. (1990) Using colour effectively in displays for computer-human interface. *Displays,* 11: 129-141.

41 Millodot, M. (1986) *Dictionary of Optometry.* London: Butterworths, p 1.

42 The dioptre (abbreviated D) is a measure of the refractive power of a lens. Specifically, it is equal to the reciprocal of the focal length in metres of the lens. So a lens with a focal length of 1 m has a power of 1D; and a lens with a focal length of 0.5 m has a power of 2D.

43 Bedford, R. E. and Wyszecki G. W. (1957) Axial chromatic aberation of the human eye. *J. Optical Society of America*, **47**: 564.

44 Murch, G. M. (1983) Visual accommodation and convergence to multi-chromatic display terminals. *Proceedings of the Society for Information Display*, **24**: 67-72.

45 Campbell, F. W. (1957) The depth of field in the human eye. *Optica Acta*, **4**: 157-164.

46 Donders, F. C. (1868), cited in Allen, R. C. and Rubin, M. L. (1981) Chromostereopsis. *Survey of Ophthalmology*, **26**: 22-27.

47 The optical axis of the eye is defined by a line drawn through the optical centers of the cornea and the lens; the visual axis by a line connecting the fovea and the object under regard.

48 This is a simplification. The lens of the eye suffers from spherical aberation which, in reality, would slightly alter the exact points of focus of the red and blue rays.

49 Vos, J. J. (1960) Some new aspects of colour stereoscopy. *J. Optical Society of America*, **50**: 785-790.

50 For a selection of references on this topic see: Bouma, H (1980) Visual reading processes and the quality of text displays. In E. Grandjean and E. Vigliani (eds.) *Ergonomic Aspects of Visual Display Terminals* pp 101-115; Lalomia, M. J. and Happ, A. J. (1987) The effective use of colour for text on the IBM 5153 colour display. *Proceedings of the Human Factors Society - 31st Annual Meeting*; Legge, G. E. and Rubin, G. S. (1986) Psychophysics of reading. IV. Wavelength effects in normal and low vision. *J. Optical Society of America*, **A**. **3**: 40-51; Legge, G. E., Parish, D. H., Luebker, A. and Wurm, L. H. (1990) Psychophysics of reading X1. Comparing color contrast and luminance contrast. *J. Optical Society of America*, **A**. **7**: 2002-2010; Matthews, M. L. (1987) The influence of colour on CRT reading performance and subjective comfort under operational conditions. *Applied Ergonomics* **18**: 323-328; Matthews, M. L. and Mertins, K. (1987) The influence of colour on visual search and subjective discomfort using CRT displays. *Proceedings of the Human Factors Society - 31st Annual Meeting 1987*; Matthews, M. L., and Mertins, K. (1988) Working with colour CRTs: pink eye, yellow fever and feeling blue. In Megaw, E. D. (ed.) *Contemporary Ergonomics* pp 228-233; Mills, C.B. and Weldon, L. J.

(1987) Reading text from computer screens. *ACM Computing Surveys* **19**: 329-358; Radl, G. W. (1980) Experimental investigations for optimal presentation-mode and colours of symbols on the CRT screen. In E. Grandjean and E. Vigliani (eds.) *Ergonomic Aspects of Visual Display Terminals* pp 127-137; Small, P. L. (1982) Factors influencing the legibility of text/background colour combinations on the IBM 3279 colour display station. IBM Hursley Park Report number HF066.

51 The EGA card has a gamut of 16 foreground and 8 background colours. The 'high intensity' colors cannot be used as backgrounds; hence for combinations using 'low intensity' foreground colors, there are 56 possible combinations (7 foreground with 8 background); and for those combinations using 'high intensity' foreground colors there are 64 color combinations (8 foreground with 8 background) giving a total of 120 combinations.

52 Travis, D. S., Bowles, S., Seton, J. and Peppe, R. (1990) Reading from color displays: a psychophysical model. *Human Factors,* **32**: 147-156.

53 Cavanagh, P. (1987) Reconstructing the third dimension: interactions between color, texture, motion, binocular disparity, and shape. *Computer Vision, Graphics, and Image Processing,* **37**: 171-195; Ingling, C. R. and Grigsby, S. C. (1990) Perceptual correlates of magnocellular and parvocellular channels: seeing form and depth in afterimages. *Vision Research,* **30**: 823-828; Livingstone, M. S. and Hubel, D. H. (1987) Psychophysical evidence for separate channels for the perception of form, color, movement, and depth. *J. Neuroscience,* **7**: 3416-3468; Lu, C. and Fender, D. H. (1972) The interaction of color and luminance in stereoscopic vision. *Investigative Ophthalmology,* **11**: 482-490; Troscianko, T. and Fahle, M. (1988) Why do isoluminant stimuli appear slower? *J. Optical Society of America* **A5**: 871-880.

54 Williams, D. R., MacLeod, D. I. A. and Hayhoe, M. (1981) Foveal tritanopia. *Vision Research,* **21**: 1341-1356.

55 Travis, D. S., Bowles, S., Seton, J. and Peppe, R. (1990) Reading from color displays: a psychophysical model. *Human Factors,* **32**: 147-156.

56 For a general review see Stromeyer, C. F. (1978) Form-color aftereffects in human vision. In Held, R., Leibowitz, H. W. and Teuber, H. L. (eds.) *Handbook of Sensory Physiology, Vol VIII Perception* pp 97-142. New York, Springer Verlag. For the specific example of visual displays see: Greenwald, M. J., Greenwald, S. L. and Blake, R. (1983) Long lasting visual after effect from viewing a computer video display. *New England Journal of Medicine,* **309**: 315; Allan, L. G., Siegal. S.,

Collins, J. C. and MacQueen, G. M. (1989) Color after effect contingent on text. *Perception and Psychophysics*, **46**: 105-113.

5

CALIBRATION AND EVALUATION

1   Overview

The scope of this chapter is using ergonomic principles to optimize the performance of users of color workstations. Its objective is to give readers the necessary information to begin 'hands on' evaluation of color workstations. A 'workstation' is a generic term comprising the visual display terminal, the human-computer interface and the environment within which these are used. Hence, it is convenient to consider the user as interacting with four broad environments: (i) The hardware environment, mainly the image quality of the display itself; (ii) The software environment, mainly the human-computer interface; (iii) The user's immediate, or 'micro' environment, such as seating and desk space; (iv) The user's extended, or 'macro', environment, such as lighting and noise.

The first two areas have been considered in detail in earlier chapters. Consequently, in this chapter, the treatment of the hardware environment is restricted to calibration methods for color displays; and the treatment of the software environment is restricted to an outline of user-centered design. The final two sections are broadly concerned with environmental ergonomics.

2   The hardware environment: evaluating the visual display

This section is intended to provide the necessary practical information for evaluating the color image quality of visual displays. The measuring techniques described have been developed on cathode ray tubes, but the principles will apply to any display technology. The measurements described are not exhaustive in that they do not cover all areas of image quality, such as text legibility, nor do they set minimum standards. Readers are referred elsewhere for such treatments[1].

The human eye is fairly insensitive to *gradual* changes in chromaticity and luminance in space and time. Because of this, on casual inspection of uncontroled colored images, such as natural scenes, color cathode ray displays appear to render scenes veridically. In fact, these gradual changes introduce significant errors when accurate color specification is required, as is often the case in industrial and scientific applications. The greatest source of error is caused by the non-linear relationship between display luminance and voltage, and even casual users of color should take account of this by correcting their display. Other sources of error are important only when color is to be carefully used and specified.

2.1   Measuring chromaticity

In order to perform color space manipulations of the type described in Chapter 3, the chromaticity co-ordinates of the display need to be specified in CIE 1931 (x, y) co-ordinates. Manufacturers of high quality displays usually include these data with the technical specifications; but chromaticities may change with time and spatial location on the screen (see below) so when accurate color specification is important, it is preferable to measure these co-ordinates yourself.

If accurate color specification is important, you will need to invest in a colorimeter. Colorimeters filter light with three filters whose spectral transmittance is identical to the CIE XYZ color matching functions described in Chapters 2 and 3. There are a number of devices available but they are not cheap (usually more than the visual display itself), and the hand-held ones may not be accurate. All devices operate in essentially the same way: you simply point the colorimeter at the screen, press a button or run a computer program, and read off the chromaticity co-ordinates.

2.2   Measuring luminance

As was pointed out in Chapter 3, one assumption underlying the color space transformations is that lights behave linearly: that is, the luminance produced by mixing two lights together is simply the algebraic sum of the two individual luminances. This assumption is generally true for lights, but it will not be true for the voltages applied to the display guns: this is because the 'linearity assumption' is violated in at least five ways with modern displays.

Before considering these violations, how is luminance measured? As with colorimetric measurements, there are now many devices on the market of the point-and-shoot variety. Photometers filter light with a filter whose spectral transmittance is identical to the CIE Y color matching function described in Chapter 2. Photometers can be purchased fairly cheaply and are adequate for measuring relative luminances; absolute measurements of luminance require more accurate equipment but these are not necessary for color space manipulations, since relative measurements are sufficient.

2.2.1 Linearity violation 1: Gamma

In an ideal display, the function relating display luminance and voltage would be linear. Mathematically, if D is the value sent to the digital-to-analog convertor and L is the luminance, then this ideal relationship could be expressed as:

$$L = m . D + c$$

where m and c are scaling constants. Moreover, if L and D are normalized to lie between zero and unity, as is usually the case, then the ideal relationship simplifies to:

$$L = D$$

In practice, the function is found to be non-linear. The actual luminance is typically modeled by a function of the form

$$L = D^\gamma$$

where γ is a constant that depends, among other things, on the luminance and contrast settings of the screen and which particular phosphor is being examined. Because of the γ exponent, the relationship is often described as a gamma function.

Think for a moment what this means to the color space transformations described in Chapter 3. Those transformations yield three RGB values; those RGB values represent proportions of the maximum luminance. So for example, RGB(0.5, 0.5, 0.5) means that each primary should be set at half of its maximum luminance. But with color displays, the programmer has control over the voltages sent to the digital to analog convertor (see Chapter 1); he has no direct control over the luminance. In order not to violate the linearity assumption, it is necessary to linearize, or 'gamma correct', the system. Otherwise, the specification RGB (0.5, 0.5, 0.5) may set each primary at only about 20% of its maximum luminance (see Figure 5.1). This is simply achieved by inverting the function, that is by computing

$$D_c = D^{1/\gamma}$$

where D_c is the gamma corrected value that should be passed to the digital to analog convertor, D is the value before gamma-correction, and γ is a constant. In a nutshell, gamma correction is the process where voltage values are computed to generate required luminances.

Where accurate color specification is not vital, a gamma may be assumed of between 2.0 and 3.5. But where accuracy is required, the function should be measured precisely with a photometer, and gamma should then be estimated formally. Linearity can then be achieved by table look-up.

Sometimes, the measured relationship is poorly described by a gamma function. If this is the case for your display, an alternative is to plot the data on a double logarithmic plot (using natural logarithms). This type of plot is usually well fit by a straight line, and is hence simple to invert. A second alternative is to perform a piecewise linear interpolation between each measured point; this is reported to give accurate results[2].

Unfortunately, the gamma function may change in the short term (day to day fluctuations) and the long term (month to month drifts). Moreover, because of the Earth's magnetic field, it may even change with screen orientation. Consequently, the screen should be calibrated exactly where it is to be used and calibrations should be performed frequently.

2.2.1.1 Measuring the gamma function
1. First, create the pattern on the screen. An ideal pattern consists of a set of horizontal or vertical stripes. During gamma correction, two of the three guns should be fixed in voltage (usually at zero, although see Section 2.2.3). The third gun is increased in predetermined steps from zero to maximum voltage. So for example, if you were calibrating the green primary in a system with 8 bits per pixel, you would set the red and blue primaries to zero and step the green primary between 0 and 255 in steps of (say) 16.

In order to equalize the power drain on the screen, when the dac value n is placed in one stripe, put the dac value (maximum dac value

- n) in the adjacent stripes. So in the example above, the stripe that you are calibrating might have the values RGB(0, 16, 0); and the adjacent stripes should have the values RGB(0, 239, 0). So long as you have a reasonable number of stripes on the screen, the power drain should be constant as you step through all the chosen dac values. Be wary of using too many stripes or else the stripe you are measuring will be so thin that you may begin to measure flare from the adjacent stripes.

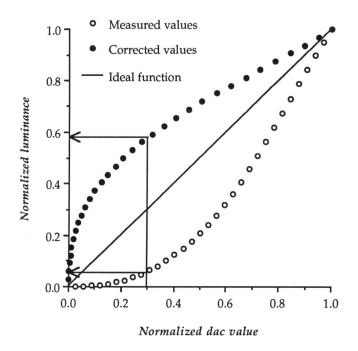

Normalized dac value

Figure 5.1: Graphical representation of display gamma correction (fictitious data). The straight line represents the ideal gamma function: the luminance of a display with this characteristic would be perfectly linear with changes in dac voltage. The open symbols represent the actual gamma function: this is obtained by measuring the luminance at each dac level for a particular display primary (the data have been normalized). The filled symbols represent the gamma corrected values. Take as an example a dac value of 0.3. In an ideal display, this would yield 30% of the luminance. However, in the display represented here, a dac value of 0.3 yields about only 5% of the luminance. By tracing the line up to the corrected function, we can see that to obtain 30% of the luminance we actually require a dac value of about 0.58. In practice, this interpolation can be achieved by simple table look-up: see Section 2.2.1.1.

2. For a fixed number of voltages, measure the associated luminance. Some real data are shown in the first two columns of Table 5.1. This represents a subset of the data; the full data set are plotted in Figures 5.2 and 5.3. For this particular 8-bit display, the dac values spanned the range from 0 to 255. The reason that there is some residual luminance (1.45 cd/m^2) for a dac value of zero is because the measurements were not carried out in a totally dark environment.

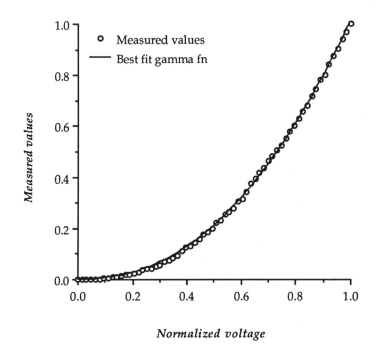

Figure 5.2: Measurement of the gamma function (real data). The open symbols show the voltage / luminance data from Table 5.1. The solid line is the best fitting gamma function. For these data the best fitting function had $\gamma = 2.26$.

3. Now normalize the values so that they range between 0 and 1. In our example, each dac value was simply divided by 255 and the resulting value placed in the third column, 'Normalized voltage'. To normalize the luminances, 1.45 was first subtracted from each value so that they began at zero, and then each value was divided by the

maximum (52.45 - 1.45 = 51.0). These normalized values are shown in the fourth column..

4. Next, fit a mathematical function to the data. There are a number of options. Figures 5.2 and 5.3 show two choices. In Figure 5.2 (from columns 3 and 4) the data are fit with a function of the form

$$y = x^{\gamma}$$

In this example, the best fit to the data were found with $\gamma = 2.26$.

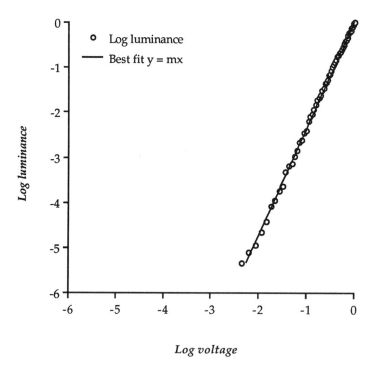

Log voltage

Figure 5.3: Measurement of the gamma function (real data). The open symbols represent the natural log of the voltage *versus* the natural log of the luminance (see Table 5.1). The straight line is the best fitting function of the form $y = mx$. For these data, m = 2.38.

Alternatively, you could take the natural logarithm of the data (Figure 5.3 and columns 5 and 6). These data may then be fit with a function of the form:

$$y = mx$$

In this example, the best fit to the data were found with m = 2.38.

5. Finally, it is necessary to invert the function. With a gamma fit, this is achieved by computing:

$$x = y^{1/\gamma}$$

For the log-log plot this is achieved by computing:

$$x = \frac{y}{m}$$

Table 5.1: Worked example of gamma correction. These are a subset of the data graphed in Figures 5.2 and 5.3.

Dac value (voltage)	Luminance (cd/m^2)	Normalized voltage	Normalized luminance	Natural log (normalized voltage)	Natural log (normalized luminance)
0	1.45	0.00	0.00	—	—
16	1.45	0.06	0.00	-2.77	—
32	1.81	0.13	0.01	-2.08	-4.95
48	2.41	0.19	0.02	-1.67	-3.96
64	3.51	0.25	0.04	-1.38	-3.21
80	4.96	0.31	0.07	-1.16	-2.68
96	7.14	0.38	0.11	-0.98	-2.19
112	9.56	0.44	0.16	-0.82	-1.84
128	12.71	0.50	0.22	-0.69	-1.51
144	15.62	0.56	0.28	-0.57	-1.28
160	20.46	0.63	0.37	-0.47	-0.99
176	23.74	0.69	0.44	-0.37	-0.83
192	28.21	0.75	0.52	-0.28	-0.64
208	33.55	0.82	0.63	-0.20	-0.46
224	39.48	0.88	0.75	-0.13	-0.29
240	46.02	0.94	0.87	-0.06	-0.13
255	52.45	1.00	1.00	0.00	0.00

6. Now given any required voltage between 0 and 1, insert this as the y value in the inverted gamma function. The resultant x value is the gamma-corrected voltage that should actually be sent to the digital-to-analog convertor.

2.2.2 Linearity violation 2: Misconvergence

In an ideal cathode ray display, the three electron beams are perfectly converged (see Chapter 1). This means that the electron guns hit the pixel at which they are aimed. In reality, all cathode ray tubes suffer some degree of misconvergence and this is especially evident around the edges of displays. For text-only applications, fairly high degrees of misconvergence may be tolerated; users perceive this as a slight blurring of the characters. However, misconvergence can disrupt reading ability: performance decrements may be demonstrated when subjects use a word processing package on a monitor with only 20% misconvergence[3]. However, where accurate color specification is important, smaller degrees of misconvergence are required. For example, screen misconvergence can help a color deficient observer pass a color vision test[4], because it can lead to a clear luminance edge around the stimulus.

Plate 14 shows examples of well converged and badly misconverged color tubes. Misconvergence can be corrected by adjusting the monitor's convergence controls to a cross-hatch pattern of white, one-pixel-width lines on the screen. Depending on the monitor, there may be a number of these controls for separate areas of the screen, or no controls at all. Ideally, the lines will look white and the red, green and blue contributions will not be separately resolved. Depending on the monitor, there may be a number of these controls for separate areas of the screen. Crts with the electron guns arranged in line, rather than the delta arrangement (see Chapter 1, Figure 1.3), are generally said to be easier to converge.

There are a number of ways of measuring misconvergence. One common equation defines misconvergence, M, in terms of the stoke width of a perfectly converged symbol (S_1) and the stroke width of the misconverged symbol (S_2) (for a definition of stroke width see Figure 5.4). The equation is:

$$M = \frac{S_2 - S_1}{S_1}$$

If misconvergence proves to be a problem only on some parts of the screen, such as the edges, a simple approach is to restrict important colored patches to those areas where it is less of a problem, such as the center of the screen.

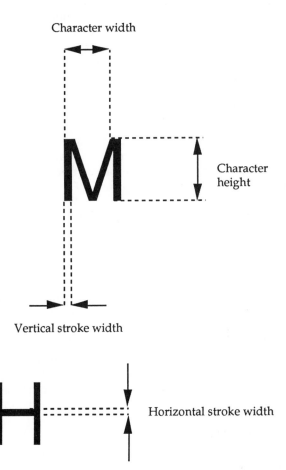

Figure 5.4: The stroke width is the width of a single line drawn on the display. Since the luminance distribution of the edge will be a blur, and not a sharp edge, the edge is defined as the 50% luminance point of the blur. The 50% point is estimated by passing a photometer over the width of the line and taking measurements at small intervals[5]. There is a separate procedure for measuring vertical and horizontal stroke widths. Vertical stroke width is measured with a capital 'M', horizontal stroke width is measured with the bar of a capital 'H'. Stroke width should be distinguished from character width and height, as shown.

2.2.3 *Linearity violation 3: Interactions between electron guns*

In an ideal system, the three primaries would be independent of each other: that is, changing the voltage to (say) the green electron gun would have no effects on either the red or the blue electron gun.

One simple way to establish this is to measure the gamma functions for each primary separately, and then to measure the same functions with a fixed input from the remaining primaries. This is most effectively achieved by setting the two other electron guns to their maximum voltage. For a particular primary, the gamma functions should be identical, apart from a scaling constant required to account for the overall change in luminance. If the gamma functions turn out to differ from each other, and accurate color specification is vital, it will be necessary to account for this interaction mathematically. This will entail measuring the gamma function for each primary for a number of fixed voltages for the remaining two guns.

2.2.4 *Linearity violation 4: Power drain*

One common problem with cathode ray displays is that the luminance at one point of the image is often affected by changing the luminance elsewhere on the image. This is analogous to an interaction between the electron guns, but is most often due to power drain.

One way to check for this is to produce a small, maximum white, square on an otherwise black screen. Measure the luminance at this point, and then fill the whole screen with the maximum white. If the luminance at the point decreases, this is probably because of an unequal power drain on the supply under the two measuring conditions. It is important not to make the square too small or else you may measure flare from other parts of the screen; this would manifest itself as an apparent increase in luminance.

2.2.5 *Linearity violation 5: Quantization errors*

The number of discrete levels of each electron gun is determined by the number of bits per pixel. With six bits, each electron gun may take on one of 64 discrete levels, and gamma correction will reduce the number of effective levels still further. In this particular example, after gamma correction each quantized step will represent a change in luminance of more than 2%. This will introduce inaccuracies when transformations in color space are required.

How many bits are enough? The answer to this depends on how much accuracy you require. Fairly compelling natural scenes may be created with only six bits, but in such scenes veridical color rendition is unimportant. Eight bits per pixel should be considered a minimum where accurate color specification is important; graphics cards are now available with fourteen bits and up and accurate work will require this precision.

2.3 Measuring spatial and temporal non-uniformity

For completeness, the chromatic and luminance measurements described above should be carried out at various screen locations. It is usually sufficient to restrict measurements to the center of the screen (i.e. the intersection of the two diagonals); and at locations on the diagonals that are 10% of the diagonal length in from the corners of the addressable area of the display. This results in five measurement locations.

2.3.1 Spatial non-uniformity

Even if identical pixel values are produced at each point on the screen, the luminance across the screen will be found to be non-uniform. Where the luminances of the three guns are affected to a different extent, ancillary differences in chromaticity will result. The effects may be reduced either by restricting the image to the central area of the monitor or by spatially correcting the different areas of the screen. This type of correction may be achieved by expressing the luminance of each spatial location as a fraction of the maximum luminance (usually found in the center). However, since it is not possible to spatially correct every pixel, this latter technique will introduce inhomogeneties of its own unless the spatial grain over which corrections are made is very small.

A second problem is spatial undersampling by the raster. This type of undersampling (which is also known as *aliasing*) is very evident on low resolution graphics monitors. What was meant to be a straight line at 30-deg to the horizontal actually looks jaggy, like a staircase (see Figure 5.5). This effect can be minimized by purchasing a display/frame buffer combination with high resolution: for example, 1024 pixels by 1280 pixels. However, even high resolution displays cannot entirely avoid the problem of spatial undersampling when very fine images are reproduced. How much spatial resolution is necessary?[6] This depends on your application. As an example, laser printers typically draw images using 300 dots per inch; a good quality terminal (for example, a Sun Workstation[7]) has a resolution of 81 pixels per inch. Magazine printing uses 150 dots per inch. If undersampling becomes a problem for one of your images, you could try increasing the size of the image and moving the observer further from the screen. Alternatively, a number of software tricks exist that antialias, or smooth, images[8].

Distortions may also be introduced by the focusing system. One example is astigmatism, a distortion that may be familiar to some of those readers who wear spectacles. In the visual system, astigmatism refers to the fact that the eye is not perfectly spherical, and hence some meridians are more in focus than others. Astigmatism affects not only the human eye, but all optical systems, including electro-optical ones. In a display system it would manifest itself by some regions of the image being more out of focus than others. The best compromise that can be made is to configure the screen so that the entire image is equally defocused. A second example is field distortion, caused by differences in magnification required as the beam passes from the center to the edge of the screen. This manifests itself as 'pin cushion' (positive) or 'barrel' (negative) distortion.

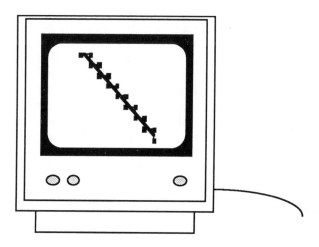

Figure 5.5: Demonstration of undersampling (or aliasing) on a crt screen. The ideal function is the straight line. This is actually reproduced by a staircase function of pixels.

2.3.2 Temporal non-uniformity

The field rate of an electronic display (typically 50 Hz in the UK and 60 Hz in the US) is not always sufficiently high to eliminate the perception of flicker and may be painfully slow in certain applications[9]. Our perception of flicker depends on a number of factors, including the luminance of the display, position in the field of view, and the observer. So for example, bright screens appear to flicker more than dim screens; perceived flicker is greater in the peripheral field of view;

and some observers may be have lower thresholds for flicker than others.

Is it possible to give some general guidelines? Researchers[10] have demonstrated that a display with a luminance of 80 cd/m^2 (a normal setting for most users) requires a frame rate of 87 Hz in order to appear flicker free to 95% of the population. Ideally, we would have a 'standard observer' for flicker, analogous to the standard observer for color vision described in Chapter 2. Work that goes some way to achieving this has been developed by Joyce Farrell at Hewlett-Packard[11]; the algorithm is presented below.

Interlacing fields may provide a solution to screen flicker (see Chapter 1), although this may introduce problems of its own: in particular, small objects may undergo illusory movement as they are drawn on different lines of the display on successive frames. Alternatively, there is a direct trade off between the field rate and the number of lines displayed. If you are willing to compromise some vertical resolution, the field rate can be increased by reducing the number of horizontal lines. For example, a 50% reduction in the number of lines displayed can yield a doubling of the field rate.

A second problem is phosphor persistence. If a relatively fast phosphor is used (for example, P-4), this should be a problem only in the most demanding applications, such as computer-based color vision tests[12]. For under these conditions the exchange of (say) a red patch with a green patch of the same luminance must not be associated with a temporal luminance artefact (see Chapter 2). If slower phosphors are used, flicker is reduced[13] but motion blur may result.

In the long term, temporal changes in chromaticity may occur as the television set warms up and as the television set ages. This will clearly be display-dependent and you will have to regularly calibrate your own monitor to check for this.

2.3.2.1 How to measure flicker from a display[14]

1. Write down the luminance from the screen with the display turned on (L_t) and the display turned off (L_r). For example, $L_t = 100$ cd/m^2 and $L_r = 10$ cd/m^2. Write down the refresh frequency of the display, f, in Hz, for example, $f = 60$ Hz. Finally, note the time constant, $TC_{10\%}$, of the phosphor from Table 5.2, and compute α from the expression:

$$\alpha = TC_{10\%} \times 0.4343$$

For example, for a slow P4 phosphor:

$TC_{10\%} = 0.00006$, and $\alpha = 0.0000261$.

Table 5.2: Time constants (spectral peak decay time to 10% point) of some common phosphors[15].

Phosphor	Time constant (seconds)
P1	0.0245
P2	0.000035 - 0.00007
P4	0.000022 - 0.00006
P7	0.4
P11	0.000034
P19	3
P20	0.00006
P22	0.006
P28	0.6
P31	0.000038

2. Compute pupil diameter, d, in mm from the formula:

$$d = 5 - 3 * \tanh [0.4 * \log_{10}(L_t \times 3.183)]$$

For example:

$$d = 5 - 3 * \tanh [0.4 * \log_{10}(100 \times 3.183)] = 2.6421 \text{ mm}.$$

Note that tanh is specified in radians and not degrees (to convert degrees to radians multiply the number of degrees by $\pi/180$). Next, computer the pupil area, A, in mm^2 from

$$A = \pi(d/2)^2$$

For example, $A = \pi(2.6421/2)^2 = 5.4826$ mm^2.

3. Compute the DC component of the temporally varying screen luminance, DC, from the formula:

$$DC = (L_t - L_r) \times A$$

For example, $DC = (100-10) \times 5.4826 = 493.434$ Trolands.

4. Compute the amplitude co-efficient of the fundamental frequency, $Amp(f)$ from the formula:

$$Amp(f) = \frac{2}{\sqrt{1 + [\alpha 2\pi f]^2}}$$

For example, $Amp(f) = \frac{2}{\sqrt{1 + [0.0000261 \times 2\pi \times 60]^2}} = 1.9999.$

5. Compute the luminance modulation of the fundamental frequency, E_{obs}, from the expression:

$$E_{obs} = DC \times Amp(f)$$

For example, $E_{obs} = 493.434 \times 1.9999 = \underline{986.82 \text{ Trolands}}.$

6. Compute the visual angle subtended by the display (see Chapter 2, Section 2.2.2.1). For example, a 40 cm diagonal display viewed from 69 cm would subtend a visual angle of 30.10 degrees.

7. To test whether a display will be flicker free to 90% of a young user population, first compute E_{pred} from the expression:

$$E_{pred} = a \times e^{bf}$$

The values of a and b may be read from Table 5.3 once you know the visual angle subtended by the display.

Table 5.3: Values of a and b that correspond to the visual angle subtended by the display

Visual angle (degrees)	a	b
10	0.1276	0.1424
30	0.1919	0.1201
50	0.5076	0.1004
70	0.53	0.0992

For a display that subtends 30 degrees, a = 0.1919 and b = 0.1201 and hence

$$E_{pred} = 0.1919 \times e^{(0.1201 \times 60)} = \underline{258.58 \text{ Trolands}}.$$

Now, if $E_{pred} > E_{obs}$ the display will not appear to flicker. Conversely, if $E_{pred} < E_{obs}$, as in our example, then the display will appear to flicker.

3 The software environment: evaluating the human-computer interface

The human-computer interface is the information technology that the user sees and interacts with. With the advent of high-quality graphics displays, it is possible to greatly improve the satisfaction and effectiveness of both novice and expert users alike with good interface design. But what does 'good interface design' look like?

The philosophy adopted here is that good interface design is *user-centered*. User-centered design has been the subject of many books in itself[16]. In order to keep this section of manageable length, and in keeping with the rest of this chapter, this section attempts to provide practical guidelines. It does not consider the various theoretical issues. Ten practical guidelines for the designer are presented in Plate 15.

3.1 Evaluating the interface

Like all decisions, design decisions are most effective when they are based on as much information as possible. Sources of this information include the designer's own intuitions, existing interface guidelines[17] and expert opinions. Computer interfaces can be compared by experimental and statistical techniques[18]. Existing theories of human-computer interaction may be used to evaluate the interface[19]. Experts in human computer interaction may be employed to consult on the design of the system at any stage.

However, the best source of information about the way the computer interface should be designed comes from the users themselves. This is because the aim of the interface is to help users do their task. This information may be obtained by asking users about their task, watching users do their task, or simply listening to users describe their task.

Because of the emphasis on the user, many users may feel that it is them, and not the system, that is being evaluated. Hence, a key technique common to all the methods that follow is to use appropriate social skills so that users feel relaxed and communicative. And finally, when you have analysed the results and feel you have identified problems with the interface, do not forget to share your ideas with the users. Not only will this make them more conducive to human factors intervention in the future, they may be able to point to flaws in your reasoning!

3.1.1 Interviews

Interviews are a useful method for obtaining general information about tasks from users and they are useful for building an initial model of the user's task. However, because the power of an interview depends on the power of the questions, interviewers need to be fairly knowledgeable before the interview begins. Additionally, interviews are time consuming and will rarely provide in-depth knowledge; hence they should be used as an ancilliary method of knowledge elicitation.

Prepare for the interview beforehand by thinking about the user and the requirements of the user's task. Gather as much information about the task as possible. As with all interviews, remember to make sure that users are relaxed. They may find it intimidating to be questioned about their job, and perhaps suspect ulterior motives. Perform the interview on the user's home ground, at the workstation itself if there is sufficient privacy. Avoid choosing a time that may be inconvenient, for example, just before lunch.

In the interview itself, remember that your task is to listen and not to talk. This can often be achieved by asking open, rather than closed, questions. For example, a quesion such as "How do you feel about the way your task is designed?" is likely to generate more information than "Do you like the way your task is designed?". Open questions begin with words and phrases such as "How...", "What...", "Why...", "Tell me about...". Closed questions use phrases such as "Did you...", "Do you...", "Can you...", "Are you...", "Have you...". Closed questions should be restricted to those situations where clarification is required. For example, the interviewer may begin with an open question such as "Tell me about the way color is used on the screen"; this might be followed up with a closed question, "Is the color green always used to signify help?".

3.1.2 Questionnaires

Questionnaires have the potential to generate a lot more information than interviews because they are fairly quick to administer and so can be given to a number of users. As with an interview, the power of a questionnaire depends on the quality of the questions: if you ask the wrong questions you will merely generate a mound of useless information. Questionnaires differ from interviews in that they are usually more rigorously structured; hence they are easier to analyse but lack the power of the supplementary question that can be used in an interview.

When producing a questionnaire, bear in mind the following points:
• *Guarantee confidentiality*: if users feel they can be identified they may avoid criticising the system.
• *Decide on the user's response*. Will the questions be a simple yes/no alternative, a rating scale, or will subjects be free to write whatever they want? Examples of these types of question are:
Yes/no
Q. Do you frequently make errors with the system?
A. ☐yes   ☐no   (tick box)

Rating scale
  Q. Do you make errors with the system?
  A ☐ frequently   ☐ sometimes   ☐ rarely   ☐ never   (tick box)
Open
  Q. Describe the types of error you make with the system.
  A. (Provide some blank space for an answer).

• *Aim for brevity*. Long questionnaires lose the user's interest and may introduce error. Questionnaires also generate an inordinate amount of data: with long questionnaires this may become unmanageable.
• *Run a pilot study*. Test out your questionnaire on a small subset of users to identify potential problems.
  If you find it difficult formulating appropriate questions, good sources have been published elsewhere[20].

3.1.3 *Observation: concurrent and retrospective protocol analysis*

Ostensibly the most direct way of evaluating an interface is to watch people use it and analyse their verbal report or 'protocol'. This can be done at the same time as users are performing the task (concurrent analysis) or after the task has been completed (retrospective analysis). An assumption is that users are able to capture their actions in language: some skills, particularly those acquired over many months of practice, may not be receptive to this.

Before beginning, remember that observation can be extremely time consuming. Your time will be used more effectively if you structure the observation. Will you be observing all users or a subset of users? If you are observing a subset of users, how will you ensure that they are representative? Will you be observing the whole task, or a subset of tasks? If you are observing a subset of tasks, it will save time if you gain some understanding of these tasks before you begin. Will you observe at the same time of day or at different times of day? For example, the system response times may be slower in the afternoon and users may have developed alternative methods to achieve the same goal.

With concurrent analysis, you simply ask the user to guide you through each stage of the process and 'think aloud'. Before you begin, tell the user that you want information on what they are doing and why they are going it. What are they trying to achieve? It sometimes helps to videotape this procedure, since this frees the interviewer from taking copious notes. (A further advantage of videotapes is that they may be a more effective means of convincing designers that users are having problems with their interface than a statistical analysis). The user should, of course, be able to concentrate on the task and so the interviewer should avoid asking too many questions; however, it is frequently necessary to ask closed questions to clarify certain actions: for example, "Why did you do that?", "Do you sometimes make errors here?".

It is an unavoidable fact that describing the activity will interfere with it: for a sobering example, try explaining your actions to a passenger when you are next driving a car! An alternative approach is to ask the user to describe their actions retrospectively. With this technique, the user is asked to perform the task, bearing in mind that they will be asked to descibe their actions afterwards. While they are recalling their behavior, the experimenter asks detailed questions. With retrospective analysis, the actions can be stopped and questioned in depth without worry that the behavior will be interfered with. Users can be asked to go back over a series of actions. Sometimes, a powerful approach is to videotape the user performing the task and then carry out a retrospective protocol analysis.

Retrospective analysis takes longer than concurrent analysis, and requires more commitment from the user. Both techniques require considerable effort in the analysis of the data. A ten-minute video may take up to an hour to analyse and longer tasks take disproportionately longer to analyse.

3.1.4 User diaries

An alternative and complementary method for evaluating the human-computer interface is to ask users to jot down any problems they have when they are using the system. This could be a set of brief notes that are written on a daily basis by a single user; or it may be a more infrequent list kept by a number of users. In order not to interfere with the task itself, these notes should be kept as short as possible; indeed the most efficient user diaries are in fact checklists, like questionnaires. And just as questionnaires should be developed by pilot experiment, the types of question asked in user diaries should be developed in the same way.

User diaries are less time consuming than protocol analysis, and provide a valuable overview of the system that other techniques may fail to extract. A common problem is that users are apt to be casual, and so may fill them in irregularly and inaccurately.

3.2   Closing the design circle: prototyping

Prototyping is simply an iterative method of software design. Rather than develop software by infrequent contact with users, prototyping methods involve the user at many stages of the design process. Rather than present the user with a finished product, the system designer presents the user with a system that is open to modification.

Because 'usability testing' involves users, it takes time. Consequently, the designer will probably make informed decisions about many aspects of the design, and concentrate usability testing on fixed areas. One example would be the type of commands required to interact with the system. In this example, a designer may have fixed the *type* of commands and yet leave the command *names* open to change. In an example of this type[21], computer novices were given a command-line interface to an electronic messaging system and told to interact with the system. Specifically, users were given the task of sending, reading, deleting and undeleting memos. Users had no idea which commands would work; they simply had to guess at commands they might expect to work. Rather than have the computer directly interpret the commands, user's responses were intercepted by an experimenter who could choose to accept or reject the user's attempt; but as far as the user was concerned the session was truly an interactive one and they had no idea that their commands were being intercepted. By analysing user's initial commands, the experimenters were able to adapt the software so that later versions could accept alternative command names. So for example, the command 'destroy' was later accepted as a synonym for 'delete'.

Prior to prototyping the interface in this way, the system could recognise only 7% of user's commands. After prototyping, it could recognise 76% of user's commands. Moreover, when experienced computer users were tested, they preferred the prototyped interface. Hence, in this example, prototyping increased both usability and acceptability of the system.

By prototyping the interface, users feel they are involved with the design of the system. This in itself will make them less likely to reject the system when it is finally implemented; but it is the design issues that are raised in prototyping that generate most benefits. The disadvantages of prototyping is that it can be costly, and it is not clear when the iterative design cycle should cease. The former problem may be a pseudo-problem: if a system is delivered to its potential users and rejected, the cost may be many magnitudes greater than usability testing would ever have been. The latter problem can be solved by setting some metric in the specification of the interface: for example, "Users shall make less than 10% errors when it meets functional and operational requirements".

4   Evaluating the environment

Environmental ergonomics is concerned with producing environmental conditions in which users can perform optimally. Its aims are to protect users from discomfort, inefficiency in performance and psychological and medical distress. In the UK, certain minimum conditions are laid down in the Offices, Shops and Railway Premises Act (1963) and the Health and Safety at Work Act (1975). The corresponding regulations in the US derive from the Fair Labor Standards Act (1938) and the Occupational Safety and Health Act (1970). These regulations should be seen as minimum requirements, if only because they contain few regulations applicable to visual displays. However, this will shortly change in Europe. In May 1990 the Council of the European Communities adopted a Directive on VDUs[22]. This directive lays down health and safety requirements for work with VDUs, and since it is a Directive, Member States have to bring into force laws, regulations and administrative provisions necessary to comply. New workstations must comply from 31 December 1992, existing workstations must comply by 31 December 1996.

In this chapter, the user's environment has been divided into the micro- and macro-environments (this division is somewhat arbitrary and elements from the two environments may overlap). The user's micro-environment comprises his immediate surroundings. Poor design of the micro-environment results in bad posture and inefficient working practices. The user's macro-environment comprises such areas as lighting and air-conditioning. Ergonomists are in general agreement that poor design of the macro-environment will lead directly to increased staff sickness and absenteeism. (This has recently come to prominence in the media under the term 'sick building syndrome'). Hence, poor environmental design reduces productivity and user well-being, and it is important that the effects of the physical environment are assessed by both of these criteria.

Many of the requirements laid down in this section derive from standard textbooks in the field or from standards bodies such as the Organisation for International Standardization (ISO).

4.1 The User's micro-environment[23]

This section reviews a set of ergonomic requirements that should be followed by workstation designers. The aim of this section is to describe potential problems and to suggest ways of overcoming them. Most of the guidelines are no more than a pair of numbers that bracket an appropriate range for most users. So for example, it is recommended that the viewing distance to the screen and documents should be between about 60 to 90 cm (Section 4.1.5). Recommendations such as these lend themselves to being evaluated by a simple checklist, and such a checklist is provided in Appendix 5. A summary of some of the micro-ergonomic requirements is presented in Figure 5.6.

The most important principle in workstation design is that of 'ease of adjustment': for example, chairs should be adjustable in height, keyboards should be detachable from computers, and the visual display should be able to tilt and swivel. Except for the rare situation where a designer is producing a bespoke workstation, a designer rarely knows the bodily dimensions of potential users. So how should recommendations be phrased?

Recommendations are usually couched in terms of the potential distribution of users. These recommendations can be found in works on static and dynamic anthropometry. Static anthropometry measures such things as height and weight; dynamic anthropometry measures such things as arm reach and strength. An assumption is made that these measures are normally distributed in the population and hence the data may be given in terms of a mean and an associated standard deviation. Because of the known anthropometric differences between men and women (men are, on the average, taller, heavier and stronger than women) the data are usually given separately for each sex.

A useful feature of presenting the data as a mean value with an associated standard deviation is that designers can build equipment for a particular set of users. So for example, the height of an adjustable desk can be designed to fit the 5th percentile female at its lowest setting and the 95th percentile male at its highest setting. There will still be a small number of very small women and very tall men for whom the desk is unsuitable; but, on the average, most users should be able to find a desk height that suits them. Tables of anthropometric data are widely available.

4.1.1 Clearances under worksurfaces

Restricted work spaces can lead to a constrained posture being adopted which may cause fatigue, tiredness and pain. How much space is enough? Users should be able to stand up, stretch and shift position during the course of their working day. This requires clearance between the knees and the worksurface to prevent the user from adopting uncomfortable or potentially harmful positions. The recommended amount of knee clearance between the underside of the desk and the seat of the chair is between 17 and 20 cm. This clearance should not be reduced by draws, desk legs or cables. It is also necessary to consider the safety aspects of getting in and out of the workstation, both of an everday nature and to escape in an emergency.

4.1.2 Seating and foot rests

Chairs supplied for work with displays should be adjustable, mainly to allow keyboard use with the hands approximately horizontal. Ideally the user's feet should rest on the floor (or on a foot rest if the person is short), so that the thighs adopt a more or less horizontal position. Seat height should be adjustable between 32-55 cm. If the chair is too high it may lead to pains in the lower back and lower leg. But providing adjustable chairs is not enough: users need to be informed of their ability to alter the chair height. Part of the problem is that adjustment controls are often difficult to find and operate.

Chairs should have backrests for pelvic and lumbar support. The backrests should be adjustable in height and angle within the range of 95 -120 degrees: this 'leaning backward position' allows relaxation of the back muscles and decreases the load on the invertebral discs. Chairs without adjustable backrests may cause pain in the lower back because of inadequate back support. Chair surfaces should smooth outwards (otherwise they may cut into the user's back or thighs). A minimum backrest height of 23 cm has been reccommended; this should be increased for display users who spend a large proportion of their working day at the display.

If a footrest is used to achieve a horizontal thigh position it should be adjustable in height between 0-5 cm and adjustable in inclination by 10-15 degrees. The width and depth of the foot rest should be great enough to cover the entire usable leg area. For safety reasons footrests should be anchored to the floor if possible and be covered with a non-slip surface.

The depth of the seat itself should allow a small person clearance for the calf and minimize thigh pressure. The width of the seat should be set to accommodate large people. Working guidelines are that the depth should not exceed 43 cm, and that the width should not be less than 40 cm[24]. Weight distribution over the chair can be equalized by the use of moulded (contoured) seating; however, this has the disadvantage of restricting movement.

For stability the chair should have a five arm base. For mobility it should be mounted on castors; but if a large degree of movement is required within the work space, as may be necessary in control rooms for example, then it may be helpful to have a groove cut into the desk (large enough for fingers) so that users can grip here when moving. Of course, this facility should not affect desk stability.

4.1.3 Desks and hand rests

If work surfaces are too low the back is bent too far forward. If they are too high the shoulders are raised and discomfort is triggered here and in the neck. Although desks have been manufactured that are adjustable in height, it is more realistic to adjust the seating and foot rest support in relation to a fixed desk height. This is mainly because users are frequently unaware of their ability to alter desk height. Partially adjustable desk tops may be helpful in allowing users to minimize strain in the neck and shoulders. If the display is too low, the user is forced to lean forward which leads to pain in the base of the neck; if it is too high, the user's chin juts forward which leads to pain in the top of the neck. Most users select a desk top height between 72-75 cm. To reduce disturbing reflections, the work surface finish should be matt, with a reflectance of between 0.4 and 0.6 (see Section 4.2.5).

Adequate area for the tasks to be carried out is also of major importance to prevent over reaching and the adoption of bad posture to carry out a task for example, holding source documents on laps. The main work of the user should be close to the midline so that the arms hang vertically. Otherwise the user's elbows will be positioned away from the body and the arms may be held forward: this leads to pain in the shoulders.

A common finding is that users twist their hands inwards while operating the keyboard; with continous keyboard use this causes pain in the outer surface of the wrist due to ulnar abduction in the hand. It has been shown that users prefer keyboards with a wrist support which prevents this position[25]. Pains in the forearm upper surface are almost certainly caused by the keyboard angle being too steep or by placing the wrist on the table or keyboard while typing. Wrist supports should not restrict the keying action, and surface height should match the height of the keyboard. If no support is used it is useful to have a free area of about 6 cm available in front of the keyboard for the resting of hands.

Forearm, hand and wrist complaints are generically termed 'repetitive strain injury' or RSI. RSI is a blanket term used to describe a range of injuries to the hands, wrists and arms. The medical terms for this are 'tenosynovitis' and 'carpal tunnel syndrome'. RSI can cause numbness in the wrists and arms and make lifting ordinary household objects, such as cans, excrutiating. Since it has been found in users who are involved in rapid typing tasks (such as journalists[26], or dealers on trading floors[27]), it has been suggested that one cause of this may be intensive use of computer keyboards. For example, users who are required to perform data entry tasks where they are required to use only a subset of keys may be especially prone to RSI. Users of manual typewriters did not suffer from RSI, the argument goes, because their work required them to take pauses, such as operating the carriage return or inserting a new sheet of paper. Ergonomists are in general agreement that RSI can be eliminated by appropriate exercise, by taking appropriate rest breaks and by appropriate design of the input task. However, this may not always be feasible in jobs where individuals are under pressure or highly committed: you cannot leave the dealing room floor every hour or so to do wrist exercises.

4.1.4 Arm reach

Screen controls, such as brightness and contrast, should be easily and safely accessible. Adequate desk area is of major importance so bad posture is not adopted while carrying out tasks. The keyboard should be positioned so that the middle row of keys is between 10-26 cm from the front of the desk to avoid shoulder pain.

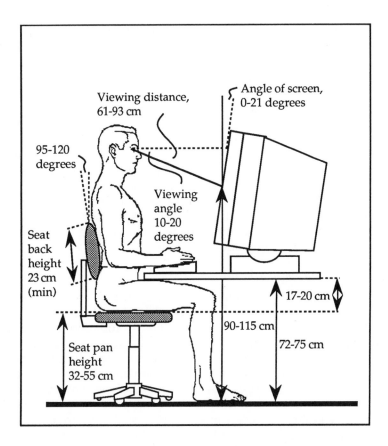

Figure 5.6: Pictorial summary of ergonomic reccommendations. (See text for details).

4.1.5 Viewing distance and field of view

In the choice of viewing distance it is important to consider the performance of the visual system itself. In particular, users should not have to frequently change their point of focus, as will happen if the source documents and the screen are placed at considerably different viewing distances. Viewing distance to the screen and documents should be between about 60 to 90 cm.

It is obvious that the user's field of view of the keyboard, screen and documents should not be obscured by each another. But this will occur if (for example) users are not provided with sufficient desk space.

4.1.6 Document holders

These are useful for supporting source documents at a suitable reading distance without taking up desk area. Their use avoids unfavorable head inclination, which may cause pain in the base or one side of the neck, and sideways body movement. Moreover, since neck strain is relieved when horizontal movements only are required from the user, benefits can be maximized by placing the document holder on the same level as the display and inclining it to a 20 degree angle which reduces the luminance of documents and places it at an optimal angle for reading without neck strain. Document holders should be adequately secured for safety reasons and to prevent movement when in use. The addition of row markers may be beneficial to some tasks.

There should be adequate provision of storage space for manuals, stationery and personal belongings. If drawers are supplied for this, they should not affect the stability of the worksurface and should not be capable of completely tipping out of the unit.

4.1.7 Are visual displays a health hazard?

This cherished question has been considered by dozens of researchers[28], and there is not adequate space to provide a full literature review here. Briefly, the 'hazards' have been reported in four broad groups: musculoskeletal, psychological, vision and radiation. It is now generally accepted that reports of musculoskeletal discomfort are caused by poor design of the micro-environment and by failing to provide users with regular rest pauses[29]. Reports of psychological stress can be traced to poor task design and/or poor introduction of information technology in the workplace[30]. Visual symptoms may be traced to poor design of the micro- and macro-environment; and current evidence suggests that long term use of visual displays does not cause visual impairment[31]. Short term visual symptoms, such as the after effects described in Chapter 4, are transitory.

On the other hand, the issue of radiation from cathode ray displays is still not fully resolved. Although the radiation levels (x-rays, ultraviolet, non-ionizing, infrared, microwave, radio frequency and ELF/VLF) emitted from cathode-ray displays are well within international regulations[32], there is some concern about the electromagnetic emissions induced by very-low frequency (VLF) and extremely-low frequency (ELF) radiations. VLF radiation is generated by the horizontal scan frequency (generally between 10 kHz and 30 kHz, see Chapter 1) and ELF radiation is generated by the vertical scan frequency (generally between 60 Hz and 75 Hz, see Chapter 1). VLF and ELF radiations, even at the low levels measured from crts, have been implicated in cases of leukemia and cancer[33]. They have also been reported to cause miscarriages in pregnant women who use crts[34].

Currently, the weight of evidence suggests that cathode-ray displays are not intrinsically a hazard to health, although there is still a question mark over magnetic field emissions. However, since the strength of the magnetic fields drops precipitately with distance from the display, a simple precaution is to sit about an arm's length from the front of a computer monitor and at least three or four feet away from the sides and backs of nearby monitors.

4.2 The user's macro-environment

4.2.1 Lighting

The major problem faced by lighting designers when designing VDU workstations is supplying enough light to illuminate printed or written material without illuminating the display screen itself and reducing screen contrast. If possible, displays should be installed in a direction parallel to luminaires[35] and windows to eliminate glare. If lighting is low and contrasts are low both the speed and precision of accommodation and convergence are reduced so the legibility of source documents will be poor. The situation is improved by supplying the work area with indirect lighting or by uplighters.

Lighting levels around the workstation should be measured at a number of intervals. One common approach is to measure at square meter intervals and draw up a contour map. A contour map provides a useful visual description of light and dark spots within the room, and may identify possible causes of lighting problems.

4.2.1.1 Illumination level

Differing levels of illumination should be avoided wherever possible. The illumination required is determined by the complexity and visual difficulty of the task, but the results of many field trials have shown that visual display users prefer lighting in the range 300-500 lux. The minimum illumination level recommended is 200 lux; further darkening does abolish screen reflections but problems then occur when the reading of documents is required. Section 4.2.5 describes how to measure illumination.

Many offices are lit by fluorescent tubes. Fluorescent tubes pulsate in brightness, they are spatially periodic and they have an uneven spectral power distribution. It has been argued that these factors place an increased computational load on the visual system and may cause headaches and eyestrain[36]. Flicker from fluorescent tubes is especially apparent when the tubes are becoming worn; it is therefore a good idea to fit the tubes with starters to prevent flashing at the end of their useful life. A second solution is to place two or more phase-shifted fluorescent tubes inside one luminary: this decreases fluctuation in light levels and is less likely to cause annoyance and fatigue through perceived flicker.

4.2.1.2 Luminance ratio relationships

As a user's line of sight changes, transient adaptive changes occur unless the luminance of every visible point in the field is the same as the central field. It has been suggested that visual effort is dependent on the spatial distribution of luminaires to which the eye must adapt and readapt. To safeguard against visual fatigue, it is commonly recommended that luminance ratios in the central visual field should not exceed 1:3 (1:10 in the periphery), and that the luminance ratio between the screen and paper should be kept at about 1:6. But it should be noted that these recommended ratios have little scientific support[37] and moreover they are often wishful thinking when measurements are carried out in the field. For example, one study found that screen to source document ratios were in the range of 1:10 to 1:87 with a median of 1:26[38]. Since little scientific evidence is available on this point, the designer of the workstation environment need not be too concerned about violating it.

In order to maximize the illuminance on working surfaces, walls and ceilings should be as light as possible. However, in order to reduce glare (see Section 4.2.1.3) walls and ceilings should be as dark as possible. The generally accepted compromise is to increase reflectance from the walls to the ceiling; see Table 5.3.

Table 5.3: Ideal reflectance values

Surface	Reflectance value
Ceiling	Greater than 0.8
Walls	0.5 - 0.7
Partitions and screens	0.4 - 0.7
Floor	0.2 - 0.4
Furniture	0.25-0.45
Desk surface	0.4 - 0.6

4.2.1.3 Glare and reflection level

Glare can be defined as a gross disturbance of adaptation caused by large luminance differences that occur both spatially and temporally. Glare is a serious problem in environments where color displays are used for critical work, because the glare can reduce the effective color gamut[39]. This is because the ambient illumination is effectively being mixed with the colors on the screen. Unless the spectral characteristics and the level of ambient illumination is known, accurate color specification becomes impossible.

Direct glare can be avoided by appropriate positioning of the luminaires or the display itself. In one study, users of CAD workstations were found to angle their screens at 8 degrees *below* the horizontal, presumably to reduce glare[40] (users generally prefer to angle their screens at 0 to 21 degrees above the horizontal; see Figure 5.6). Indirect glare is usually caused by reflections from glossy or high reflectance surfaces, such as light desktops or clothing. To reduce indirect glare, worksurfaces should be within the range 0.4 to 0.6 and the surface should be matt.

Screen reflections fall into two broad categories: specular and diffuse reflections. Specular reflections are mirror like images; since screens are usually convex, reflections are optically projected and appear behind the screen. Diffuse reflections produce a veiling luminance over the screen, reducing the contrast of the information underneath. Both situations can be improved by using diffuse, indirect lighting and by using negative polarity displays (black text on a white background)[41]. Glare on screens can be decreased by fitting the display with an antireflection coating, or a polarization or micromesh filter, although these may alter the spectral composition of the display phosphors.

Of course, direct glare from windows can be reduced and eliminated by the appropriate use of window blinds, shades or louvres. If slatted blinds are used, it is preferable to use vertical rather than horizontal ('venetian') blinds. This is because, even when fully closed, horizontal blinds still allow direct sunlight to pass through the holes for the draw cords.

4.2.2 Climate

4.2.2.1 Air conditioning
The purpose of air conditioning is to provide a uniform and consistent working environment. However, its existence frequently causes problems. First, it often produces draughts around the legs and the neck; for this reason the speed of air movement should be less than 0.15 m/s and never exceed 0.2 m/s. Air movement less than this leads to complaints that the room is airless. Second, air conditioning may dry the mucous membranes leading to an increased chance of infection. A third finding is that air conditioning creates negative ions (ions are molecules of atmospheric gas that have taken on a negative or a positive charge). Some work has been carried out into the investigation

of ions in the air and their effect on well being[42] and there are claims that their presence causes irritability and tension.

Poor air conditioning has been identified as a possible cause of 'sick building syndrome'. This syndrome, which covers various symptoms (mainly high staff turnover, staff illness and lost productivity), can be seen largely as a failure to respond to the demands placed on a building by the installation of high technology. The causes of sick building syndrome have been identified as poor ventilation, inadequate filtration and contamination of air handling systems. The build up of dirt becomes a breeding ground for bacteria and fungi. The use of traditional duct air conditioning is seen as the major contributor to sick building syndrome because of difficulty in its maintainance and keeping it clean.

Compared with other environments, air in 'sick buildings' has been found to contain relatively more allergenic fungi and bacteria and pathogenic bacteria, tobacco smoke and carbon monoxide. The situation has been helped by providing underfloor air conditioning: that is, driving air through a raised tiled floor, which is much easier to clean. The provision of this in an office building in London, along with uplighters instead of fluorescent lighting and good interior design, led to the phrase 'healthy building' being coined[43].

4.2.2.2 Temperature

Room temperature is proportional to the power consumption of the equipment, room lighting and room occupancy. Designers can go some way to improving the situation by using machines with low thermal emission, and ensuring that the dissipated heat from machines is not directed towards any users. The number of machines in a room should be kept low and be evenly distributed.

Ideally the temperature should be maintained at 21 degrees C in winter, and between 20 degrees C to 24 degrees C in summer. Higher temperatures cause tiredness; lower ones induce a need for movement and a reduction in attention. However, much relies on personal preferences and there may be a sex difference with women on average prefering a 2 degrees C higher temperature than men[44].

4.2.2.3 Humidity

Relative humidity is a measure of the amount of water vapor present in the air. This value should fall between 45-55%. Values below this may lead to eye discomfort, and values below 30% are unhygenic, since they causes a drying of the mucous membranes of the eyes and nose which increases the chance of infection. There is a possibility that the skin rash complained of by some VDT users is caused and aggravated by a dry atmosphere. At the other extreme, values above 70% are considered uncomfortable.

4.2.3 *Noise*

The degree to which noise affects the user's task depends on a number of criteria, and not simply the loudness and the duration of the noise. It may depend on past experience with the noise and the predictability and necessity of the noise, as well as the time of year, the time of day, the type of task and the type of environment[45]. Interestingly, performance of simple, routine tasks is often unaffected by noise; indeed, some noise has been shown to actually *improve* performance[46]. In fact, noise appears to disrupt only those tasks that place a high load on the user's processing of information.

However, the threshold for annoyance by noise is considerably lower than the threshold for affecting performance. Noise levels between 60-70 dBA result in widespread complaints, with levels between 70-75 dBA resulting in threats of legal action. Part of the problem in setting guidelines in this area is that the relationship between noise annoyance and noise level is not a simple one. The low intermittent rattle of a window frame may be substantially more annoying than the continous drone of the traffic outside. However, in general, noise levels around 55 dBA are generally found acceptable; where telephone speech is an operational requirement, this level should be considered a maximum.

In offices, noise sources may include voices, telephones and general office equipment. The main noise from visual displays comes from the cooling fan; although the noise level is low, its frequency may be annoying. The noise from printers may be reduced by enclosing the printer in an acoustic cover.

4.2.4 *Cable management*

The trailing leads from machines are both a hazard and an eyesore. Cable management concerns the capability of coping with cables from machines efficiently, economically and safely in an aesthetically acceptable way. The solutions must be capable of adaptation and allow for growth as new technology is brought in as well as providing easy access for maintenance. Ease of maintenance will also be aided by the separation of mains and data channels. Some solutions to the problems of cable management are: flat wire under carpets; floor and/or skirting trunking; suspended booms or trays; wall mounted dado trunking; suspended ceilings possibly with flexible cable drops; and raised floors with pillars and panels.

On a more local level, clip on cable managers supplied with furniture and adequate provision of cable ties may provide a small-scale solution.

4.2.5 *How to measure features of the macro-environment*

1. Luminance is the amount of light per unit area leaving a surface. The SI units are cd/m^2. Luminance is simply measured by pointing a photometer at the surface and noting the reading.

2. Illuminance is the amount of light striking a surface from a point source. The SI units are lux.

3. Reflectance is defined as the ratio of reflected to incident light. For a perfectly diffuse surface, the formula is:

$$\text{Reflectance} = \frac{\pi \times \text{luminance}}{\text{illuminance}}$$

where luminance is measured in cd/m^2 and illuminance is measured in lux. Reflectance itself is unitless.

When the surface being considered is not perfectly diffuse, the luminance factor is measured instead of the reflectance. The luminance factor is defined as:

$$\text{Luminance factor} = \frac{\text{Test object luminance}}{\text{Reflectance standard luminance}}$$

The luminance of the test object and the reflectance standard should be measured in exactly the same place under exactly the same conditions. The reflectance standard is usually provided with the photometer. Ideally, its reflectance is 100%; in practice, it is usually less than this (the exact value will be specified with the sample). When the reflectance is less than 100%, the measured luminance factor should be multiplied by the actual reflectance to give an accurate luminance factor.

4. Air movement is generally measured with a hot wire anemometer.

5. Humidity and temperature may be measured with hygrometers.

6. Noise is measured with a sound level meter.

7. Contrast is commonly defined as the ratio of two luminances. At least three definitions are available:

$$\text{Michelson contrast} = \frac{L_{max} - L_{min}}{L_{max} + L_{min}}$$

$$\text{Contrast ratio} = \frac{L_{max}}{L_{min}}$$

Contrast = $\dfrac{L_{max} - L_{min}}{L_{min}}$

where L_{max} represents the maximum luminance and L_{min} represents the minimum luminance. Michelson contrast is sometimes referred to as *contrast modulation*; its use should be restricted to comparing conditions where the average or mean luminance does not change. To compute character or object contrasts on a cathode-ray tube (crt) across conditions where mean luminance may vary use the second or third equations.

A second form of the third equation is sometimes used; this allows distinction between negative contrast screens (dark text on light background) and positive contrast screens (light text on a dark background). For measuring the contrast of text and foreground luminances, this equation is preferred because of its simplicity:

Contrast = $\dfrac{L_{object} - L_{bg}}{L_{bg}}$

where L_{object} is the luminance of the object or character and L_{bg} is the luminance of the background.

5   Calibration and evaluation: key points

• *The luminance* versus *voltage function for color displays is non-linear. Correct this non-linearity by measurements of the display gamma function.*
• *Be aware of other sources of display artefact such as misconvergence, interactions between electron guns, power drain and quantization errors.*
• *Base design decisions on interviews, questionnairres, diaries and observation of the users of the system.*
• *Prototype the design.*
• *Make sure that the immediate and the extended workstation environment meets ergonomic standards.*

6   Further reading

Brainard, D. H. (1989) Calibration of a computer controled color monitor. *Color Research and Application*, 14: 23-34.

An excellent paper on the procedures and problems involved in calibrating color displays.

Cowan, W. B. (1983) Discreteness artefacts in raster display systems. In Mollon, J. D. and Sharpe, L. T. (eds.) *Color Vision: Physiology and Psychophysics*, pp 145-153. London: Academic Press.

Summarizes the image problems introduced by the frame buffer and display controler.

Harris, J. P., Makepeace, A. P. W. and Troscianko, T. S. (1987) Cathode ray tube displays in psychophysiological research. *J. Psychophysiology*, 4: 413-429.

A clear, practical review of crt artefacts.

Post, D. L. and Calhoun, C. S. (1989) An evaluation of methods for producing desired colors on CRT monitors. *Color Research and Application*, **14**: 172-186.

A comparison of seven different methods of analysing the data obtained from gamma correction. Introduces a 'measure and adjust' algorithm for producing precise chromaticities on displays.

Savoy, R. L. (1986) Making quantized images appear smooth: tricks of the trade in vision research. *Behavior, Research Methods, Instruments and Computers*, **18**: 507-517.

Tips on avoiding quantization problems, set out as a number of 'case studies'.

Stanislaw, H. and Olzak, L. A. (1990) Parametric methods for gamma and inverse gamma correction, with extensions to halftoning. *Behavior, Research Methods, Instruments and Computers*, **22**: 402-408.

More methods for achieving accurate gamma correction.

Watson, A. B., Nielson, K. R. K., Poirson, A., Fitzhugh, A., Bilson, A., Nguyen, K. and Ahumada, A. J. (1986) Use of a raster frame buffer in vision research. *Behavior, Research Methods, Instruments and Computers*, **18**: 587-594.

This paper includes a discussion of the use of look-up tables for gamma correction and should be accessible to non-vision scientists.

7   Notes and References

1 The standard reference work is Cakir, A., Hart, D. J. and Stewart, T. F. M. (1980) *Visual Display Terminals*. New York: Wiley. Recent minimum requirements can be found in ISO 9241/3 Visual Display Terminals used for Office tasks: Image Quality.

2 Post, D. L. and Calhoun, C. S. (1989) An evaluation of methods for producing desired colours on CRT monitors. *Color Research and Application*, 14: 172-186.

3 Milner, N. P., Knowles, J. L. and Lovett, S. P. (1988) An ergonomic investigation of misconvergence on colour visual display terminals. *British Telecom Technology Journal*, 6: 24-36.

4 Vingrys, A. J. and King-Smith, P.E. (1986) Factors in using color video monitors for assessment of visual thresholds. *Color Research and Application*, 11 (Supplement): S57-S62.

5 See Keller, P. A. (1986) Resolution measurement techniques for data display cathode ray tubes. *Displays*, 7: 17-29.

6 For a paper comparing display resolution with visual resolution see Murch, G. M. and Beaton, R. J. (1988) Matching display resolution and addressability to human visual capacity. *Displays*, 9:23-26. For methods of measuring display resolution see Keller, P. A. (1986) Resolution measurement techniques for data display cathode ray tubes. *Displays*, 7: 17-29.

7 Sun Workstation is a registered trademark of Sun Microsystems, Inc.

8 See for example, Covington, M. A. (1990) Smooth views. *Byte*, 15 (May), 279-283.

9 Rodieck, R. W. (1983) Raster-based colour stimulators. In Mollon, J. D. and Sharpe, L. T. (eds.) *Colour Vision: Physiology and Psychophysics*, pp 131-144. London: Academic Press.

10 Bauer, D., Bonacker, M. and Cavonius, C. R. (1983) Frame repitition rate for flicker-free viewing of bright VDU screens. *Displays*, 4: 31-33.

11 Farrell, J. E., Casson, E. J., Haynie, C. R. and Benson, B. L. (1988) Designing flicker-free video display terminals. *Displays*, 9: 115-122.

12 Vingrys, A. J., King-Smith, P.E. (1986) Factors in using color video monitors for assessment of visual thresholds. *Color Research and Application*, 11 (Supplement): S57-S62 demonstrate that the green phosphor of their television set (a Sony Trinitron) decays more slowly than the red.

13 Bauer, D. (1987) Use of slow phosphors to eliminate flicker in VDUs with bright background. *Displays*, 8: 29-32.

14 This algorithm has been derived by Joyce Farrell at Hewlett Packard. I thank her for allowing me to describe it here. For a fuller exposition see Farrell, J. E., Casson, E. J., Haynie, C. R. and Benson, B. L. (1988) Designing flicker-free video display terminals. *Displays*, 9: 115-122.

15 From, Sherr, S. (1979) *Electronic Displays*. New York: Wiley, page 82.

16 For an excellent example, see Shneiderman, B. (1987) *Designing the User Interface*. Reading, Mass.: Addison-Wesley.

17 See, for example, Smith, S. L. and Mosier, J. N. (1986) *Guidelines for designing User Interface Software* (Technical Report ESD-TR-86-278), Hanscom Air Force Base, MA: USAF Electronic System Division. (NTIS No. AD A1777 198).

18 Monk, A. (1985) Statistical evaluation of behavioural data. In A. Monk (ed.) *Fundamentals of Human-Computer Interaction*. London: Academic Press.

19 For one example see Card, S., Moran, T. and Newell, A. (1983) *The Psychology of Human Computer Interaction*. Hillsdale, NJ: Lawrence Erlbaum. This model of human-computer interaction was used in the development of the Xerox 'Star' interface; see Bewley, W. L., Roberts, T. L., Schroit, D. and Verplank, W. L. (1983) Human Factors Testing in the Design of Xerox's 8010 'STAR' office workstation. *Human Factors in Computing Systems*. CHI '83 Proceedings, 72-77.

20 See for example, Clegg, C. *et al.* (1988) *People and Computers: How to Evaluate your Company's new Technology*. Chichester: Ellis Horwood.

21 Good, M. D., Whiteside, J. A., Wixon, D. R. and Jones, S. J. (1984). Building a user-derived interface. *Communications of the ACM*, 27: 1032-1043.

22 The text of the Directive can be found in the *Official J. European Communities*, L156/14, dated 26 June 1990.

23 Unless otherwise stated, these guidelines have been extracted from: AT&T Bell Laboratories (1983) *Video Display Terminals*. Short Hill, NJ; Cakir, A., Hart, D. J. and Stewart, T. F. M. (1980) *Visual Display Terminals*. New York: Wiley; and Granjean, E. (1987) Design of VDT wokstations. In G. Salvendy (ed.), *Handbook of Human Factors*, Wiley: New York, pp 1359-1397.

24 Grandjean E., Hunting W., Wotzka G., Sharer R. (1983) An ergonomic investigation of multipurpose chairs. *Human Factors* **15**: 247-255.

25 Grandjean E., Nishiyama K., Hunting W., Piderman M. A. (1982) Laboratory study on preferred and imposed settings of a VDT workstation. *Behaviour and Information Technology*, **1**, 289-304.

26 *Financial Times*, 19 January 1989, p 11.

27 *The Independent*, 10 September 1990, p 13.

28 Pearce, B. (1984) *Health Hazards of VDTs?* John Wiley: Chichester. 244 pages.

29 Arndt, R. (1983) Working posture and musculoskeletal problems of VDT operators: Review and reappraisal. *AIHA Journal*, **44**.

30 Dickerson, O. B. and Baker, W. E. (1984) Health considerations at the information work place. In *VDTs: Usability Issues and Health Concerns*, Stamford Conference, Prentice-Hall.

31 Association of Ophthalmologists of Quebec (1982) *CRT Display terminals and their effects on ocular health*. Quebec: Laval University.

32 IBM report that their displays emit less that 0.1% of the most stringent worldwide safety standards; IBM, *Health and Safety Aspects of Visual Displays*, IBM, New York.

33 Brodeur, P. (1990) The magnetic field menace. *MacWorld*, July, 136-145.

34 A comprehensive review can be found in: Blackwell, R. and Chang, A. (1988) Video display terminals and pregnancy. A review. *British J. Obstetrics and Gynaecology*, **95**: 446-453.

35 A luminaire is a complete lighting unit consisting of a lamp or lamps together with the parts designed to distribute the light, to position and protect the lamps, and to connect the lamps to the power supply.

36 Wilkins, A. J. (1990) Visual display units versus visual computation. In *Applying Visual Psychophysics to User Interface Design*, British Telecom Research Laboratories, Ipswich.

37 It is clear from Chapter 2 that the visual system can operate within a vast range of contrast ratios. For a specific critique of established recommendations see Brass, J, (1982) Discarding ESI in favor of brightness contrast engineering - A "wide-angle" view. *Lighting Design and Applications*, **12**(11): 30-34.

38 Laubli T., Hunting W. and Granjean E. (1981) Postural and visual loads at VDT workplaces *Ergonomics* **24**: 933-944.

39 De Corte, W. (1988) Colour solid of CRT phosphors when ambient illumination is present. *Displays*, **9**: 107-114. See especially Figure 2 of this paper.

40 Van der Heiden, G. and Krueger, H. (1984) Evaluation of ergonomic features of the Computer Vision Instaview Graphics Terminal. (Report). Zurich: Department of Ergonomics of the Swiss Federal Institute of Technology. This report shows that the micro-ergonomic preferences of users of CAD workstations are essentially the same as those of users of conventional VDTs.

41 Bauer, D., Bonacker, M. and Cavonius, C. R. (1981) Influence of vdu screen brightness on the visibility of reflected images. *Displays*, **2**: 242-244.

42 Tom, G., Poole, M. F., Galla, J. and Berrier, J. (1981) The influence of negative ions on human performance and mood. *Human Factors*, **23**: 633-636.

43 Crawford, D. (1989) Access to health. *The Valuer*, November, 312-313.

44 Bell, C. R. (1974) *Men at Work.* Allen and Unwin.

45 Sperry, W. (1978) Aircraft and airport noise. In D. Lipscomb and A. Taylor (eds.) *Noise control: Handbook of Principles and Practices.* New York: Van Nostrand Reinhold.

46 For a review of this area see Gawron, V. (1982) Performance effects of noise intensity, psychological set, and task type and complexity. *Human Factors*, **24**: 225-243.

APPENDICES

Appendix 1: Color space transformations using matrix algebra

Those readers familiar with linear equations but unfamiliar with matrix algebra may find the following notes helpful.

A matrix of the form:

$$\begin{bmatrix} R \\ G \\ B \end{bmatrix} = \begin{bmatrix} a0 & a1 & a2 \\ a3 & a4 & a5 \\ a6 & a7 & a8 \end{bmatrix} \begin{bmatrix} X \\ Y \\ Z \end{bmatrix}$$

may be simply translated as:

$$R = a0X + a1Y + a2Z$$
$$G = a3X + a4Y + a5Z$$
$$B = a6X + a7Y + a8Z$$

All of the matrix manipulations in Chapter 3 involve either (1) multiplying two 3x3 matrices together or (2) multiplying a 3x3 matrix by a column vector or (3) inverting a matrix. This appendix describes how to realize these manipulations (note that the multiplication symbol in this appendix is *). Most of the popular spreadsheet programs (such as Lotus 1-2-3 or Microsoft Excel) have commands to perform these transformations.

1. *To multiply two 3x3 matrices, **A** and **B**, together:*

If

$$\left[\; \mathbf{A} \;\right] = \begin{bmatrix} a0 \; a1 \; a2 \\ a3 \; a4 \; a5 \\ a6 \; a7 \; a8 \end{bmatrix}$$

And

$$\left[\; \mathbf{B} \;\right] = \begin{bmatrix} b0 \; b1 \; b2 \\ b3 \; b4 \; b5 \\ b6 \; b7 \; b8 \end{bmatrix}$$

Then

$$\left[\; \mathbf{AB} \;\right] = \begin{bmatrix} a0 \; a1 \; a2 \\ a3 \; a4 \; a5 \\ a6 \; a7 \; a8 \end{bmatrix} \begin{bmatrix} b0 \; b1 \; b2 \\ b3 \; b4 \; b5 \\ b6 \; b7 \; b8 \end{bmatrix} = \begin{bmatrix} ab0 \; ab1 \; ab2 \\ ab3 \; ab4 \; ab5 \\ ab6 \; ab7 \; ab8 \end{bmatrix}$$

where

$$ab0 = a0 * b0 + a1 * b3 + a2 * b6$$
$$ab1 = a0 * b1 + a1 * b4 + a2 * b7$$
$$ab2 = a0 * b2 + a1 * b5 + a2 * b8$$
$$ab3 = a3 * b0 + a4 * b3 + a5 * b6$$
$$ab4 = a3 * b1 + a4 * b4 + a5 * b7$$
$$ab5 = a3 * b2 + a4 * b5 + a5 * b8$$
$$ab6 = a6 * b0 + a7 * b3 + a8 * b6$$
$$ab7 = a6 * b1 + a7 * b4 + a8 * b7$$
$$ab8 = a6 * b2 + a7 * b5 + a8 * b8$$

2. *To multiply a 3x3 matrix, **A**, by a column vector, **B**:*

If

$$\left[\; \mathbf{A} \;\right] = \begin{bmatrix} a0 \; a1 \; a2 \\ a3 \; a4 \; a5 \\ a6 \; a7 \; a8 \end{bmatrix}$$

And

$$\left[\begin{array}{c} B \end{array}\right] = \left[\begin{array}{c} b0 \\ b1 \\ b2 \end{array}\right]$$

Then

$$\left[\begin{array}{c} AB \end{array}\right] = \left[\begin{array}{ccc} a0 & a1 & a2 \\ a3 & a4 & a5 \\ a6 & a7 & a8 \end{array}\right]\left[\begin{array}{c} b0 \\ b1 \\ b2 \end{array}\right] = \left[\begin{array}{c} ab0 \\ ab1 \\ ab2 \end{array}\right]$$

where

$$ab0 = a0 * b0 + a1 * b1 + a2 * b2$$
$$ab1 = a3 * b0 + a4 * b1 + a5 * b2$$
$$ab2 = a6 * b0 + a7 * b1 + a8 * b2$$

3. *To invert a 3x3 matrix:*

One of the elegant features of matrix notation is that if

$$\left[\begin{array}{c} R \\ G \\ B \end{array}\right] = \left[\begin{array}{c} A \end{array}\right]\left[\begin{array}{c} X \\ Y \\ Z \end{array}\right]$$

then

$$\left[\begin{array}{c} X \\ Y \\ Z \end{array}\right] = \left[\begin{array}{c} A^{-1} \end{array}\right]\left[\begin{array}{c} R \\ G \\ B \end{array}\right]$$

where A^{-1} is the inverse of A. It is this simplicity of notation that makes matrix algebra so useful in color space manipulations.

If

$$\left[\begin{array}{c} A \end{array}\right] = \left[\begin{array}{ccc} a0 & a1 & a2 \\ a3 & a4 & a5 \\ a6 & a7 & a8 \end{array}\right]$$

Then to compute the inverse of this matrix, A^{-1}, first compute the determinant of the matrix, D:

$D = (a0 * a4 * a8) - (a0 * a5 * a7) + (a1 * a5 * a6) - (a1 * a3 * a8) + (a2 * a3 * a7)$
$- (a2 * a4 * a6)$

Then

$$\left[A^{-1} \right] = \begin{bmatrix} b0 & b1 & b2 \\ b3 & b4 & b5 \\ b6 & b7 & b8 \end{bmatrix}$$

where

$$b0 = \frac{a4 * a8 - a7 * a5}{D}$$

$$b1 = \frac{-(a1 * a8 - a7 * a2)}{D}$$

$$b2 = \frac{a1 * a5 - a2 * a4}{D}$$

$$b3 = \frac{-(a3 * a8 - a6 * a5)}{D}$$

$$b4 = \frac{a0 * a8 - a6 * a2}{D}$$

$$b5 = \frac{-(a0 * a5 - a3 * a2)}{D}$$

$$b6 = \frac{a3 * a7 - a4 * a6}{D}$$

$$b7 = \frac{-(a0 * a7 - a6 * a1)}{D}$$

$$b8 = \frac{a0 * a4 - a3 * a1}{D}$$

Appendix 2: 'C' functions to implement color space manipulations

This Appendix provides 'C' functions that allow you to transform RGB color space to a number of other color spaces, and *vice versa*. It is assumed that the functions are contained in a file called colspace.h.

Certain definitions are required at the top of colspace.h, namely cie_xyz[] and cie_white[]. These contain the CIE (x, y) co-ordinates of the three phosphors and the white point of the monitor that is being used. The current values will almost certainly be wrong for your monitor.

An important assumption is that the chromaticity co-ordinates of the white point do not change with luminance. In terms of the monitor's RGB color space, this means that (for example) RGB(0.1, 0.1, 0.1) yields the same chromaticity co-ordinates as RGB(.9, .9, .9) (of course, the luminance will differ). This will only be true if you have gamma corrected the monitor correctly. Poor gamma correction will introduce large errors to programs that use these functions.

The author makes no warranties, either express or implied, regarding this computer software, its merchantability, or its fitness for any particular purpose.

adjoint

Function:	Calculates the adjoint of a 3x3 matrix
Syntax:	#include <colspace.h>
	void adjoint(double x[9], double y[9]);
Prototype in:	colspace.h
Remarks:	Given a 3x3 matrix in the array x, adjoint returns the adjoint of this matrix in the array y.
Return value:	None.
Portability:	Compiles ok under Microsoft C and Turbo C.

cie_rgb

Function:	Computes RGB co-ordinates from a CIE 1931 (x, y) vector.
Syntax:	#include <colspace.h>
	void cie_rgb(double cie[3], double rgb[3]);
Prototype in:	colspace.h
Remarks:	Given the CIE vector in cie[], cie_rgb computes the corresponding RGB co-ordinates for the display specified by the arrays cie_xyz[] and cie_white. CIE x

should be specified in cie[0], CIE y in cie[1] and CIE Y (i.e. the luminance) in cie[2]. For the return vector, R corresponds to rgb[0], G to rgb[1] and B to rgb[2]. These values are between 0 and 1.

Return value: None.
See also: rgb_cie
Example: See cie_rgb

det

Function: Computes the determinant of a 3x3 matrix.
Syntax: #include <colspace.h>
double det(double x[9]);
Prototype in: colspace.h
Remarks: Given a 3x3 matrix in the array x, det returns the determinant of the matrix.
Return value: det returns the determinant of a matrix as a double.
See also: inverse

hsv_rgb

Function: Computes RGB given hue/saturation/value.
Syntax: #include <colspace.h>
void hsv_rgb(double hsv[3], double rgb[3]);
Prototype in: colspace.h
Remarks: Given the hue, saturation and value vector in hsv[], hsv_rgb computes the RGB values. Hue corresponds to hsv[0], saturation to hsv[1] and value to hsv[2]. Hue should be specified between between 0 and 360; saturation and value should be specified between 0 and 1. For the return vector, R corresponds to rgb[0], G to rgb[1] and B to rgb[2]. These values are between 0 and 1.
Return value: None.
See also: rgb_hsv, rgb_hcs

init_tristim_lum

Function: Initializes the tristimulus matrix for a display.
Syntax: #include <colspace.h>
int init_tristim_matrix(double lum[3]);
Prototype in: colspace.h
Remarks: Writes the 3x3 tristimulus matrix (CIE (X, Y, Z)) of the display in the array tristim[]. This array is used to compute color co-ordinates in other color spaces.

The function requires the definition of one other array, cie_xyz[], that contains the CIE (x, y) coordinates of the three primaries. The function needs to be provided with the relative luminances of the three primaries in the order red, green, blue. These values should add up to unity. When programs are being written for a user whose photometric matches are known, this function should be used in preference to init_tristim_matrix. **NB: This function must be called before any color space manipulations are performed.**

Return value: Returns NULL if the array lum[] does not sum to unity.

See also: init_tristim_matrix

Example: See init_tristim_matrix.

init_tristim_matrix

Function: Initialises the tristimulus matrix for a display.

Syntax: #include <colspace.h>
                 int init_tristim_matrix(void);

Prototype in: colspace.h

Remarks: Writes the 3x3 tristimulus matrix (CIE (X, Y, Z)) of the display in the array tristim[]. This array is used to compute color co-ordinates in other color spaces. The function requires the definition of two other arrays, cie_xyz[] and cie_white[]. These contain the CIE (x, y) co-ordinates of the three primaries and the white point.**NB: This function must be called before any color space manipulations are performed.**

Return value: Returns NULL if the array cie_xyz[] cannot be inverted (i.e. if the determinant is zero).

See also: init_tristim_lum

Example:
```
#include <stdio.h>
#include "colspace.h"

main()
{
    double vector[3], result[3];
    int ch = 0, i;
    double lum[3];

    if (init_tristim_matrix() == NULL)
    {
        printf("Couldn't initialize
                program\n");
```

```
        exit(1);
    }
    printf("Tristimulus matrix is:\n");

    printf("Xr = %g, Xg = %g Xb = %g\n",
        tristim[0], tristim[1], tristim[2]);
    printf("Yr = %g, Yg = %g Yb = %g\n",
        tristim[3], tristim[4], tristim[5]);
    printf("Zr = %g, Zg = %g Zb = %g\n",
        tristim[6], tristim[7], tristim[8]);

    printf("Type in rgb relative
        luminances: ");
    scanf("%lf %lf %lf", &lum[0], &lum[1],
        &lum[2]);

    if (init_tristim_lum(lum) == NULL)
    {
        printf("Those luminances do not add
            up to unity\n");
        exit(1);
    }
    printf("Tristimulus matrix is:\n");

    printf("Xr = %g, Xg = %g Xb = %g\n",
        tristim[0], tristim[1], tristim[2]);
    printf("Yr = %g, Yg = %g Yb = %g\n",
        tristim[3], tristim[4], tristim[5]);
    printf("Zr = %g, Zg = %g Zb = %g\n",
        tristim[6], tristim[7], tristim[8]);
}
```

inverse

Function:	inverts a 3x3 matrix.
Syntax:	#include <colspace.h>
	int inverse(double x[9], double y[9]);
Prototype in:	colspace.h
Remarks:	Given a 3x3 matrix in the array x, inverse returns the inverse of this matrix in the array y. The matrix elements are numbered from left to right starting with element 0 at the top left.
Return value:	inverse returns a NULL if the matrix cannot be inverted (i.e the determinant is zero).
See also:	det

matrix_multiply

Function:	Multiplies two 3x3 matrices together.

Syntax:	#include <colspace.h> void matrix_multiply (double x[9], double y[9], double z[9]);
Prototype in:	colspace.h
Remarks:	Given a two 3x3 matrices in the arrays x and y, matrix_multiply returns their product in the matrix z. The matrix elements are numbered from left to right starting with element 0 at the top left.
Return value:	None.
See also:	vect_mult

mb_rgb

Function:	Computes RGB co-ordinates from a cone difference vector.
Syntax:	#include <colspace.h> void mb_rgb(double mb[3], double rgb[3]);
Prototype in:	colspace.h
Remarks:	Given the cone difference vector in mb[], mb_rgb computes the corresponding RGB co-ordinates for the display specified by the arrays cie_xyz[] and cie_white[]. The cone co-ordinates used are those of Smith & Pokorny. S/(M+L) modulation should be specified in mb[0], M/(M+L) modulation in mb[1] and luminance (i.e. M+L) modulation in mb[2]. For the return vector, R corresponds to rgb[0], G to rgb[1] and B to rgb[2]. These values are between 0 and 1.
Return value:	None.
See also:	rgb_mb

rgb_cie

Function:	Computes CIE 1931 (x, y) co-ordinates from RGB vector.
Syntax:	#include <colspace.h> void rgb_cie(double rgb[3], double cie[3]);
Prototype in:	colspace.h
Remarks:	Given the RGB vector in rgb[], rgb_cie computes the corresponding CIE co-ordinates for the display specified by the arrays cie_xyz[] and cie_white[]. R corresponds to rgb[0], G to rgb[1] and B to rgb[2]. The return vector gives CIE x in cie[0], CIE y in cie[1] and CIE Y (i.e. the luminance) in cie[2]. RGB values must be between 0 and 1.

Return value:	None.
See also:	cie_rgb
Example:	

```c
#include <stdio.h>
#include <colspace.h>

main()
{
    double vector[3], result[3];
    int ch = 0, i;

    if (init_tristim_matrix() == NULL)
    {
        printf("Couldn't initialize
            program\n");
        exit(1);
    }
    printf("Tristimulus matrix is:\n");

    printf("Xr = %g, Xg = %g Xb = %g\n",
        tristim[0], tristim[1], tristim[2]);
    printf("Yr = %g, Yg = %g Yb = %g\n",
        tristim[3], tristim[4], tristim[5]);
    printf("Zr = %g, Zg = %g Zb = %g",
        tristim[6], tristim[7], tristim[8]);

    while(ch != '1' && ch != '2')
    {
        printf("\n1. rgb -> cie\n2. cie ->
            rgb\n Which transform?");
        ch = getche();
    }
    printf("\nType in vector: ");
        scanf("%lf %lf %lf", &vector[0],
            &vector[1], &vector[2]);

    switch(ch)
    {
        case '1':     rgb_cie(vector, result);
                      break;
        case '2':     cie_rgb(vector, result);
                      break;
    }

    printf("vector [%g %g %g] transforms to
        [%g %g %g]\n", vector[0], vector[1],
            vector[2], result[0], result[1],
            result[2]);
}
```

rgb_hsv

Function:	Computes hue/saturation/value from an RGB vector.
Syntax:	#include <colspace.h> int rgb_hsv(double rgb[3], double hsv[3]);
Prototype in:	colspace.h
Remarks:	Given the RGB vector in rgb[], rgb_hsv computes the corresponding hue, saturation and value. R corresponds to rgb[0], G to rgb[1] and B to rgb[2]. The return vector gives hue (between 0 and 360) in hsv[0], saturation (between 0 and 1) in hsv[1] and value (between 0 and 1) in hsv[2]. RGB values must be between 0 and 1.
Return value:	rgb_hsv returns NULL if RGB values are all zero, or if the computed saturation is zero.
See also:	hsv_rgb, rgb_hcs

rgb_mb

Function:	Computes cone difference co-ordinates from an RGB vector.
Syntax:	#include <colspace.h> int rgb_mb(double rgb[3], double mb[3]);
Prototype in:	colspace.h
Remarks:	Given the RGB vector in rgb[], rgb_mb computes the corresponding cone difference co-ordinates for the display specified by the arrays cie_xyz[] and cie_white[]. The cone co-ordinates are computed from the Smith & Pokorny cone fundamentals. R corresponds to rgb[0], G to rgb[1] and B to rgb[2]. The return vector gives S/(M+L) modulation in mb[0], M/(M+L) modulation in mb[1] and luminance (that is M+L) in mb[2]. RGB values must be between 0 and 1.
Return value:	rgb_mb returns NULL if the luminance (i.e. M+L) is zero.
See also:	mb_rgb
Example:	#include <stdio.h> #include "colspace.h" main() { double vector[3], result[3], rgb[3];

```
if (init_tristim_matrix() == NULL)
{
    printf("Couldn't initialize
        program\n");
    exit(1);
}

for(;;)
{
    printf("\nType in cie vector: ");
    scanf("%lf %lf %lf", &vector[0],
        &vector[1], &vector[2]);

    cie_rgb(vector, rgb);
    rgb_mb(rgb, result);

    printf("vector [%g %g %g] transforms
        to [%g %g %g]\n", vector[0],
        vector[1], vector[2], result[0],
        result[1], result[2]);
}
}
```

rgb_sml

Function:	Computes cone co-ordinates from an RGB vector.
Syntax:	#include <colspace.h>
	void rgb_sml(double rgb[3], double sml[3]);
Prototype in:	colspace.h
Remarks:	Given the RGB vector in rgb[], rgb_sml computes the corresponding cone co-ordinates for the display specified by the arrays cie_xyz[] and cie_white[]. The cone co-ordinates are computed from the Smith & Pokorny cone fundamentals. R corresponds to rgb[0], G to rgb[1] and B to rgb[2]. The return vector gives S cone modulation in sml[0], M cone modulation in sml[1] and L cone modulation in sml[2]. RGB values must be between 0 and 1.
Return value:	None.
See also:	sml_rgb, rgb_est, est_rgb

rgb_yiq

Function:	Computes yiq from an RGB vector.
Syntax:	#include <colspace.h>
	int rgb_yiq(double rgb[3], double yiq[3]);
Prototype in:	colspace.h

Remarks:	Given the RGB vector in rgb[], rgb_yiq computes the corresponding luminance, in-phase and quadrature signals. R corresponds to rgb[0], G to rgb[1] and B to rgb[2]. The return vector (with all values between 0 and 1) gives luminance in yiq[0], in-phase in in yiq[1] and quadrature in yiq[2]. RGB values must be between 0 and 1. Note that this color space is valid only for a predefined set of phosphors (the NTSC set).
Return value:	None
See also:	yiq_rgb

sml_rgb

Function:	Computes RGB co-ordinates from a cone vector.
Syntax:	#include <colspace.h>
	void sml_rgb(double sml[3], double rgb[3]);
Prototype in:	colspace.h
Remarks:	Given the cone vector in sml[], sml_rgb computes the corresponding RGB co-ordinates for the display specified by the arrays cie_xyz[] and cie_white[]. The cone co-ordinates used are those of Smith & Pokorny. S cone modulation should be specified in sml[0], M cone modulation in sml[1] and L cone modulation in sml[2]. For the return vector, R corresponds to rgb[0], G to rgb[1] and B to rgb[2]. These values are between 0 and 1.
Return value:	None.
See also:	rgb_sml, rgb_est, est_rgb

vect_mult

Function:	Multiplies a 3x3 matrix by a column vector.
Syntax:	#include <colspace.h>
	void vect_mult(double x[9], double y[3], double z[3]);
Prototype in:	colspace.h
Remarks:	Given a 3x3 matrix in the array x and a column vector in the array y, vect_mult returns the product in the array z.
Return value:	None.
See also:	matrix_multiply

yiq_rgb

Function:	Computes RGB given yiq.
Syntax:	#include <colspace.h>

	void yiq_rgb(double yiq[3], double rgb[3]);
Prototype in:	colspace.h
Remarks:	Given the luminance, in-phase and quadrature signals in yiq[], yiq_rgb computes the RGB values. Luminance corresponds to yiq[0], the in-phase signal to yiq[1] and the quadrature signal yiq[2]. For the return vector, R corresponds to rgb[0], G to rgb[1] and B to rgb[2]. These values are between 0 and 1.
Return value:	None.
Portability:	Compiles ok under Microsoft C and Turbo C.
See also:	rgb_yiq

```c
#include <math.h>
#include <stdio.h>

#define sqr(a)  (a*a)
#define PI   3.1415926536

/*
 * Next matrix in form    xR xG xB
 *                        yR yG yB
 *                        zR zG zB
 * where x y and z are the chromaticity co-ordinates,
 * not tristim values,of the display primaries. Put the
 * values for your monitor in here.
 */
double cie_xyz[9] = { .6281, .2859, .1535,
                      .3476, .6091, .0640,
                      .0243, .1050, .7825 };

/*
 * Next matrix contains cie x, y and z of white formed
 * by three primaries. Put the values for your monitor
 * in here.
 */
double cie_white[3] = { .2965, .3102, .3933 };


/*
 * Next matrix will contain tristimulus values when
 * init_tristim_matrix()
 * or init_tristim_lum() is called
 */
double tristim[9] = { 0.0, 0.0, 0.0,
                      0.0, 0.0, 0.0,
                      0.0, 0.0, 0.0 };

/*
 * Following matrix is Smith-Pokorny fundamentals
 */
double sp_vals[9] = {0.000000, 0.00000, 0.01608,
                     -0.15514, 0.45684, 0.03286,
                     0.15514, 0.54312, -0.03286};

/*
 * Next matrix contains RGB -> YIQ values
 * Eqns are   Y = 0.30R + 0.59G + 0.11B
 *            I = 0.60R - 0.28G - 0.32B
 *            Q = 0.21R - 0.52G + 0.31B
 */
double yiq_vals[9] = {.30, .59, .11,
                      .60, -.28, -.32,
                      .21, -.52, .31 };
```

```
/*
 * Function prototypes
 */

int inverse(double[9], double[9]);
double det(double[9]);
void matrix_multiply(double[9], double[9], double[9]);
void vect_mult(double[9], double[3], double[3]);
void adjoint(double[9], double[9]);
int init_tristim_matrix(void);
int init_tristim_lum(double[3]);
void rgb_cie(double[3], double[3]);
void cie_rgb(double[3], double[3]);
void rgb_sml(double[3], double[3]);
void sml_rgb(double[3], double[3]);
int rgb_mb(double[3], double[3]);
void mb_rgb(double[3], double[3]);
int rgb_hsv(double[3], double[3]);
void hsv_rgb(double[3], double[3]);
void rgb_yiq(double[3], double[3]);
void yiq_rgb(double[3], double[3]);

/*
 * Compute inverse of matrix fstmat[], returned in array
 * secmat[]. Returns a NULL if unsucessful (i.e. if
 * determinant is zero)
 */
int inverse(double fstmat[9], double secmat[9])
{
  double d;

  if ((d = det(fstmat)) == 0) {
    return(NULL);
  }

  secmat[0] = (fstmat[4] * fstmat[8] - fstmat[7] *
    fstmat[5]) / d;
  secmat[1] = (- (fstmat[1] * fstmat[8] - fstmat[7] *
    fstmat[2])) / d;
  secmat[2] = (fstmat[1] * fstmat[5] - fstmat[2] *
    fstmat[4]) / d;
  secmat[3] = (- (fstmat[3] * fstmat[8] - fstmat[6] *
    fstmat[5])) / d;
  secmat[4] = (fstmat[0] * fstmat[8] - fstmat[6] *
    fstmat[2]) / d;
  secmat[5] = (- (fstmat[0] * fstmat[5] - fstmat[3] *
    fstmat[2])) / d;
  secmat[6] = (fstmat[3] * fstmat[7] - fstmat[4] *
    fstmat[6]) / d;
  secmat[7] = (- (fstmat[0] * fstmat[7] - fstmat[6] *
    fstmat[1])) / d;
```

```c
      secmat[8] = (fstmat[0] * fstmat[4] - fstmat[3] *
      fstmat[1]) / d;
      return(1);
}

/*
 * Compute determinant of a matrix
 */
double det(double mat[9])
{
   return(mat[0] * mat[4] * mat[8] - mat[0] * mat[5] *
   mat[7] + mat[1] * mat[5] * mat[6] - mat[1] * mat[3] *
   mat[8] + mat[2] * mat[3] * mat[7] - mat[2] * mat[4] *
   mat[6]);
}

/*
 * Given 3x3 matrix[] and a column vector[], this
 * function returns result[]
 */
void vect_mult(double matrix[9], double vector[3],
double result[3])
{
   int i;

   for (i = 0; i < 3; i++)
      result[i] = matrix[i*3] * vector[0] +
         matrix[(i*3)+1] * vector[1] + matrix[(i*3)+2] *
         vector[2];
}
/*
 * Multiply two 3x3 matrices together, mat1 and mat2,
 * and put the result in the matrix mat3
 */
void matrix_multiply(double mat1[9], double mat2[9],
double mat3[9])
{
   int i, j, k;

   for (i = 0; i < 9; i++)
   {
      j = (i < 3) ? i: i%3;
      k = (i / 3) * 3;
      mat3[i] = mat1[k] * mat2[j] + mat1[k+1] * mat2[j+3]
      + mat1[k+2] * mat2[j+6];
   }
}
/*
 * Get the adjoint of a matrix fstmat, put in secmat
 */
void adjoint(double fstmat[9], double secmat[9])
{
```

```c
    secmat[0] = fstmat[0];
    secmat[1] = fstmat[3];
    secmat[2] = fstmat[6];
    secmat[3] = fstmat[1];
    secmat[4] = fstmat[4];
    secmat[5] = fstmat[7];
    secmat[6] = fstmat[2];
    secmat[7] = fstmat[5];
    secmat[8] = fstmat[8];
}

/*
    init_tristim_matrix()

This function generates the basic tristimulus matrix to
initialize the program
*/

int init_tristim_matrix(void)
{
    double wht_vect[3], cie_vect[3];
    int i, j;

    if ((inverse(cie_xyz, tristim)) == NULL)
        return(NULL);
/*
 * Compute tristimulus values of the white for unit Y
 */
    wht_vect[0] = cie_white[0] / cie_white[1];
    wht_vect[1] = 1.0;
    wht_vect[2] = cie_white[2] / cie_white[1];

    vect_mult(tristim, wht_vect, cie_vect);
    for (i = 0; i < 9; i++)
    {
        j = i < 3 ? i : i%3;
        tristim[i] = cie_xyz[i] * cie_vect[j];
    }
    return(1);
}
/*
    init_tristim_lum()

This function generates the basic tristimulus matrix to
initialize the program given three relative luminances
in the order red, green, blue. Use this function as an
alternative to init_tristim_matrix()
*/

int init_tristim_lum(double lum[3])
{
    int i;
```

```c
  double sum = 0.0;

  for(i=0; i < 3; i++)
    sum+=lum[i];
/*
 * Check that function has been sent sensible
 * luminance values
 */
  if(sum > 1.0 || sum < 1.0)
    return(NULL);

  for(i=0; i < 9; i++)
    tristim[i] = 0.0;
/* red gun */
  tristim[0] = cie_xyz[0] * lum[0] / cie_xyz[3];
  tristim[3] = lum[0];
  tristim[6] = cie_xyz[6] * lum[0] / cie_xyz[3];

/* green gun */
  tristim[1] = cie_xyz[1] * lum[1] / cie_xyz[4];
  tristim[4] = lum[1];
  tristim[7] = cie_xyz[7] * lum[1] / cie_xyz[4];

/* blue gun */
  tristim[2] = cie_xyz[2] * lum[2] / cie_xyz[5];
  tristim[5] = lum[2];
  tristim[8] = cie_xyz[8] * lum[2] / cie_xyz[5];

  return(1);
}
/*
 * Given RGB, this function returns CIE
 * co-ordinates (x, y, Y)
 */
void rgb_cie(double rgb_vect[3], double cie_vect[3])
{
  double temp_vect[3];
  int i;

  vect_mult(tristim, rgb_vect, temp_vect);

  for (i = 0; i < 2; i++)
    cie_vect[i] = temp_vect[i] / (temp_vect[0] +
      temp_vect[1] + temp_vect[2]);

  cie_vect[2] = temp_vect[1];   /* Luminance */
}
/*
 * Given cie xyY vector, this function returns RGB
```

```
 * co-ordinates
 */
void cie_rgb(double cie_vect[3], double rgb_vect[3])
{
  double inv_tristim[9], tristim_vect[3];

  tristim_vect[0] = cie_vect[0] * cie_vect[2] /
    cie_vect[1];
  tristim_vect[1] = cie_vect[2];
  tristim_vect[2] = (1.0 - cie_vect[0] - cie_vect[1]) *
    cie_vect[2] / cie_vect[1];
  inverse(tristim, inv_tristim);
  vect_mult(inv_tristim, tristim_vect, rgb_vect);
}
/*
 * Given RGB, this function returns Smith-Pokorny
 * co-ordinates
 */
void rgb_sml(double phosphor_vect[3], double
cone_vect[3])
{
  double cone_RGB[9];
  matrix_multiply(sp_vals, tristim, cone_RGB);
  vect_mult(cone_RGB, phosphor_vect, cone_vect);
}
/*
 * Given Smith-Pokorny SML, this function returns RGB
 */
void sml_rgb(double cone_vect[3], double
phosphor_vect[3])
{
  double cone_RGB[9], RGB_cone[9];
  matrix_multiply(sp_vals, tristim, cone_RGB);
  inverse(cone_RGB, RGB_cone);
  vect_mult(RGB_cone, cone_vect, phosphor_vect);
}

/*
 * Given RGB, this function returns MacLeod-Boynton
 * s, m and luminance
 */
int rgb_mb(double phosphor_vect[3], double cone_vect[3])
{
  double lum;

  rgb_sml(phosphor_vect, cone_vect);
  lum = cone_vect[1] + cone_vect[2];
  if (lum == 0)
  return (NULL);
  cone_vect[0] /= lum;
  cone_vect[1] /= lum;
  cone_vect[2] = lum;
```

```
}
/*
 * Given MacLeod-Boynton s, m and luminance, this
 * function returns RGB
 */
void mb_rgb(double cone_vect[3], double
phosphor_vect[3])
{
  double sp_cone_vect[3];

  sp_cone_vect[0] = cone_vect[0] * cone_vect[2];
  sp_cone_vect[1] = cone_vect[1] * cone_vect[2];
  sp_cone_vect[2] = (1.0 - cone_vect[1]) * cone_vect[2];

  sml_rgb(sp_cone_vect, phosphor_vect);
}
/*
 * Given RGB, this function returns HSV
 */
#define bigger(a,b)   ((a > b)? a : b)
#define smaller(a,b)  ((a < b)? a : b)

int rgb_hsv(double rgb[3], double hsv[3])
{
  double min, max, r_rel, g_rel, b_rel;

  hsv[0] = hsv[1] = hsv[2] = 0;

  max = bigger(rgb[0], bigger(rgb[1],rgb[2]));
/* get largest rgb value */
  min = smaller(rgb[0], smaller(rgb[1],rgb[2]));
/* get smallest rgb value */

  /*
   * Compute value; if max is zero, silly input
   */
  if (!max)
    return(NULL);
  else
    hsv[2] = max;

  /*
   * Compute saturation
   */
  if ((hsv[1] = (max - min) / max) == 0)
    return(NULL);

  /*
   * Now compute the hue
   */
  r_rel = (max - rgb[0]) / (max - min);
  g_rel = (max - rgb[1]) / (max - min);
```

```
  b_rel = (max - rgb[2]) / (max - min);

  if (rgb[0] == max) {
    if (rgb[1] == min)
      hsv[0] = 5 + b_rel;
    else
      hsv[0] = 1 - g_rel;
  }
  else if (rgb[1] == max) {
    if (rgb[2] == min)
      hsv[0] = r_rel + 1;
    else
      hsv[0] = 3 - b_rel;
  }
  else {
    if (rgb[0] == min)
      hsv[0] = 3 + g_rel;
    else
      hsv[0] = 5 - r_rel;
  }

  hsv[0] *= 60;          /* hue, convert to degrees */
  return(1);
}
/*
 * Given HSV, this function returns RGB
 */
void hsv_rgb(double hsv[3], double rgb[3])
{
  double sub_color, hue_step, main_color, var1, var2,
var3;

  hue_step = hsv[0] / 60;
  if (hue_step == 6)
    hue_step = 0;
  main_color = (int) hue_step;
  sub_color = hue_step - main_color;

  var1 = (1 - hsv[1]) * hsv[2];
  var2 = (1 - (hsv[1] * sub_color)) * hsv[2];
  var3 = (1 - (hsv[1] * (1 - sub_color))) * hsv[2];

  switch (main_color)
  {
    case 0:       rgb[0] = hsv[2];
                  rgb[1] = var3;
                  rgb[2] = var1;
    case 1:       rgb[0] = var2;
                  rgb[1] = hsv[2];
                  rgb[2] = var1;
    case 2:       rgb[0] = var1;
                  rgb[1] = hsv[2];
```

```
                       rgb[2]  = var3;
       case 3:         rgb[0]  = var1;
                       rgb[1]  = var2;
                       rgb[2]  = hsv[2];
       case 4:         rgb[0]  = var3;
                       rgb[1]  = var1;
                       rgb[2]  = hsv[2];
       case 5:         rgb[0]  = hsv[2];
                       rgb[1]  = var1;
                       rgb[2]  = var2;
  }
}
/*
 * Given RGB, this function returns YIQ
 */
void rgb_yiq(double rgb[3], double yiq[3])
{
  vect_mult(yiq_vals, rgb, yiq);
}
/*
 * Given YIQ, this function returns RGB
 */
void yiq_rgb(double yiq[3], double rgb[3])
{
  double inv_rgb[9];

  inverse(yiq_vals, inv_rgb);
  vect_mult(inv_rgb, yiq, rgb);
}
```

Appendix 3: CIE co-ordinates of Munsell colors

2.5R

Value	Chroma	CIE x	CIE y	Y
9	6	0.3665	0.3183	0.7866
9	4	0.3445	0.3179	0.7866
9	2	0.3210	0.3168	0.7866
8	10	0.4125	0.3160	0.5910
8	8	0.3900	0.3171	0.5910
8	6	0.3671	0.3175	0.5910
8	4	0.3460	0.3177	0.5910
8	2	0.3236	0.3169	0.5910
7	16	0.4885	0.3039	0.4306
7	14	0.4660	0.3082	0.4306
7	12	0.4435	0.3119	0.4306
7	10	0.4183	0.3144	0.4306
7	8	0.3961	0.3160	0.4306
7	6	0.3728	0.3170	0.4306
7	4	0.3499	0.3171	0.4306
7	2	0.3284	0.3170	0.4306
6	18	0.5262	0.2928	0.3005
6	16	0.5041	0.2983	0.3005
6	14	0.4790	0.3041	0.3005
6	12	0.4568	0.3082	0.3005
6	10	0.4320	0.3118	0.3005
6	8	0.4065	0.3144	0.3005
6	6	0.3832	0.3158	0.3005
6	4	0.3566	0.3163	0.3005
6	2	0.3318	0.3166	0.3005
5	20	0.5784	0.2719	0.1977
5	18	0.5540	0.2804	0.1977
5	16	0.5300	0.2880	0.1977
5	14	0.5047	0.2950	0.1977
5	12	0.4820	0.3002	0.1977
5	10	0.4533	0.3058	0.1977
5	8	0.4252	0.3101	0.1977
5	6	0.3960	0.3130	0.1977
5	4	0.3660	0.3148	0.1977
5	2	0.3360	0.3158	0.1977
4	18	0.5898	0.2622	0.1200
4	16	0.5620	0.2724	0.1200
4	14	0.5369	0.2810	0.1200
4	12	0.5072	0.2897	0.1200
4	10	0.4774	0.2969	0.1200
4	8	0.4472	0.3031	0.1200
4	6	0.4141	0.3085	0.1200
4	4	0.3806	0.3125	0.1200

4	2	0.3461	0.3150	0.1200
3	16	0.6116	0.2456	0.06555
3	14	0.5828	0.2579	0.06555
3	12	0.5536	0.2691	0.06555
3	10	0.5191	0.2811	0.06555
3	8	0.4821	0.2918	0.06555
3	6	0.4409	0.3009	0.06555
3	4	0.4021	0.3076	0.06555
3	2	0.3591	0.3130	0.06555
2	14	0.5734	0.2083	0.03126
2	12	0.5438	0.2254	0.03126
2	10	0.5122	0.2428	0.03126
2	8	0.4776	0.2593	0.03126
2	6	0.4390	0.2760	0.03126
2	4	0.4021	0.2900	0.03126
2	2	0.3614	0.3033	0.03126
1	10	0.5058	0.1900	0.01210
1	8	0.4812	0.2103	0.01210
1	6	0.4515	0.2329	0.01210
1	4	0.4166	0.2569	0.01210
1	2	0.3768	0.2816	0.01210

5.0R

Value	Chroma	CIE x	CIE y	Y
9	6	0.3734	0.3256	0.7866
9	4	0.3495	0.3226	0.7866
9	2	0.3240	0.3188	0.7866
8	10	0.4249	0.3270	0.5910
8	8	0.4001	0.3263	0.5910
8	6	0.3743	0.3248	0.5910
8	4	0.3510	0.3224	0.5910
8	2	0.3254	0.3186	0.5910
7	14	0.4848	0.3238	0.4306
7	12	0.4595	0.3252	0.4306
7	10	0.4320	0.3260	0.4306
7	8	0.4067	0.3256	0.4306
7	6	0.3805	0.3244	0.4306
7	4	0.3552	0.3222	0.4306
7	2	0.3306	0.3190	0.4306
6	18	0.5552	0.3138	0.3005
6	16	0.5297	0.3179	0.3005
6	14	0.5020	0.3212	0.3005
6	12	0.4760	0.3234	0.3005
6	10	0.4480	0.3250	0.3005
6	8	0.4187	0.3251	0.3005
6	6	0.3921	0.3244	0.3005
6	4	0.3628	0.3221	0.3005
6	2	0.3343	0.3190	0.3005
5	20	0.6142	0.2970	0.1977
5	18	0.5918	0.3038	0.1977

5	16	0.5637	0.3102	0.1977
5	14	0.5341	0.3158	0.1977
5	12	0.5071	0.3194	0.1977
5	10	0.4747	0.3227	0.1977
5	8	0.4413	0.3240	0.1977
5	6	0.4078	0.3238	0.1977
5	4	0.3740	0.3220	0.1977
5	2	0.3392	0.3192	0.1977
4	18	0.6329	0.2881	0.1200
4	16	0.6039	0.2978	0.1200
4	14	0.5734	0.3057	0.1200
4	12	0.5385	0.3129	0.1200
4	10	0.5043	0.3176	0.1200
4	8	0.4690	0.3209	0.1200
4	6	0.4229	0.3226	0.1200
4	4	0.3916	0.3223	0.1200
4	2	0.3508	0.3200	0.1200
3	16	0.6250	0.2660	0.06555
3	14	0.6204	0.2789	0.06555
3	12	0.5884	0.2904	0.06555
3	10	0.5500	0.3024	0.06555
3	8	0.5064	0.3114	0.06555
3	6	0.4592	0.3168	0.06555
3	4	0.4148	0.3190	0.06555
3	2	0.3645	0.3190	0.06555
2	14	0.6302	0.2287	0.03126
2	12	0.5930	0.2465	0.03126
2	10	0.5557	0.2633	0.03126
2	8	0.5143	0.2800	0.03126
2	6	0.4642	0.2934	0.03126
2	4	0.4184	0.3032	0.03126
2	2	0.3692	0.3111	0.03126
1	10	0.5604	0.2100	0.01210
1	8	0.5282	0.2297	0.01210
1	6	0.4885	0.2515	0.01210
1	4	0.4420	0.2728	0.01210
1	2	0.3908	0.2929	0.01210

7.5R

Value	Chroma	CIE x	CIE y	Y
9	6	0.3812	0.3348	0.7866
9	4	0.3551	0.3283	0.7866
9	2	0.3263	0.3210	0.7866
8	10	0.4388	0.3419	0.5910
8	8	0.4118	0.3385	0.5910
8	6	0.3830	0.3335	0.5910
8	4	0.3564	0.3279	0.5910
8	2	0.3277	0.3211	0.5910
7	16	0.5341	0.3452	0.4306
7	14	0.5059	0.3450	0.4306

7	12	0.4777	0.3435	0.4306
7	10	0.4470	0.3413	0.4306
7	8	0.4196	0.3382	0.4306
7	6	0.3888	0.3336	0.4306
7	4	0.3611	0.3282	0.4306
7	2	0.3335	0.3220	0.4306
6	18	0.5829	0.3396	0.3005
6	16	0.5560	0.3420	0.3005
6	14	0.5265	0.3431	0.3005
6	12	0.4961	0.3428	0.3005
6	10	0.4655	0.3412	0.3005
6	8	0.4318	0.3383	0.3005
6	6	0.4000	0.3340	0.3005
6	4	0.3692	0.3291	0.3005
6	2	0.3381	0.3228	0.3005
5	20	0.6388	0.3216	0.1977
5	18	0.6161	0.3277	0.1977
5	16	0.5901	0.3331	0.1977
5	14	0.5590	0.3370	0.1977
5	12	0.5280	0.3389	0.1977
5	10	0.4927	0.3399	0.1977
5	8	0.4563	0.3387	0.1977
5	6	0.4180	0.3348	0.1977
5	4	0.3806	0.3294	0.1977
5	2	0.3425	0.3229	0.1977
4	20	0.6806	0.2988	0.1200
4	18	0.6538	0.3100	0.1200
4	16	0.6260	0.3192	0.1200
4	14	0.5959	0.3269	0.1200
4	12	0.5603	0.3321	0.1200
4	10	0.5235	0.3351	0.1200
4	8	0.4850	0.3359	0.1200
4	6	0.4415	0.3340	0.1200
4	4	0.3990	0.3300	0.1200
4	2	0.3538	0.3236	0.1200
3	16	0.6817	0.2872	0.06555
3	14	0.6492	0.3012	0.06555
3	12	0.6158	0.3129	0.06555
3	10	0.5730	0.3240	0.06555
3	8	0.5251	0.3297	0.06555
3	6	0.4738	0.3316	0.06555
3	4	0.4240	0.3302	0.06555
3	2	0.3690	0.3248	0.06555
2	14	0.6791	0.2520	0.03126
2	12	0.6392	0.2704	0.03126
2	10	0.5952	0.2874	0.03126
2	8	0.5433	0.3027	0.03126
2	6	0.4875	0.3123	0.03126
2	4	0.4335	0.3169	0.03126
2	2	0.3751	0.3181	0.03126
1	10	0.6111	0.2290	0.01210
1	8	0.5722	0.2487	0.01210

1	6	0.5235	0.2698	0.01210
1	4	0.4660	0.2888	0.01210
1	2	0.4020	0.3034	0.01210

10.0R

Value	Chroma	CIE x	CIE y	Y
9	6	0.3880	0.3439	0.7866
9	4	0.3600	0.3348	0.7866
9	2	0.3284	0.3233	0.7866
8	10	0.4490	0.3589	0.5910
8	8	0.4212	0.3526	0.5910
8	6	0.3910	0.3442	0.5910
8	4	0.3621	0.3349	0.5910
8	2	0.3301	0.3237	0.5910
7	16	0.5519	0.3729	0.4306
7	14	0.5234	0.3700	0.4306
7	12	0.4930	0.3559	0.4306
7	10	0.4600	0.3596	0.4306
7	8	0.4308	0.3533	0.4306
7	6	0.3984	0.3452	0.4306
7	4	0.3671	0.3360	0.4306
7	2	0.3360	0.3253	0.4306
6	18	0.6009	0.3720	0.3005
6	16	0.5741	0.3713	0.3005
6	14	0.5468	0.3697	0.3005
6	12	0.5150	0.3667	0.3005
6	10	0.4812	0.3619	0.3005
6	8	0.4449	0.3550	0.3005
6	6	0.4103	0.3473	0.3005
6	4	0.3768	0.3381	0.3005
6	2	0.3417	0.3268	0.3005
5	18	0.6297	0.3642	0.3005
5	16	0.6037	0.3657	0.1977
5	14	0.5771	0.3664	0.1977
5	12	0.5481	0.3660	0.1977
5	10	0.5113	0.3630	0.1977
5	8	0.4713	0.3575	0.1977
5	6	0.4299	0.3499	0.1977
5	4	0.3879	0.3398	0.1977
5	2	0.3465	0.3278	0.1977
4	16	0.6409	0.3533	0.1200
4	14	0.6154	0.3568	0.1200
4	12	0.5801	0.3588	0.1200
4	10	0.5418	0.3580	0.1200
4	8	0.4995	0.3557	0.1200
4	6	0.4535	0.3500	0.1200
4	4	0.4078	0.3412	0.1200
4	2	0.3582	0.3294	0.1200
3	14	0.6703	0.3249	0.06555
3	12	0.6322	0.3361	0.06555

3	10	0.5871	0.3440	0.06555
3	8	0.5393	0.3477	0.06555
3	6	0.4854	0.3467	0.06555
3	4	0.4308	0.3412	0.06555
3	2	0.3728	0.3314	0.06555
2	14	0.7165	0.2734	0.03126
2	12	0.6732	0.2937	0.03126
2	10	0.6247	0.3120	0.03126
2	8	0.5713	0.3259	0.03126
2	6	0.5095	0.3331	0.03126
2	4	0.4481	0.3330	0.03126
2	2	0.3811	0.3274	0.03126
1	10	0.6661	0.2499	0.01210
1	8	0.6178	0.2713	0.01210
1	6	0.5584	0.2921	0.01210
1	4	0.4933	0.3068	0.01210
1	2	0.4128	0.3154	0.01210

2.5YR

Value	Chroma	CIE x	CIE y	Y
9	6	0.3927	0.3550	0.7866
9	4	0.3641	0.3422	0.7866
9	2	0.3320	0.3273	0.7866
8	12	0.4852	0.3847	0.5910
8	10	0.4552	0.3761	0.5910
8	8	0.4275	0.3662	0.5910
8	6	0.3960	0.3547	0.5910
8	4	0.3667	0.3429	0.5910
8	2	0.3334	0.3276	0.5910
7	20	0.5824	0.4046	0.4306
7	18	0.5695	0.4024	0.4306
7	16	0.5522	0.3989	0.4306
7	14	0.5297	0.3938	0.4306
7	12	0.5001	0.3861	0.4306
7	10	0.4671	0.3768	0.4306
7	8	0.4371	0.3679	0.4306
7	6	0.4053	0.3570	0.4306
7	4	0.3715	0.3439	0.4306
7	2	0.3392	0.3298	0.4306
6	18	0.5879	0.4021	0.3005
6	16	0.5698	0.3990	0.3005
6	14	0.5488	0.3947	0.3005
6	12	0.5215	0.3887	0.3005
6	10	0.4891	0.3806	0.3005
6	8	0.4533	0.3708	0.3005
6	6	0.4180	0.3600	0.3005
6	4	0.3806	0.3467	0.3005
6	2	0.3453	0.3321	0.3005
5	16	0.5933	0.3989	0.1977
5	14	0.5731	0.3953	0.1977

5	12	0.5482	0.3909	0.1977
5	10	0.5175	0.3844	0.1977
5	8	0.4795	0.3758	0.1977
5	6	0.4365	0.3640	0.1977
5	4	0.3925	0.3494	0.1977
5	2	0.3506	0.3337	0.1977
4	12	0.5809	0.3910	0.1200
4	10	0.5475	0.3856	0.1200
4	8	0.5071	0.3777	0.1200
4	6	0.4612	0.3674	0.1200
4	4	0.4141	0.3539	0.1200
4	2	0.3624	0.3367	0.1200
3	10	0.5941	0.3818	0.06555
3	8	0.5475	0.3771	0.06555
3	6	0.4954	0.3692	0.06555
3	4	0.4360	0.3563	0.06555
3	2	0.3757	0.3391	0.06555
2	8	0.5995	0.3590	0.03126
2	6	0.5280	0.3581	0.03126
2	4	0.4598	0.3508	0.03126
2	2	0.3852	0.3365	0.03126
1	8	0.6721	0.3058	0.01210
1	6	0.6048	0.3270	0.01210
1	4	0.5311	0.3371	0.01210
1	2	0.4258	0.3344	0.01210

5.0YR

Value	Chroma	CIE x	CIE y	Y
9	6	0.3948	0.3659	0.7866
9	4	0.3668	0.3509	0.7866
9	2	0.3353	0.3325	0.7866
8	14	0.5088	0.4145	0.5910
8	12	0.4849	0.4050	0.5910
8	10	0.4576	0.3938	0.5910
8	8	0.4310	0.3820	0.5910
8	6	0.3988	0.3663	0.5910
8	4	0.3690	0.3510	0.5910
8	2	0.3373	0.3330	0.5910
7	20	0.5657	0.4298	0.4306
7	18	0.5564	0.4267	0.4306
7	16	0.5437	0.4228	0.4306
7	14	0.5252	0.4168	0.4306
7	12	0.5007	0.4081	0.4306
7	10	0.4711	0.3972	0.4306
7	8	0.4402	0.3842	0.4306
7	6	0.4091	0.3701	0.4306
7	4	0.3750	0.3530	0.4306
7	2	0.3421	0.3349	0.4306
6	18	0.5715	0.4270	0.3005
6	16	0.5597	0.4239	0.3005

6	14	0.5423	0.4188	0.3005
6	12	0.5199	0.4119	0.3005
6	10	0.4921	0.4022	0.3005
6	8	0.4592	0.3900	0.3005
6	6	0.4229	0.3750	0.3005
6	4	0.3840	0.3564	0.3005
6	2	0.3474	0.3373	0.3005
5	14	0.5642	0.4201	0.1977
5	12	0.5422	0.4141	0.1977
5	10	0.5161	0.4064	0.1977
5	8	0.4830	0.3960	0.1977
5	6	0.4420	0.3808	0.1977
5	4	0.3968	0.3614	0.1977
5	2	0.3530	0.3395	0.1977
4	12	0.5729	0.4169	0.1200
4	10	0.5432	0.4097	0.1200
4	8	0.5070	0.3994	0.1200
4	6	0.4651	0.3859	0.1200
4	4	0.4187	0.3679	0.1200
4	2	0.3651	0.3442	0.1200
3	8	0.5456	0.4040	0.06555
3	6	0.4966	0.3908	0.06555
3	4	0.4376	0.3715	0.06555
3	2	0.3771	0.3476	0.06555
2	6	0.5426	0.3925	0.03126
2	4	0.4674	0.3738	0.03126
2	2	0.3880	0.3476	0.03126
1	4	0.5660	0.3795	0.01210
1	2	0.4377	0.3580	0.01210

7.5YR

Value	Chroma	CIE x	CIE y	Y
9	8	0.4220	0.3930	0.7866
9	6	0.3950	0.3763	0.7866
9	4	0.3679	0.3585	0.7866
9	2	0.3380	0.3377	0.7866
8	20	0.5391	0.4518	0.5910
8	18	0.5316	0.4480	0.5910
8	16	0.5195	0.4424	0.5910
8	14	0.5025	0.4338	0.5910
8	12	0.4816	0.4232	0.5910
8	10	0.4568	0.4100	0.5910
8	8	0.4306	0.3952	0.5910
8	6	0.4000	0.3770	0.5910
8	4	0.3699	0.3586	0.5910
8	2	0.3395	0.3379	0.5910
7	18	0.5417	0.4492	0.4306
7	16	0.5319	0.4449	0.4306
7	14	0.5174	0.4381	0.4306
7	12	0.4970	0.4282	0.4306

7	10	0.4704	0.4151	0.4306
7	8	0.4415	0.3996	0.4306
7	6	0.4107	0.3820	0.4306
7	4	0.3772	0.3613	0.4306
7	2	0.3437	0.3397	0.4306
6	16	0.5468	0.4478	0.3005
6	14	0.5320	0.4412	0.3005
6	12	0.5145	0.4331	0.3005
6	10	0.4904	0.4220	0.3005
6	8	0.4596	0.4064	0.3005
6	6	0.4242	0.3876	0.3005
6	4	0.3860	0.3652	0.3005
6	2	0.3487	0.3421	0.3005
5	14	0.5506	0.4450	0.1977
5	12	0.5335	0.4378	0.1977
5	10	0.5108	0.4276	0.1977
5	8	0.4820	0.4141	0.1977
5	6	0.4440	0.3954	0.1977
5	4	0.3991	0.3714	0.1977
5	2	0.3540	0.3445	0.1977
4	10	0.5356	0.4342	0.1200
4	8	0.5038	0.4204	0.1200
4	6	0.4655	0.4029	0.1200
4	4	0.4208	0.3809	0.1200
4	2	0.3662	0.3504	0.1200
3	8	0.5390	0.4306	0.06555
3	6	0.4930	0.4116	0.06555
3	4	0.4378	0.3865	0.06555
3	2	0.3771	0.3549	0.06555
2	6	0.5475	0.4271	0.03126
2	4	0.4690	0.3964	0.03126
2	2	0.3889	0.3590	0.03126
1	2	0.4430	0.3775	0.01210

10.0YR

Value	Chroma	CIE x	CIE y	Y
9	8	0.4199	0.4069	0.7866
9	6	0.3941	0.3877	0.7866
9	4	0.3677	0.3668	0.7866
9	2	0.3392	0.3430	0.7866
8	20	0.5245	0.4709	0.5910
8	18	0.5179	0.4670	0.5910
8	16	0.5079	0.4613	0.5910
8	14	0.4940	0.4530	0.5910
8	12	0.4753	0.4414	0.5910
8	10	0.4527	0.4268	0.5910
8	8	0.4280	0.4102	0.5910
8	6	0.3994	0.3896	0.5910
8	4	0.3701	0.3674	0.5910
8	2	0.3407	0.3434	0.5910
7	18	0.5276	0.4700	0.4306

7	16	0.5188	0.4650	0.4306
7	14	0.5074	0.4581	0.4306
7	12	0.4900	0.4480	0.4306
7	10	0.4667	0.4335	0.4306
7	8	0.4399	0.4164	0.4306
7	6	0.4102	0.3960	0.4306
7	4	0.3778	0.3719	0.4306
7	2	0.3443	0.3454	0.4306
6	14	0.5200	0.4623	0.3005
6	12	0.5050	0.4536	0.3005
6	10	0.4843	0.4416	0.3005
6	8	0.4570	0.4249	0.3005
6	6	0.4240	0.4030	0.3005
6	4	0.3861	0.3767	0.3005
6	2	0.3491	0.3483	0.3005
5	12	0.5211	0.4600	0.1977
5	10	0.5025	0.4489	0.1977
5	8	0.4770	0.4338	0.1977
5	6	0.4428	0.4128	0.1977
5	4	0.3995	0.3840	0.1977
5	2	0.3546	0.3514	0.1977
4	10	0.5250	0.4573	0.1200
4	8	0.4965	0.4414	0.1200
4	6	0.4618	0.4213	0.1200
4	4	0.4189	0.3948	0.1200
4	2	0.3660	0.3590	0.1200
3	8	0.5305	0.4559	0.06555
3	6	0.4872	0.4326	0.06555
3	4	0.4341	0.4018	0.06555
3	2	0.3747	0.3630	0.06555
2	4	0.4676	0.4168	0.03126
2	2	0.3872	0.3688	0.03126
1	2	0.4446	0.3982	0.01210

2.5Y

Value	Chroma	CIE x	CIE y	Y
9	12	0.4569	0.4527	0.7866
9	10	0.4370	0.4369	0.7866
9	8	0.4154	0.4186	0.7866
9	6	0.3910	0.3972	0.7866
9	4	0.3655	0.3738	0.7866
9	2	0.3390	0.3472	0.7866
8	20	0.5091	0.4900	0.5910
8	18	0.5033	0.4855	0.5910
8	16	0.4957	0.4800	0.5910
8	14	0.4842	0.4712	0.5910
8	12	0.4678	0.4589	0.5910
8	10	0.4469	0.4423	0.5910
8	8	0.4231	0.4231	0.5910
8	6	0.3969	0.4009	0.5910

8	4	0.3684	0.3751	0.5910
8	2	0.3406	0.3484	0.5910
7	16	0.5049	0.4843	0.4306
7	14	0.4950	0.4773	0.4306
7	12	0.4806	0.4666	0.4306
7	10	0.4606	0.4516	0.4306
7	8	0.4353	0.4312	0.4306
7	6	0.4073	0.4073	0.4306
7	4	0.3761	0.3800	0.4306
7	2	0.3436	0.3507	0.4306
6	14	0.5061	0.4829	0.3005
6	12	0.4928	0.4730	0.3005
6	10	0.4760	0.4607	0.3005
6	8	0.4517	0.4421	0.3005
6	6	0.4203	0.4176	0.3005
6	4	0.3840	0.3867	0.3005
6	2	0.3480	0.3540	0.3005
5	12	0.5082	0.4812	0.1977
5	10	0.4905	0.4683	0.1977
5	8	0.4685	0.4524	0.1977
5	6	0.4380	0.4292	0.1977
5	4	0.3968	0.3954	0.1977
5	2	0.3534	0.3570	0.1977
4	10	0.5120	0.4800	0.1200
4	8	0.4865	0.4625	0.1200
4	6	0.4542	0.4391	0.1200
4	4	0.4138	0.4076	0.1200
4	2	0.3633	0.3654	0.1200
3	6	0.4784	0.4531	0.06555
3	4	0.4277	0.4166	0.06555
3	2	0.3703	0.3700	0.06555
2	4	0.4627	0.4392	0.03126
2	2	0.3825	0.3785	0.03126
1	2	0.4362	0.4177	0.01210

5.0Y

Value	Chroma	CIE x	CIE y	Y
9	20	0.4830	0.5092	0.7866
9	18	0.4782	0.5049	0.7866
9	16	0.4711	0.4977	0.7866
9	14	0.4602	0.4869	0.7866
9	12	0.4455	0.4719	0.7866
9	10	0.4275	0.4529	0.7866
9	8	0.4080	0.4319	0.7866
9	6	0.3858	0.4071	0.7866
9	4	0.3621	0.3799	0.7866
9	2	0.3378	0.3504	0.7866
8	18	0.4847	0.5069	0.5910
8	16	0.4791	0.5012	0.5910
8	14	0.4699	0.4920	0.5910

8	12	0.4562	0.4788	0.5910
8	10	0.4376	0.4601	0.5910
8	8	0.4158	0.4378	0.5910
8	6	0.3913	0.4117	0.5910
8	4	0.3650	0.3826	0.5910
8	2	0.3394	0.3518	0.5910
7	16	0.4875	0.5047	0.4306
7	14	0.4791	0.4965	0.4306
7	12	0.4677	0.4857	0.4306
7	10	0.4509	0.4696	0.4306
7	8	0.4271	0.4462	0.4306
7	6	0.4009	0.4198	0.4306
7	4	0.3718	0.3885	0.4306
7	2	0.3419	0.3540	0.4306
6	14	0.4905	0.5038	0.3005
6	12	0.4780	0.4920	0.3005
6	10	0.4639	0.4790	0.3005
6	8	0.4426	0.4588	0.3005
6	6	0.4140	0.4305	0.3005
6	4	0.3794	0.3955	0.3005
6	2	0.3457	0.3580	0.3005
5	12	0.4932	0.5019	0.1977
5	10	0.4777	0.4876	0.1977
5	8	0.4579	0.4692	0.1977
5	6	0.4302	0.4435	0.1977
5	4	0.3915	0.4057	0.1977
5	2	0.3500	0.3620	0.1977
4	8	0.4745	0.4810	0.1200
4	6	0.4451	0.4550	0.1200
4	4	0.4069	0.4188	0.1200
4	2	0.3590	0.3701	0.1200
3	6	0.4670	0.4711	0.06555
3	4	0.4191	0.4283	0.06555
3	2	0.3646	0.3748	0.06555
2	4	0.4543	0.4573	0.03126
2	2	0.3757	0.3839	0.03126
1	2	0.4230	0.4265	0.01210

7.5Y

Value	Chroma	CIE x	CIE y	Y
9	18	0.4663	0.5188	0.7866
9	16	0.4595	0.5104	0.7866
9	14	0.4503	0.4993	0.7866
9	12	0.4369	0.4829	0.7866
9	10	0.4201	0.4622	0.7866
9	8	0.4019	0.4392	0.7866
9	6	0.3811	0.4123	0.7866
9	4	0.3591	0.3832	0.7866
9	2	0.3365	0.3527	0.7866
8	18	0.4709	0.5220	0.5910

8	16	0.4658	0.5158	0.5910
8	14	0.4574	0.5062	0.5910
8	12	0.4455	0.4917	0.5910
8	10	0.4283	0.4712	0.5910
8	8	0.4088	0.4466	0.5910
8	6	0.3862	0.4175	0.5910
8	4	0.3622	0.3861	0.5910
8	2	0.3379	0.3540	0.5910
7	16	0.4728	0.5215	0.4306
7	14	0.4652	0.5128	0.4306
7	12	0.4547	0.5005	0.4306
7	10	0.4400	0.4830	0.4306
7	8	0.4184	0.4568	0.4306
7	6	0.3943	0.4264	0.4306
7	4	0.3677	0.3925	0.4306
7	2	0.3396	0.3558	0.4306
6	14	0.4754	0.5220	0.3005
6	12	0.4638	0.5087	0.3005
6	10	0.4512	0.4943	0.3005
6	8	0.4321	0.4719	0.3005
6	6	0.4060	0.4400	0.3005
6	4	0.3745	0.4004	0.3005
6	2	0.3431	0.3601	0.3005
5	12	0.4767	0.5208	0.1977
5	10	0.4632	0.5057	0.1977
5	8	0.4450	0.4850	0.1977
5	6	0.4199	0.4551	0.1977
5	4	0.3850	0.4120	0.1977
5	2	0.3470	0.3640	0.1977
4	8	0.4595	0.4990	0.1200
4	6	0.4331	0.4688	0.1200
4	4	0.3982	0.4272	0.1200
4	2	0.3542	0.3727	0.1200
3	6	0.4526	0.4889	0.06555
3	4	0.4086	0.4379	0.06555
3	2	0.3589	0.3778	0.06555
2	4	0.4401	0.4723	0.03126
2	2	0.3660	0.3858	0.03126
1	2	0.4042	0.4287	0.01210

10.0Y

Value	Chroma	CIE x	CIE y	Y
9	18	0.4540	0.5320	0.7866
9	16	0.4477	0.5225	0.7866
9	14	0.4393	0.5101	0.7866
9	12	0.4271	0.4920	0.7866
9	10	0.4120	0.4694	0.7866
9	8	0.3957	0.4450	0.7866
9	6	0.3761	0.4155	0.7866
9	4	0.3558	0.3852	0.7866

9	2	0.3349	0.3537	0.7866
8	18	0.4570	0.5366	0.5910
8	16	0.4525	0.5295	0.5910
8	14	0.4450	0.5181	0.5910
8	12	0.4341	0.5020	0.5910
8	10	0.4190	0.4791	0.5910
8	8	0.4008	0.4520	0.5910
8	6	0.3803	0.4216	0.5910
8	4	0.3581	0.3883	0.5910
8	2	0.3359	0.3552	0.5910
7	16	0.4582	0.5375	0.4306
7	14	0.4516	0.5277	0.4306
7	12	0.4420	0.5131	0.4306
7	10	0.4289	0.4937	0.4306
7	8	0.4090	0.4641	0.4306
7	6	0.3864	0.4305	0.4306
7	4	0.3624	0.3951	0.4306
7	2	0.3369	0.3569	0.4306
6	14	0.4593	0.5392	0.3005
6	12	0.4488	0.5237	0.3005
6	10	0.4372	0.5068	0.3005
6	8	0.4201	0.4812	0.3005
6	6	0.3960	0.4452	0.3005
6	4	0.3679	0.4033	0.3005
6	2	0.3398	0.3611	0.3005
5	12	0.4590	0.5390	0.1977
5	10	0.4468	0.5209	0.1977
5	8	0.4307	0.4967	0.1977
5	6	0.4072	0.4621	0.1977
5	4	0.3762	0.4158	0.1977
5	2	0.3422	0.3648	0.1977
4	8	0.4430	0.5153	0.1200
4	6	0.4190	0.4795	0.1200
4	4	0.3871	0.4321	0.1200
4	2	0.3476	0.3732	0.1200
3	6	0.4345	0.5026	0.06555
3	4	0.3961	0.4452	0.06555
3	2	0.3513	0.3789	0.06555
2	4	0.4188	0.4789	0.03126
2	2	0.3556	0.3848	0.03126
1	2	0.3802	0.4212	0.01210

2.5GY

Value	Chroma	CIE x	CIE y	Y
9	18	0.4354	0.5508	0.7866
9	16	0.4288	0.5383	0.7866
9	14	0.4212	0.5237	0.7866
9	12	0.4108	0.5028	0.7866
9	10	0.3973	0.4761	0.7866
9	8	0.3834	0.4490	0.7866

9	6	0.3670	0.4178	0.7866
9	4	0.3499	0.3866	0.7866
9	2	0.3321	0.3539	0.7866
8	18	0.4371	0.5557	0.5910
8	16	0.4327	0.5475	0.5910
8	14	0.4261	0.5344	0.5910
8	12	0.4154	0.5133	0.5910
8	10	0.4021	0.4869	0.5910
8	8	0.3858	0.4550	0.5910
8	6	0.3690	0.4230	0.5910
8	4	0.3504	0.3887	0.5910
8	2	0.3327	0.3555	0.5910
7	16	0.4366	0.5578	0.4306
7	14	0.4309	0.5459	0.4306
7	12	0.4213	0.5270	0.4306
7	10	0.4091	0.5030	0.4306
7	8	0.3919	0.4684	0.4306
7	6	0.3728	0.4316	0.4306
7	4	0.3534	0.3953	0.4306
7	2	0.3328	0.3569	0.4306
6	14	0.4354	0.5594	0.3005
6	12	0.4269	0.5414	0.3005
6	10	0.4159	0.5190	0.3005
6	8	0.4006	0.4885	0.3005
6	6	0.3799	0.4470	0.3005
6	4	0.3572	0.4038	0.3005
6	2	0.3342	0.3607	0.3005
5	12	0.4333	0.5602	0.1977
5	10	0.4224	0.5369	0.1977
5	8	0.4088	0.5068	0.1977
5	6	0.3879	0.4646	0.1977
5	4	0.3621	0.4143	0.1977
5	2	0.3352	0.3636	0.1977
4	8	0.4174	0.5300	0.1200
4	6	0.3968	0.4857	0.1200
4	4	0.3708	0.4329	0.1200
4	2	0.3382	0.3706	0.1200
3	6	0.4069	0.5110	0.06555
3	4	0.3772	0.4484	0.06555
3	2	0.3412	0.3768	0.06555
2	4	0.3881	0.4752	0.03126
2	2	0.3421	0.3803	0.03126
1	2	0.3540	0.4088	0.01210

5.0GY

Value	Chroma	CIE x	CIE y	Y
9	18	0.4108	0.5699	0.7866
9	16	0.4058	0.5541	0.7866
9	14	0.3993	0.5329	0.7866
9	12	0.3911	0.5082	0.7866

9	10	0.3810	0.4791	0.7866
9	8	0.3698	0.4497	0.7866
9	6	0.3572	0.4179	0.7866
9	4	0.3437	0.3861	0.7866
9	2	0.3284	0.3534	0.7866
8	20	0.4127	0.5855	0.5910
8	18	0.4104	0.5785	0.5910
8	16	0.4061	0.5641	0.5910
8	14	0.4011	0.5468	0.5910
8	12	0.3924	0.5199	0.5910
8	10	0.3816	0.4879	0.5910
8	8	0.3696	0.4542	0.5910
8	6	0.3573	0.4214	0.5910
8	4	0.3433	0.3872	0.5910
8	2	0.3284	0.3542	0.5910
7	16	0.4076	0.5783	0.4306
7	14	0.4027	0.5615	0.4306
7	12	0.3949	0.5367	0.4306
7	10	0.3852	0.5051	0.4306
7	8	0.3722	0.4669	0.4306
7	6	0.3581	0.4291	0.4306
7	4	0.3437	0.3929	0.4306
7	2	0.3284	0.3559	0.4306
6	14	0.4042	0.5788	0.3005
6	12	0.3980	0.5564	0.3005
6	10	0.3891	0.5264	0.3005
6	8	0.3772	0.4880	0.3005
6	6	0.3622	0.4438	0.3005
6	4	0.3461	0.4008	0.3005
6	2	0.3288	0.3592	0.3005
5	12	0.4011	0.5802	0.1977
5	10	0.3928	0.5485	0.1977
5	8	0.3815	0.5093	0.1977
5	6	0.3663	0.4614	0.1977
5	4	0.3482	0.4097	0.1977
5	2	0.3289	0.3612	0.1977
4	10	0.3983	0.5850	0.1200
4	8	0.3868	0.5384	0.1200
4	6	0.3718	0.4852	0.1200
4	4	0.3538	0.4284	0.1200
4	2	0.3312	0.3678	0.1200
3	8	0.3924	0.5832	0.06555
3	6	0.3750	0.5109	0.06555
3	4	0.3554	0.4429	0.06555
3	2	0.3319	0.3729	0.06555
2	6	0.3839	0.5748	0.03126
2	4	0.3582	0.4650	0.03126
2	2	0.3309	0.3743	0.03126
1	4	0.3765	0.5942	0.01210
1	2	0.3359	0.3982	0.01210

7.5GY

Value	Chroma	CIE x	CIE y	Y
9	18	0.3602	0.5920	0.7866
9	16	0.3581	0.5654	0.7866
9	14	0.3551	0.5339	0.7866
9	12	0.3518	0.5042	0.7866
9	10	0.3471	0.4735	0.7866
9	8	0.3414	0.4415	0.7866
9	6	0.3351	0.4111	0.7866
9	4	0.3274	0.3793	0.7866
9	2	0.3198	0.3500	0.7866
8	20	0.3592	0.6235	0.5910
8	18	0.3585	0.6063	0.5910
8	16	0.3569	0.5798	0.5910
8	14	0.3546	0.5490	0.5910
8	12	0.3511	0.5144	0.5910
8	10	0.3463	0.4791	0.5910
8	8	0.3408	0.4452	0.5910
8	6	0.3339	0.4129	0.5910
8	4	0.3266	0.3809	0.5910
8	2	0.3194	0.3502	0.5910
7	18	0.3555	0.6242	0.4306
7	16	0.3549	0.6000	0.4306
7	14	0.3532	0.5700	0.4306
7	12	0.3502	0.5328	0.4306
7	10	0.3461	0.4950	0.4306
7	8	0.3406	0.4558	0.4306
7	6	0.3341	0.4191	0.4306
7	4	0.3267	0.3848	0.4306
7	2	0.3190	0.3516	0.4306
6	16	0.3498	0.6282	0.3005
6	14	0.3498	0.5985	0.3005
6	12	0.3488	0.5596	0.3005
6	10	0.3463	0.5196	0.3005
6	8	0.3418	0.4768	0.3005
6	6	0.3351	0.4321	0.3005
6	4	0.3275	0.3922	0.3005
6	2	0.3193	0.3550	0.3005
5	14	0.3429	0.6335	0.1977
5	12	0.3450	0.5949	0.1977
5	10	0.3451	0.5490	0.1977
5	8	0.3412	0.4976	0.1977
5	6	0.3354	0.4483	0.1977
5	4	0.3274	0.3994	0.1977
5	2	0.3188	0.3560	0.1977
4	12	0.3348	0.6468	0.1200
4	10	0.3395	0.5913	0.1200
4	8	0.3400	0.5348	0.1200
4	6	0.3355	0.4739	0.1200
4	4	0.3281	0.4157	0.1200

4	2	0.3185	0.3604	0.1200
3	10	0.3266	0.6448	0.06555
3	8	0.3341	0.5700	0.06555
3	6	0.3333	0.4967	0.06555
3	4	0.3270	0.4288	0.06555
3	2	0.3180	0.3644	0.06555
2	8	0.3160	0.6509	0.03126
2	6	0.3260	0.5379	0.03126
2	4	0.3248	0.4457	0.03126
2	2	0.3165	0.3650	0.03126
1	4	0.3133	0.5380	0.01210
1	2	0.3154	0.3840	0.01210

10.0GY

Value	Chroma	CIE x	CIE y	Y
9	18	0.3032	0.5748	0.7866
9	16	0.3079	0.5440	0.7866
9	14	0.3115	0.5129	0.7866
9	12	0.3139	0.4829	0.7866
9	10	0.3155	0.4558	0.7866
9	8	0.3157	0.4259	0.7866
9	6	0.3153	0.4008	0.7866
9	4	0.3144	0.3711	0.7866
9	2	0.3124	0.3454	0.7866
8	24	0.2781	0.6840	0.5910
8	22	0.2846	0.6564	0.5910
8	20	0.2918	0.6255	0.5910
8	18	0.2987	0.5919	0.5910
8	16	0.3043	0.5578	0.5910
8	14	0.3091	0.5247	0.5910
8	12	0.3124	0.4926	0.5910
8	10	0.3140	0.4601	0.5910
8	8	0.3149	0.4284	0.5910
8	6	0.3150	0.4014	0.5910
8	4	0.3140	0.3727	0.5910
8	2	0.3121	0.3459	0.5910
7	22	0.2728	0.6893	0.4306
7	20	0.2816	0.6563	0.4306
7	18	0.2905	0.6186	0.4306
7	16	0.2981	0.5835	0.4306
7	14	0.3047	0.5458	0.4306
7	12	0.3092	0.5095	0.4306
7	10	0.3123	0.4732	0.4306
7	8	0.3140	0.4387	0.4306
7	6	0.3142	0.4058	0.4306
7	4	0.3133	0.3764	0.4306
7	2	0.3117	0.3469	0.4306
6	20	0.2648	0.7004	0.3005
6	18	0.2763	0.6616	0.3005
6	16	0.2872	0.6199	0.3005

6	14	0.2962	0.5802	0.3005
6	12	0.3037	0.5358	0.3005
6	10	0.3086	0.4949	0.3005
6	8	0.3116	0.4563	0.3005
6	6	0.3128	0.4175	0.3005
6	4	0.3124	0.3822	0.3005
6	2	0.3112	0.3496	0.3005
5	18	0.2549	0.7179	0.1977
5	16	0.2702	0.6700	0.1977
5	14	0.2838	0.6208	0.1977
5	12	0.2940	0.5751	0.1977
5	10	0.3028	0.5237	0.1977
5	8	0.3080	0.4759	0.1977
5	6	0.3108	0.4301	0.1977
5	4	0.3111	0.3881	0.1977
5	2	0.3110	0.3508	0.1977
4	16	0.2422	0.7360	0.1200
4	14	0.2590	0.6858	0.1200
4	12	0.2758	0.6282	0.1200
4	10	0.2908	0.5672	0.1200
4	8	0.3008	0.5095	0.1200
4	6	0.3069	0.4550	0.1200
4	4	0.3100	0.4018	0.1200
4	2	0.3109	0.3550	0.1200
3	14	0.2283	0.7423	0.06555
3	12	0.2531	0.6700	0.06555
3	10	0.2724	0.6026	0.06555
3	8	0.2887	0.5361	0.06555
3	6	0.2992	0.4717	0.06555
3	4	0.3053	0.4123	0.06555
3	2	0.3088	0.3578	0.06555
2	12	0.1907	0.7798	0.03126
2	10	0.2307	0.6814	0.03126
2	8	0.2628	0.5837	0.03126
2	6	0.2852	0.4972	0.03126
2	4	0.2986	0.4240	0.03126
2	2	0.3069	0.3580	0.03126
1	6	0.2232	0.6392	0.01210
1	4	0.2722	0.4903	0.01210
1	2	0.3006	0.3720	0.01210

2.5G

Value	Chroma	CIE x	CIE y	Y
9	16	0.2630	0.4966	0.7866
9	14	0.2711	0.4726	0.7866
9	12	0.2786	0.4491	0.7866
9	10	0.2851	0.4275	0.7866
9	8	0.2912	0.4054	0.7866
9	6	0.2966	0.3846	0.7866
9	4	0.3018	0.3606	0.7866

9	2	0.3058	0.3400	0.7866
8	24	0.2091	0.6033	0.5910
8	22	0.2221	0.5799	0.5910
8	20	0.2339	0.5561	0.5910
8	18	0.2451	0.5309	0.5910
8	16	0.2563	0.5045	0.5910
8	14	0.2661	0.4780	0.5910
8	12	0.2743	0.4554	0.5910
8	10	0.2829	0.4301	0.5910
8	8	0.2896	0.4065	0.5910
8	6	0.2952	0.3851	0.5910
8	4	0.3009	0.3614	0.5910
8	2	0.3053	0.3404	0.5910
7	26	0.1689	0.6549	0.4306
7	24	0.1875	0.6265	0.4306
7	22	0.2029	0.6017	0.4306
7	20	0.2181	0.5744	0.4306
7	18	0.2328	0.5467	0.4306
7	16	0.2448	0.5203	0.4306
7	14	0.2568	0.4931	0.4306
7	12	0.2672	0.4667	0.4306
7	10	0.2775	0.4395	0.4306
7	8	0.2861	0.4129	0.4306
7	6	0.2933	0.3873	0.4306
7	4	0.2992	0.3644	0.4306
7	2	0.3047	0.3413	0.4306
6	28	0.1145	0.7122	0.3005
6	26	0.1340	0.6871	0.3005
6	24	0.1536	0.6605	0.3005
6	22	0.1739	0.6318	0.3005
6	20	0.1922	0.6035	0.3005
6	18	0.2102	0.5737	0.3005
6	16	0.2278	0.5430	0.3005
6	14	0.2426	0.5133	0.3005
6	12	0.2574	0.4814	0.3005
6	10	0.2690	0.4530	0.3005
6	8	0.2799	0.4239	0.3005
6	6	0.2892	0.3963	0.3005
6	4	0.2967	0.3695	0.3005
6	2	0.3039	0.3437	0.3005
5	28	0.0794	0.7385	0.1977
5	26	0.0992	0.7155	0.1977
5	24	0.1188	0.6918	0.1977
5	22	0.1377	0.6674	0.1977
5	20	0.1579	0.6392	0.1977
5	18	0.1782	0.6095	0.1977
5	16	0.2005	0.5759	0.1977
5	14	0.2211	0.5411	0.1977
5	12	0.2385	0.5071	0.1977
5	10	0.2565	0.4705	0.1977
5	8	0.2710	0.4380	0.1977
5	6	0.2841	0.4045	0.1977

5	4	0.2943	0.3735	0.1977
5	2	0.3030	0.3445	0.1977
4	26	0.0528	0.7502	0.1200
4	24	0.0760	0.7250	0.1200
4	22	0.1009	0.6975	0.1200
4	20	0.1230	0.6706	0.1200
4	18	0.1446	0.6431	0.1200
4	16	0.1682	0.6111	0.1200
4	14	0.1909	0.5779	0.1200
4	12	0.2128	0.5425	0.1200
4	10	0.2355	0.5006	0.1200
4	8	0.2561	0.4597	0.1200
4	6	0.2735	0.4215	0.1200
4	4	0.2891	0.3821	0.1200
4	2	0.3012	0.3470	0.1200
3	22	0.0390	0.7468	0.06555
3	20	0.0720	0.7127	0.06555
3	18	0.1049	0.6766	0.06555
3	16	0.1341	0.6420	0.06555
3	14	0.1626	0.6052	0.06555
3	12	0.1902	0.5642	0.06555
3	10	0.2170	0.5211	0.06555
3	8	0.2435	0.4752	0.06555
3	6	0.2642	0.4342	0.06555
3	4	0.2836	0.3915	0.06555
3	2	0.2999	0.3500	0.06555
2	16	0.0329	0.7358	0.03126
2	14	0.0820	0.6860	0.03126
2	12	0.1307	0.6308	0.03126
2	10	0.1773	0.5698	0.03126
2	8	0.2192	0.5042	0.03126
2	6	0.2493	0.4522	0.03126
2	4	0.2763	0.3998	0.03126
2	2	0.2978	0.3507	0.03126
1	8	0.0620	0.6896	0.01210
1	6	0.1711	0.5619	0.01210
1	4	0.2454	0.4489	0.01210
1	2	0.2910	0.3634	0.01210

5.0G

Value	Chroma	CIE x	CIE y	Y
9	12	0.2528	0.4160	0.7866
9	10	0.2639	0.4001	0.7866
9	8	0.2735	0.3854	0.7866
9	6	0.2832	0.3697	0.7866
9	4	0.2933	0.3519	0.7866
9	2	0.3017	0.3357	0.7866
8	22	0.1821	0.4940	0.5910
8	20	0.1956	0.4806	0.5910
8	18	0.2103	0.4652	0.5910

8	16	0.2240	0.4500	0.5910
8	14	0.2368	0.4348	0.5910
8	12	0.2489	0.4191	0.5910
8	10	0.2613	0.4026	0.5910
8	8	0.2723	0.3865	0.5910
8	6	0.2822	0.3702	0.5910
8	4	0.2924	0.3523	0.5910
8	2	0.3009	0.3359	0.5910
7	26	0.1397	0.5312	0.4306
7	24	0.1521	0.5200	0.4306
7	22	0.1659	0.5074	0.4306
7	20	0.1805	0.4933	0.4306
7	18	0.1967	0.4771	0.4306
7	16	0.2111	0.4616	0.4306
7	14	0.2262	0.4450	0.4306
7	12	0.2416	0.4267	0.4306
7	10	0.2554	0.4087	0.4306
7	8	0.2687	0.3901	0.4306
7	6	0.2801	0.3721	0.4306
7	4	0.2902	0.3548	0.4306
7	2	0.3001	0.3366	0.4306
6	28	0.0908	0.5695	0.3005
6	26	0.1079	0.5560	0.3005
6	24	0.1252	0.5408	0.3005
6	22	0.1432	0.5252	0.3005
6	20	0.1609	0.5091	0.3005
6	18	0.1785	0.4924	0.3005
6	16	0.1960	0.4751	0.3005
6	14	0.2130	0.4571	0.3005
6	12	0.2293	0.4390	0.3005
6	10	0.2466	0.4181	0.3005
6	8	0.2612	0.3990	0.3005
6	6	0.2748	0.3795	0.3005
6	4	0.2868	0.3595	0.3005
6	2	0.2988	0.3382	0.3005
5	28	0.0609	0.5898	0.1977
5	26	0.0784	0.5761	0.1977
5	24	0.0953	0.5628	0.1977
5	22	0.1144	0.5463	0.1977
5	20	0.1318	0.5321	0.1977
5	18	0.1489	0.5171	0.1977
5	16	0.1695	0.4981	0.1977
5	14	0.1912	0.4773	0.1977
5	12	0.2104	0.4578	0.1977
5	10	0.2329	0.4331	0.1977
5	8	0.2511	0.4107	0.1977
5	6	0.2690	0.3860	0.1977
5	4	0.2841	0.3628	0.1977
5	2	0.2978	0.3392	0.1977
4	26	0.0407	0.6010	0.1200
4	24	0.0614	0.5857	0.1200
4	22	0.0841	0.5684	0.1200

4	20	0.1018	0.5543	0.1200
4	18	0.1188	0.5400	0.1200
4	16	0.1402	0.5214	0.1200
4	14	0.1627	0.5015	0.1200
4	12	0.1843	0.4807	0.1200
4	10	0.2115	0.4532	0.1200
4	8	0.2359	0.4266	0.1200
4	6	0.2581	0.3992	0.1200
4	4	0.2781	0.3704	0.1200
4	2	0.2959	0.3417	0.1200
3	22	0.0340	0.6011	0.06555
3	20	0.0620	0.5802	0.06555
3	18	0.0882	0.5605	0.06555
3	16	0.1120	0.5414	0.06555
3	14	0.1382	0.5197	0.06555
3	12	0.1660	0.4948	0.06555
3	10	0.1935	0.4682	0.06555
3	8	0.2228	0.4380	0.06555
3	6	0.2471	0.4100	0.06555
3	4	0.2711	0.3780	0.06555
3	2	0.2935	0.3439	0.06555
2	16	0.0277	0.5986	0.03126
2	14	0.0688	0.5691	0.03126
2	12	0.1120	0.5358	0.03126
2	10	0.1560	0.4981	0.03126
2	8	0.1979	0.4583	0.03126
2	6	0.2318	0.4231	0.03126
2	4	0.2640	0.3845	0.03126
2	2	0.2918	0.3450	0.03126
1	8	0.0559	0.5710	0.01210
1	6	0.1468	0.4996	0.01210
1	4	0.2290	0.4218	0.01210
1	2	0.2833	0.3564	0.01210

7.5G

Value	Chroma	CIE x	CIE y	Y
9	12	0.2419	0.3985	0.7866
9	10	0.2545	0.3855	0.7866
9	8	0.2652	0.3738	0.7866
9	6	0.2763	0.3607	0.7866
9	4	0.2882	0.3461	0.7866
9	2	0.2987	0.3323	0.7866
8	20	0.1845	0.4492	0.5910
8	18	0.1980	0.4372	0.5910
8	16	0.2120	0.4252	0.5910
8	14	0.2254	0.4125	0.5910
8	12	0.2380	0.4002	0.5910
8	10	0.2515	0.3867	0.5910
8	8	0.2639	0.3733	0.5910
8	6	0.2754	0.3608	0.5910

8	4	0.2874	0.3464	0.5910
8	2	0.2981	0.3326	0.5910
7	26	0.1303	0.4858	0.4306
7	24	0.1415	0.4778	0.4306
7	22	0.1539	0.4683	0.4306
7	20	0.1688	0.4570	0.4306
7	18	0.1841	0.4448	0.4306
7	16	0.1982	0.4330	0.4306
7	14	0.2139	0.4199	0.4306
7	12	0.2295	0.4058	0.4306
7	10	0.2445	0.3914	0.4306
7	8	0.2595	0.3764	0.4306
7	6	0.2728	0.3622	0.4306
7	4	0.2850	0.3482	0.4306
7	2	0.2972	0.3333	0.4306
6	28	0.0858	0.5127	0.3005
6	26	0.1010	0.5018	0.3005
6	24	0.1159	0.4910	0.3005
6	22	0.1325	0.4795	0.3005
6	20	0.1485	0.4677	0.3005
6	18	0.1654	0.4551	0.3005
6	16	0.1832	0.4414	0.3005
6	14	0.2001	0.4278	0.3005
6	12	0.2171	0.4138	0.3005
6	10	0.2350	0.3979	0.3005
6	8	0.2510	0.3829	0.3005
6	6	0.2662	0.3672	0.3005
6	4	0.2807	0.3522	0.3005
6	2	0.2958	0.3344	0.3005
5	28	0.0585	0.5224	0.1977
5	26	0.0730	0.5131	0.1977
5	24	0.0878	0.5039	0.1977
5	22	0.1050	0.4927	0.1977
5	20	0.1212	0.4817	0.1977
5	18	0.1372	0.4705	0.1977
5	16	0.1571	0.4561	0.1977
5	14	0.1776	0.4415	0.1977
5	12	0.1964	0.4271	0.1977
5	10	0.2200	0.4082	0.1977
5	8	0.2395	0.3915	0.1977
5	6	0.2598	0.3724	0.1977
5	4	0.2775	0.3545	0.1977
5	2	0.2945	0.3355	0.1977
4	26	0.0392	0.5258	0.1200
4	24	0.0581	0.5151	0.1200
4	22	0.0770	0.5040	0.1200
4	20	0.0928	0.4942	0.1200
4	18	0.1086	0.4842	0.1200
4	16	0.1293	0.4703	0.1200
4	14	0.1500	0.4562	0.1200
4	12	0.1706	0.4419	0.1200
4	10	0.1989	0.4219	0.1200

4	8	0.2232	0.4022	0.1200
4	6	0.2467	0.3822	0.1200
4	4	0.2702	0.3602	0.1200
4	2	0.2919	0.3371	0.1200
3	22	0.0332	0.5206	0.06555
3	20	0.0568	0.5082	0.06555
3	18	0.0798	0.4954	0.06555
3	16	0.1023	0.4818	0.06555
3	14	0.1262	0.4667	0.06555
3	12	0.1516	0.4505	0.06555
3	10	0.1800	0.4310	0.06555
3	8	0.2088	0.4101	0.06555
3	6	0.2346	0.3901	0.06555
3	4	0.2618	0.3667	0.06555
3	2	0.2890	0.3391	0.06555
2	16	0.0276	0.5153	0.03126
2	14	0.0629	0.4973	0.03126
2	12	0.1022	0.4759	0.03126
2	10	0.1442	0.4505	0.03126
2	8	0.1842	0.4244	0.03126
2	6	0.2200	0.3983	0.03126
2	4	0.2540	0.3705	0.03126
2	2	0.2869	0.3400	0.03126
1	8	0.0530	0.4943	0.01210
1	6	0.1344	0.4505	0.01210
1	4	0.2159	0.3967	0.01210
1	2	0.2758	0.3484	0.01210

10.0G

Value	Chroma	CIE x	CIE y	Y
9	12	0.2325	0.3796	0.7866
9	10	0.2457	0.3702	0.7866
9	8	0.2574	0.3618	0.7866
9	6	0.2703	0.3513	0.7866
9	4	0.2840	0.3402	0.7866
9	2	0.2965	0.3293	0.7866
8	20	0.1734	0.4164	0.5910
8	18	0.1866	0.4086	0.5910
8	16	0.2012	0.3992	0.5910
8	14	0.2148	0.3903	0.5910
8	12	0.2282	0.3811	0.5910
8	10	0.2430	0.3710	0.5910
8	8	0.2564	0.3611	0.5910
8	6	0.2693	0.3512	0.5910
8	4	0.2828	0.3403	0.5910
8	2	0.2957	0.3293	0.5910
7	24	0.1310	0.4377	0.4306
7	22	0.1434	0.4306	0.4306
7	20	0.1589	0.4220	0.4306
7	18	0.1734	0.4135	0.4306

7	16	0.1881	0.4049	0.4306
7	14	0.2033	0.3956	0.4306
7	12	0.2195	0.3854	0.4306
7	10	0.2352	0.3748	0.4306
7	8	0.2513	0.3635	0.4306
7	6	0.2662	0.3526	0.4306
7	4	0.2803	0.3415	0.4306
7	2	0.2945	0.3297	0.4306
6	26	0.0941	0.4520	0.3005
6	24	0.1070	0.4458	0.3005
6	22	0.1230	0.4378	0.3005
6	20	0.1382	0.4299	0.3005
6	18	0.1551	0.4208	0.3005
6	16	0.1722	0.4113	0.3005
6	14	0.1895	0.4015	0.3005
6	12	0.2060	0.3914	0.3005
6	10	0.2247	0.3796	0.3005
6	8	0.2420	0.3679	0.3005
6	6	0.2591	0.3558	0.3005
6	4	0.2749	0.3443	0.3005
6	2	0.2929	0.3303	0.3005
5	28	0.0572	0.4590	0.1977
5	26	0.0690	0.4542	0.1977
5	24	0.0811	0.4491	0.1977
5	22	0.0958	0.4428	0.1977
5	20	0.1120	0.4360	0.1977
5	18	0.1275	0.4288	0.1977
5	16	0.1469	0.4192	0.1977
5	14	0.1671	0.4089	0.1977
5	12	0.1852	0.3992	0.1977
5	10	0.2095	0.3853	0.1977
5	8	0.2297	0.3730	0.1977
5	6	0.2519	0.3587	0.1977
5	4	0.2711	0.3455	0.1977
5	2	0.2910	0.3310	0.1977
4	26	0.0400	0.4545	0.1200
4	24	0.0553	0.4492	0.1200
4	22	0.0702	0.4440	0.1200
4	20	0.0850	0.4388	0.1200
4	18	0.1006	0.4330	0.1200
4	16	0.1212	0.4245	0.1200
4	14	0.1398	0.4168	0.1200
4	12	0.1602	0.4070	0.1200
4	10	0.1876	0.3933	0.1200
4	8	0.2124	0.3799	0.1200
4	6	0.2374	0.3655	0.1200
4	4	0.2628	0.3498	0.1200
4	2	0.2880	0.3327	0.1200
3	22	0.0333	0.4444	0.06555
3	20	0.0528	0.4393	0.06555
3	18	0.0718	0.4340	0.06555
3	16	0.0925	0.4275	0.06555

3	14	0.1161	0.4192	0.06555
3	12	0.1411	0.4095	0.06555
3	10	0.1688	0.3974	0.06555
3	8	0.1970	0.3841	0.06555
3	6	0.2240	0.3699	0.06555
3	4	0.2525	0.3537	0.06555
3	2	0.2844	0.3337	0.06555
2	16	0.0285	0.4327	0.03126
2	14	0.0599	0.4270	0.03126
2	12	0.0934	0.4183	0.03126
2	10	0.1321	0.4059	0.03126
2	8	0.1705	0.3911	0.03126
2	6	0.2092	0.3739	0.03126
2	4	0.2442	0.3559	0.03126
2	2	0.2820	0.3341	0.03126
1	8	0.0511	0.4158	0.01210
1	6	0.1249	0.4019	0.01210
1	4	0.2040	0.3724	0.01210
1	2	0.2689	0.3407	0.01210

2.5BG

Value	Chroma	CIE x	CIE y	Y
9	10	0.2382	0.3568	0.7866
9	8	0.2509	0.3507	0.7866
9	6	0.2652	0.3433	0.7866
9	4	0.2805	0.3349	0.7866
9	2	0.2947	0.3267	0.7866
8	18	0.1759	0.3782	0.5910
8	16	0.1915	0.3732	0.5910
8	14	0.2057	0.3681	0.5910
8	12	0.2196	0.3630	0.5910
8	10	0.2352	0.3566	0.5910
8	8	0.2500	0.3500	0.5910
8	6	0.2647	0.3429	0.5910
8	4	0.2791	0.3351	0.5910
8	2	0.2940	0.3268	0.5910
7	22	0.1334	0.3870	0.4306
7	20	0.1490	0.3827	0.4306
7	18	0.1626	0.3788	0.4306
7	16	0.1788	0.3739	0.4306
7	14	0.1932	0.3694	0.4306
7	12	0.2102	0.3636	0.4306
7	10	0.2264	0.3576	0.4306
7	8	0.2439	0.3508	0.4306
7	6	0.2608	0.3430	0.4306
7	4	0.2764	0.3354	0.4306
7	2	0.2927	0.3269	0.4306
6	22	0.1120	0.3860	0.3005
6	20	0.1269	0.3829	0.3005
6	18	0.1428	0.3790	0.3005

6	16	0.1600	0.3748	0.3005
6	14	0.1779	0.3699	0.3005
6	12	0.1954	0.3645	0.3005
6	10	0.2148	0.3584	0.3005
6	8	0.2332	0.3522	0.3005
6	6	0.2526	0.3448	0.3005
6	4	0.2702	0.3369	0.3005
6	2	0.2902	0.3268	0.3005
5	24	0.0738	0.3851	0.1977
5	22	0.0861	0.3832	0.1977
5	20	0.1005	0.3814	0.1977
5	18	0.1165	0.3785	0.1977
5	16	0.1348	0.3750	0.1977
5	14	0.1559	0.3708	0.1977
5	12	0.1735	0.3668	0.1977
5	10	0.1980	0.3606	0.1977
5	8	0.2205	0.3537	0.1977
5	6	0.2448	0.3452	0.1977
5	4	0.2659	0.3369	0.1977
5	2	0.2880	0.3270	0.1977
4	24	0.0510	0.3800	0.1200
4	22	0.0636	0.3788	0.1200
4	20	0.0768	0.3773	0.1200
4	18	0.0915	0.3754	0.1200
4	16	0.1102	0.3720	0.1200
4	14	0.1283	0.3688	0.1200
4	12	0.1492	0.3649	0.1200
4	10	0.1738	0.3600	0.1200
4	8	0.2006	0.3540	0.1200
4	6	0.2278	0.3463	0.1200
4	4	0.2552	0.3375	0.1200
4	2	0.2840	0.3270	0.1200
3	20	0.0482	0.3695	0.06555
3	18	0.0648	0.3682	0.06555
3	16	0.0843	0.3667	0.06555
3	14	0.1051	0.3648	0.06555
3	12	0.1288	0.3620	0.06555
3	10	0.1552	0.3580	0.06555
3	8	0.1845	0.3531	0.06555
3	6	0.2132	0.3468	0.06555
3	4	0.2437	0.3386	0.06555
3	2	0.2799	0.3271	0.06555
2	14	0.0555	0.3588	0.03126
2	12	0.0851	0.3576	0.03126
2	10	0.1190	0.3551	0.03126
2	8	0.1557	0.3517	0.03126
2	6	0.1971	0.3452	0.03126
2	4	0.2343	0.3378	0.03126
2	2	0.2765	0.3271	0.03126
1	8	0.0476	0.3458	0.01210
1	6	0.1169	0.3452	0.01210
1	4	0.1883	0.3406	0.01210

1	2	0.2600	0.3289	0.01210

5.0BG

Value	Chroma	CIE x	CIE y	Y
9	10	0.2301	0.3405	0.7866
9	8	0.2437	0.3378	0.7866
9	6	0.2599	0.3338	0.7866
9	4	0.2768	0.3287	0.7866
9	2	0.2930	0.3232	0.7866
8	16	0.1814	0.3450	0.5910
8	14	0.1958	0.3432	0.5910
8	12	0.2101	0.3412	0.5910
8	10	0.2264	0.3383	0.5910
8	8	0.2419	0.3352	0.5910
8	6	0.2588	0.3318	0.5910
8	4	0.2752	0.3278	0.5910
8	2	0.2919	0.3228	0.5910
7	20	0.1380	0.3412	0.4306
7	18	0.1515	0.3410	0.4306
7	16	0.1675	0.3401	0.4306
7	14	0.1838	0.3390	0.4306
7	12	0.1997	0.3379	0.4306
7	10	0.2163	0.3361	0.4306
7	8	0.2354	0.3335	0.4306
7	6	0.2543	0.3302	0.4306
7	4	0.2712	0.3269	0.4306
7	2	0.2898	0.3225	0.4306
6	20	0.1168	0.3344	0.3005
6	18	0.1325	0.3345	0.3005
6	16	0.1491	0.3345	0.3005
6	14	0.1662	0.3343	0.3005
6	12	0.1844	0.3337	0.3005
6	10	0.2037	0.3329	0.3005
6	8	0.2236	0.3311	0.3005
6	6	0.2441	0.3290	0.3005
6	4	0.2648	0.3262	0.3005
6	2	0.2872	0.3219	0.3005
5	22	0.0781	0.3211	0.1977
5	20	0.0904	0.3231	0.1977
5	18	0.1046	0.3244	0.1977
5	16	0.1243	0.3261	0.1977
5	14	0.1448	0.3275	0.1977
5	12	0.1614	0.3280	0.1977
5	10	0.1850	0.3280	0.1977
5	8	0.2100	0.3280	0.1977
5	6	0.2360	0.3270	0.1977
5	4	0.2591	0.3246	0.1977
5	2	0.2841	0.3210	0.1977
4	20	0.0675	0.3075	0.1200
4	18	0.0828	0.3108	0.1200

4	16	0.0992	0.3141	0.1200
4	14	0.1170	0.3170	0.1200
4	12	0.1379	0.3198	0.1200
4	10	0.1618	0.3219	0.1200
4	8	0.1890	0.3234	0.1200
4	6	0.2182	0.3240	0.1200
4	4	0.2480	0.3232	0.1200
4	2	0.2799	0.3208	0.1200
3	18	0.0580	0.2940	0.06555
3	16	0.0735	0.2979	0.06555
3	14	0.0940	0.3027	0.06555
3	12	0.1158	0.3071	0.06555
3	10	0.1410	0.3118	0.06555
3	8	0.1703	0.3159	0.06555
3	6	0.2020	0.3188	0.06555
3	4	0.2343	0.3200	0.06555
3	2	0.2742	0.3192	0.06555
2	12	0.0769	0.2880	0.03126
2	10	0.1050	0.2956	0.03126
2	8	0.1405	0.3037	0.03126
2	6	0.1843	0.3110	0.03126
2	4	0.2234	0.3150	0.03126
2	2	0.2697	0.3175	0.03126
1	6	0.1093	0.2860	0.01210
1	4	0.1753	0.3201	0.01210
1	2	0.2500	0.3141	0.01210

7.5BG

Value	Chroma	CIE x	CIE y	Y
9	10	0.2215	0.3226	0.7866
9	8	0.2361	0.3225	0.7866
9	6	0.2543	0.3220	0.7866
9	4	0.2728	0.3208	0.7866
9	2	0.2911	0.3188	0.7866
8	16	0.1721	0.3168	0.5910
8	14	0.1868	0.3179	0.5910
8	12	0.2010	0.3188	0.5910
8	10	0.2184	0.3196	0.5910
8	8	0.2352	0.3198	0.5910
8	6	0.2525	0.3198	0.5910
8	4	0.2718	0.3200	0.5910
8	2	0.2900	0.3183	0.5910
7	18	0.1427	0.3076	0.4306
7	16	0.1584	0.3101	0.4306
7	14	0.1751	0.3129	0.4306
7	12	0.1914	0.3148	0.4306
7	10	0.2094	0.3165	0.4306
7	8	0.2292	0.3178	0.4306
7	6	0.2490	0.3186	0.4306
7	4	0.2671	0.3189	0.4306

7	2	0.2878	0.3182	0.4306
6	18	0.1248	0.2981	0.3005
6	16	0.1408	0.3017	0.3005
6	14	0.1585	0.3052	0.3005
6	12	0.1762	0.3081	0.3005
6	10	0.1961	0.3110	0.3005
6	8	0.2171	0.3138	0.3005
6	6	0.2384	0.3155	0.3005
6	4	0.2604	0.3169	0.3005
6	2	0.2849	0.3172	0.3005
5	18	0.0982	0.2828	0.1977
5	16	0.1167	0.2880	0.1977
5	14	0.1364	0.2932	0.1977
5	12	0.1537	0.2976	0.1977
5	10	0.1776	0.3032	0.1977
5	8	0.2030	0.3082	0.1977
5	6	0.2292	0.3125	0.1977
5	4	0.2550	0.3150	0.1977
5	2	0.2812	0.3161	0.1977
4	18	0.0768	0.2667	0.1977
4	16	0.0992	0.2718	0.1200
4	14	0.1092	0.2774	0.1200
4	12	0.1298	0.2840	0.1200
4	10	0.1540	0.2910	0.1200
4	8	0.1815	0.2985	0.1200
4	6	0.2113	0.3052	0.1200
4	4	0.2429	0.3108	0.1200
4	2	0.2764	0.3148	0.1200
3	16	0.0691	0.2559	0.06555
3	14	0.0874	0.2627	0.06555
3	12	0.1086	0.2706	0.06555
3	10	0.1326	0.2784	0.06555
3	8	0.1620	0.2872	0.06555
3	6	0.1928	0.2958	0.06555
3	4	0.2272	0.3041	0.06555
3	2	0.2699	0.3120	0.06555
2	12	0.0724	0.2478	0.03126
2	10	0.0991	0.2582	0.03126
2	8	0.1325	0.2710	0.03126
2	6	0.1747	0.2853	0.03126
2	4	0.2162	0.2981	0.03126
2	2	0.2651	0.3098	0.03126
1	6	0.1059	0.2485	0.01210
1	4	0.1702	0.2768	0.01210
1	2	0.2430	0.3023	0.01210

10.0BG

Value	Chroma	CIE x	CIE y	Y
9	6	0.2501	0.3118	0.7866
9	4	0.2700	0.3140	0.7866

9	2	0.2907	0.3159	0.7866
8	14	0.1788	0.2936	0.5910
8	12	0.1937	0.2978	0.5910
8	10	0.2120	0.3025	0.5910
8	8	0.2302	0.3063	0.5910
8	6	0.2489	0.3099	0.5910
8	4	0.2686	0.3130	0.5910
8	2	0.2894	0.3152	0.5910
7	16	0.1489	0.2768	0.4306
7	14	0.1671	0.2832	0.4306
7	12	0.1841	0.2892	0.4306
7	10	0.2035	0.2956	0.4306
7	8	0.2235	0.3014	0.4306
7	6	0.2448	0.3069	0.4306
7	4	0.2642	0.3109	0.4306
7	2	0.2869	0.3143	0.4306
6	18	0.1181	0.2581	0.3005
6	16	0.1337	0.2651	0.3005
6	14	0.1518	0.2729	0.3005
6	12	0.1698	0.2802	0.3005
6	10	0.1909	0.2881	0.3005
6	8	0.2116	0.2950	0.3005
6	6	0.2335	0.3015	0.3005
6	4	0.2578	0.3078	0.3005
6	2	0.2837	0.3132	0.3005
5	16	0.1108	0.2489	0.1977
5	14	0.1308	0.2582	0.1977
5	12	0.1485	0.2662	0.1977
5	10	0.1716	0.2760	0.1977
5	8	0.1970	0.2860	0.1977
5	6	0.2234	0.2952	0.1977
5	4	0.2512	0.3040	0.1977
5	2	0.2796	0.3111	0.1977
4	16	0.0888	0.2298	0.1200
4	14	0.1033	0.2376	0.1200
4	12	0.1248	0.2484	0.1200
4	10	0.1480	0.2600	0.1200
4	8	0.1760	0.2730	0.1200
4	6	0.2065	0.2863	0.1200
4	4	0.2384	0.2984	0.1200
4	2	0.2740	0.3091	0.1200
3	14	0.0798	0.2151	0.06555
3	12	0.1018	0.2281	0.06555
3	10	0.1250	0.2411	0.06555
3	8	0.1551	0.2571	0.06555
3	6	0.1861	0.2722	0.06555
3	4	0.2221	0.2886	0.06555
3	2	0.2660	0.3050	0.06555
2	10	0.0929	0.2133	0.03126
2	8	0.1258	0.2331	0.03126
2	6	0.1669	0.2570	0.03126
2	4	0.2096	0.2790	0.03126

2	2	0.2606	0.3010	0.03126
1	6	0.1074	0.2129	0.01210
1	4	0.1658	0.2496	0.01210
1	2	0.2362	0.2882	0.01210

2.5B

Value	Chroma	CIE x	CIE y	Y
9	4	0.2680	0.3073	0.7866
9	2	0.2909	0.3125	0.7866
8	12	0.1877	0.2752	0.5910
8	10	0.2066	0.2839	0.5910
8	8	0.2264	0.2923	0.5910
8	6	0.2462	0.3000	0.5910
8	4	0.2668	0.3067	0.5910
8	2	0.2897	0.3124	0.5910
7	16	0.1435	0.2472	0.4206
7	14	0.1624	0.2581	0.4206
7	12	0.1797	0.2672	0.4206
7	10	0.1994	0.2775	0.4206
7	8	0.2208	0.2871	0.4206
7	6	0.2418	0.2960	0.4206
7	4	0.2629	0.3038	0.4206
7	2	0.2867	0.3110	0.4206
6	16	0.1294	0.2348	0.3005
6	14	0.1480	0.2459	0.3005
6	12	0.1660	0.2561	0.3005
6	10	0.1879	0.2682	0.3005
6	8	0.2080	0.2789	0.3005
6	6	0.2312	0.2899	0.3005
6	4	0.2571	0.3008	0.3005
6	2	0.2835	0.3097	0.3005
5	16	0.1090	0.2166	0.1977
5	14	0.1283	0.2292	0.1977
5	12	0.1461	0.2406	0.1977
5	10	0.1697	0.2549	0.1977
5	8	0.1947	0.2687	0.1977
5	6	0.2210	0.2823	0.1977
5	4	0.2492	0.2954	0.1977
5	2	0.2791	0.3071	0.1977
4	16	0.0900	0.1973	0.1200
4	14	0.1027	0.2057	0.1200
4	12	0.1247	0.2209	0.1200
4	10	0.1463	0.2354	0.1200
4	8	0.1737	0.2524	0.1200
4	6	0.2048	0.2708	0.1200
4	4	0.2360	0.2872	0.1200
4	2	0.2727	0.3038	0.1200
3	12	0.0989	0.1963	0.06555
3	10	0.1220	0.2132	0.06555
3	8	0.1511	0.2331	0.06555

3	6	0.1826	0.2536	0.06555
3	4	0.2183	0.2748	0.06555
3	2	0.2636	0.2983	0.06555
2	10	0.0911	0.1828	0.03126
2	8	0.1230	0.2076	0.03126
2	6	0.1621	0.2358	0.03126
2	4	0.2060	0.2649	0.03126
2	2	0.2578	0.2940	0.03126
1	6	0.1118	0.1908	0.01210
1	4	0.1649	0.2324	0.01210
1	2	0.2322	0.2781	0.01210

5.0B

Value	Chroma	CIE x	CIE y	Y
9	4	0.2675	0.3005	0.7866
9	2	0.2919	0.3102	0.7866
8	8	0.2237	0.2761	0.5910
8	6	0.2457	0.2888	0.5910
8	4	0.2671	0.2998	0.5910
8	2	0.2908	0.3096	0.5910
7	14	0.1615	0.2307	0.4306
7	12	0.1778	0.2430	0.4306
7	10	0.1986	0.2579	0.4306
7	8	0.2204	0.2729	0.4306
7	6	0.2410	0.2854	0.4306
7	4	0.2633	0.2972	0.4306
7	2	0.2875	0.3078	0.4306
6	16	0.1310	0.2048	0.3005
6	14	0.1496	0.2193	0.3005
6	12	0.1685	0.2339	0.3005
6	10	0.1883	0.2487	0.3005
6	8	0.2088	0.2635	0.3005
6	6	0.2320	0.2789	0.3005
6	4	0.2579	0.2938	0.3005
6	2	0.2842	0.3063	0.3005
5	16	0.1132	0.1863	0.1977
5	14	0.1320	0.2021	0.1977
5	12	0.1505	0.2172	0.1977
5	10	0.1729	0.2347	0.1977
5	8	0.1958	0.2519	0.1977
5	6	0.2215	0.2701	0.1977
5	4	0.2493	0.2879	0.1977
5	2	0.2794	0.3032	0.1977
4	14	0.1098	0.1785	0.1200
4	12	0.1299	0.1963	0.1200
4	10	0.1512	0.2148	0.1200
4	8	0.1759	0.2345	0.1200
4	6	0.2060	0.2572	0.1200
4	4	0.2363	0.2782	0.1200
4	2	0.2723	0.2992	0.1200

3	12	0.1042	0.1681	0.06555
3	10	0.1259	0.1879	0.06555
3	8	0.1527	0.2119	0.06555
3	6	0.1835	0.2375	0.06555
3	4	0.2176	0.2632	0.06555
3	2	0.2617	0.2921	0.06555
2	10	0.0965	0.1558	0.03126
2	8	0.1245	0.1827	0.03126
2	6	0.1617	0.2162	0.03126
2	4	0.2048	0.2518	0.03126
2	2	0.2559	0.2874	0.03126
1	6	0.1212	0.1745	0.01210
1	4	0.1667	0.2168	0.01210
1	2	0.2291	0.2677	0.01210

7.5B

Value	Chroma	CIE x	CIE y	Y
9	4	0.2688	0.2961	0.7866
9	2	0.2937	0.3087	0.7866
8	8	0.2252	0.2668	0.5910
8	6	0.2472	0.2821	0.5910
8	4	0.2688	0.2956	0.5910
8	2	0.2922	0.3077	0.5910
7	12	0.1818	0.2303	0.4306
7	10	0.2016	0.2466	0.4306
7	8	0.2225	0.2631	0.4306
7	6	0.2436	0.2787	0.4306
7	4	0.2651	0.2927	0.4306
7	2	0.2888	0.3058	0.4306
6	16	0.1376	0.1879	0.3005
6	14	0.1556	0.2043	0.3005
6	12	0.1734	0.2203	0.3005
6	10	0.1934	0.2374	0.3005
6	8	0.2132	0.2537	0.3005
6	6	0.2352	0.2708	0.3005
6	4	0.2602	0.2881	0.3005
6	2	0.2854	0.3037	0.3005
5	16	0.1230	0.1711	0.1977
5	14	0.1404	0.1878	0.1977
5	12	0.1584	0.2042	0.1977
5	10	0.1792	0.2230	0.1977
5	8	0.2007	0.2417	0.1977
5	6	0.2248	0.2612	0.1977
5	4	0.2511	0.2808	0.1977
5	2	0.2803	0.3000	0.1977
4	14	0.1204	0.1655	0.1200
4	12	0.1393	0.1837	0.1200
4	10	0.1601	0.2028	0.1200
4	8	0.1821	0.2232	0.1200
4	6	0.2102	0.2470	0.1200

4	4	0.2388	0.2704	0.1200
4	2	0.2733	0.2947	0.1200
3	12	0.1131	0.1542	0.06555
3	10	0.1343	0.1756	0.06555
3	8	0.1583	0.1987	0.06555
3	6	0.1875	0.2258	0.06555
3	4	0.2200	0.2536	0.06555
3	2	0.2616	0.2857	0.06555
2	10	0.1051	0.1422	0.03126
2	8	0.1313	0.1692	0.03126
2	6	0.1658	0.2026	0.03126
2	4	0.2063	0.2400	0.03126
2	2	0.2545	0.2799	0.03126
1	8	0.0968	0.1280	0.01210
1	6	0.1303	0.1639	0.01210
1	4	0.1716	0.2048	0.01210
1	2	0.2291	0.2579	0.01210

10.0B

Value	Chroma	CIE x	CIE y	Y
9	4	0.2712	0.2924	0.7866
9	2	0.2949	0.3076	0.7866
8	8	0.2294	0.2587	0.5910
8	6	0.2512	0.2760	0.5910
8	4	0.2718	0.2911	0.5910
8	2	0.2935	0.3062	0.5910
7	12	0.1883	0.2203	0.4306
7	10	0.2078	0.2382	0.4306
7	8	0.2277	0.2559	0.4306
7	6	0.2478	0.2728	0.4306
7	4	0.2685	0.2886	0.4306
7	2	0.2908	0.3039	0.4306
6	16	0.1454	0.1778	0.3005
6	14	0.1629	0.1947	0.3005
6	12	0.1803	0.2114	0.3005
6	10	0.2000	0.2298	0.3005
6	8	0.2189	0.2468	0.3005
6	6	0.2399	0.2650	0.3005
6	4	0.2637	0.2840	0.3005
6	2	0.2871	0.3012	0.3005
5	18	0.1203	0.1505	0.1977
5	16	0.1326	0.1632	0.1977
5	14	0.1492	0.1797	0.1977
5	12	0.1666	0.1964	0.1977
5	10	0.1860	0.2149	0.1977
5	8	0.2067	0.2344	0.1977
5	6	0.2299	0.2548	0.1977
5	4	0.2547	0.2757	0.1977
5	2	0.2821	0.2966	0.1977
4	16	0.1155	0.1416	0.1200

4	14	0.1310	0.1580	0.1200
4	12	0.1487	0.1760	0.1200
4	10	0.1681	0.1954	0.1200
4	8	0.1893	0.2160	0.1200
4	6	0.2157	0.2407	0.1200
4	4	0.2429	0.2648	0.1200
4	2	0.2753	0.2910	0.1200
3	14	0.1065	0.1285	0.06555
3	12	0.1228	0.1460	0.06555
3	10	0.1432	0.1675	0.06555
3	8	0.1658	0.1905	0.06555
3	6	0.1933	0.2173	0.06555
3	4	0.2246	0.2467	0.06555
3	2	0.2631	0.2801	0.06555
2	10	0.1157	0.1346	0.03126
2	8	0.1396	0.1603	0.03126
2	6	0.1716	0.1937	0.03126
2	4	0.2102	0.2313	0.03126
2	2	0.2558	0.2725	0.03126
1	8	0.1077	0.1218	0.01210
1	6	0.1392	0.1563	0.01210
1	4	0.1783	0.1974	0.01210
1	2	0.2309	0.2491	0.01210

2.5PB

Value	Chroma	CIE x	CIE y	Y
9	2	0.2975	0.3063	0.7866
8	6	0.2562	0.2709	0.5910
8	4	0.2758	0.2879	0.5910
8	2	0.2957	0.3047	0.5910
7	10	0.2162	0.2309	0.4306
7	8	0.2352	0.2498	0.4306
7	6	0.2538	0.2677	0.4306
7	4	0.2729	0.2848	0.4306
7	2	0.2932	0.3025	0.4306
6	14	0.1754	0.1868	0.3005
6	12	0.1913	0.2038	0.3005
6	10	0.2095	0.2225	0.3005
6	8	0.2274	0.2406	0.3005
6	6	0.2465	0.2599	0.3005
6	4	0.2684	0.2804	0.3005
6	2	0.2897	0.2991	0.3005
5	18	0.1363	0.1410	0.1977
5	16	0.1495	0.1559	0.1977
5	14	0.1642	0.1728	0.1977
5	12	0.1793	0.1894	0.1977
5	10	0.1968	0.2078	0.1977
5	8	0.2157	0.2278	0.1977
5	6	0.2365	0.2488	0.1977
5	4	0.2600	0.2720	0.1977

5	2	0.2847	0.2942	0.1977
4	18	0.1218	0.1208	0.1200
4	16	0.1336	0.1349	0.1200
4	14	0.1473	0.1513	0.1200
4	12	0.1634	0.1698	0.1200
4	10	0.1805	0.1888	0.1200
4	8	0.1995	0.2094	0.1200
4	6	0.2235	0.2343	0.1200
4	4	0.2487	0.2597	0.1200
4	2	0.2782	0.2876	0.1200
3	14	0.1251	0.1218	0.06555
3	12	0.1398	0.1395	0.06555
3	10	0.1576	0.1600	0.06555
3	8	0.1780	0.1833	0.06555
3	6	0.2022	0.2101	0.06555
3	4	0.2312	0.2405	0.06555
3	2	0.2663	0.2756	0.06555
2	12	0.1166	0.1076	0.03126
2	10	0.1332	0.1278	0.03126
2	8	0.1540	0.1530	0.03126
2	6	0.1825	0.1857	0.03126
2	4	0.2175	0.2245	0.03126
2	2	0.2592	0.2675	0.03126
1	8	0.1273	0.1157	0.01210
1	6	0.1539	0.1491	0.01210
1	4	0.1895	0.1911	0.01210
1	2	0.2360	0.2420	0.01210

5.0PB

Value	Chroma	CIE x	CIE y	Y
9	2	0.2991	0.3057	0.7866
8	6	0.2614	0.2670	0.5910
8	4	0.2798	0.2861	0.5910
8	2	0.2974	0.3039	0.5910
7	10	0.2254	0.2267	0.4306
7	8	0.2427	0.2458	0.4306
7	6	0.2596	0.2643	0.4306
7	4	0.2773	0.2828	0.4306
7	2	0.2952	0.3011	0.4306
6	14	0.1873	0.1822	0.3005
6	12	0.2026	0.1999	0.3005
6	10	0.2197	0.2188	0.3005
6	8	0.2360	0.2365	0.3005
6	6	0.2533	0.2558	0.3005
6	4	0.2734	0.2778	0.3005
6	2	0.2923	0.2978	0.3005
5	18	0.1518	0.1365	0.1977
5	16	0.1638	0.1521	0.1977
5	14	0.1773	0.1689	0.1977
5	12	0.1918	0.1858	0.1977

5	10	0.2080	0.2041	0.1977
5	8	0.2255	0.2239	0.1977
5	6	0.2447	0.2449	0.1977
5	4	0.2662	0.2687	0.1977
5	2	0.2882	0.2923	0.1977
4	20	0.1288	0.1027	0.1200
4	18	0.1392	0.1167	0.1200
4	16	0.1504	0.1317	0.1200
4	14	0.1627	0.1479	0.1200
4	12	0.1773	0.1659	0.1200
4	10	0.1925	0.1843	0.1200
4	8	0.2103	0.2050	0.1200
4	6	0.2325	0.2300	0.1200
4	4	0.2562	0.2560	0.1200
4	2	0.2816	0.2842	0.1200
3	18	0.1228	0.0895	0.06555
3	16	0.1318	0.1024	0.06555
3	14	0.1431	0.1184	0.06555
3	12	0.1557	0.1356	0.06555
3	10	0.1718	0.1562	0.06555
3	8	0.1908	0.1799	0.06555
3	6	0.2122	0.2052	0.06555
3	4	0.2393	0.2361	0.06555
3	2	0.2708	0.2719	0.06555
2	14	0.1253	0.0873	0.03126
2	12	0.1363	0.1048	0.03126
2	10	0.1500	0.1240	0.03126
2	8	0.1685	0.1491	0.03126
2	6	0.1942	0.1811	0.03126
2	4	0.2263	0.2192	0.03126
2	2	0.2638	0.2624	0.03126
1	10	0.1285	0.0870	0.01210
1	8	0.1447	0.1124	0.01210
1	6	0.1678	0.1447	0.01210
1	4	0.2012	0.1867	0.01210
1	2	0.2427	0.2368	0.01210

7.5PB

Value	Chroma	CIE x	CIE y	Y
9	2	0.3015	0.3052	0.7866
8	6	0.2702	0.2648	0.5910
8	4	0.2856	0.2846	0.5910
8	2	0.3003	0.3034	0.5910
7	10	0.2410	0.2224	0.4306
7	8	0.2546	0.2418	0.4306
7	6	0.2687	0.2612	0.4306
7	4	0.2833	0.2809	0.4306
7	2	0.2982	0.3003	0.4306
6	14	0.2119	0.1799	0.3005
6	12	0.2241	0.1975	0.3005

6	10	0.2378	0.2168	0.3005
6	8	0.2505	0.2347	0.3005
6	6	0.2638	0.2531	0.3005
6	4	0.2798	0.2752	0.3005
6	2	0.2955	0.2963	0.3005
5	20	0.1794	0.1239	0.1977
5	18	0.1862	0.1365	0.1977
5	16	0.1945	0.1511	0.1977
5	14	0.2042	0.1661	0.1977
5	12	0.2157	0.1830	0.1977
5	10	0.2285	0.2020	0.1977
5	8	0.2417	0.2204	0.1977
5	6	0.2563	0.2417	0.1977
5	4	0.2739	0.2666	0.1977
5	2	0.2918	0.2908	0.1977
4	26	0.1659	0.0825	0.1200
4	24	0.1684	0.0899	0.1200
4	22	0.1713	0.0980	0.1200
4	20	0.1742	0.1058	0.1200
4	18	0.1798	0.1185	0.1200
4	16	0.1861	0.1316	0.1200
4	14	0.1941	0.1468	0.1200
4	12	0.2037	0.1629	0.1200
4	10	0.2158	0.1811	0.1200
4	8	0.2304	0.2023	0.1200
4	6	0.2471	0.2266	0.1200
4	4	0.2657	0.2528	0.1200
4	2	0.2861	0.2819	0.1200
3	34	0.1608	0.0480	0.06555
3	32	0.1612	0.0511	0.06555
3	30	0.1621	0.0556	0.06555
3	28	0.1632	0.0609	0.06555
3	26	0.1642	0.0655	0.06555
3	24	0.1658	0.0711	0.06555
3	22	0.1677	0.0782	0.06555
3	20	0.1702	0.0867	0.06555
3	18	0.1730	0.0948	0.06555
3	16	0.1765	0.1048	0.06555
3	14	0.1824	0.1188	0.06555
3	12	0.1903	0.1353	0.06555
3	10	0.2005	0.1536	0.06555
3	8	0.2149	0.1761	0.06555
3	6	0.2311	0.2010	0.06555
3	4	0.2520	0.2319	0.06555
3	2	0.2777	0.2687	0.06555
2	38	0.1623	0.0280	0.03126
2	36	0.1628	0.0310	0.03126
2	34	0.1630	0.0340	0.03126
2	32	0.1635	0.0373	0.03126
2	30	0.1640	0.0409	0.03126
2	28	0.1647	0.0451	0.03126
2	26	0.1653	0.0492	0.03126

2	24	0.1660	0.0538	0.03126
2	22	0.1670	0.0594	0.03126
2	20	0.1685	0.0666	0.03126
2	18	0.1701	0.0742	0.03126
2	16	0.1728	0.0839	0.03126
2	14	0.1762	0.0955	0.03126
2	12	0.1813	0.1094	0.03126
2	10	0.1882	0.1258	0.03126
2	8	0.2005	0.1495	0.03126
2	6	0.2189	0.1790	0.03126
2	4	0.2420	0.2148	0.03120
2	2	0.2712	0.2582	0.03120
1	38	0.1680	0.0140	0.01210
1	36	0.1681	0.0160	0.01210
1	34	0.1682	0.0180	0.01210
1	32	0.1682	0.0202	0.01210
1	30	0.1684	0.0234	0.01210
1	28	0.1686	0.0270	0.01210
1	26	0.1689	0.0309	0.01210
1	24	0.1691	0.0352	0.01210
1	22	0.1696	0.0402	0.01210
1	20	0.1701	0.0454	0.01210
1	18	0.1709	0.0518	0.01210
1	16	0.1720	0.0583	0.01210
1	14	0.1738	0.0688	0.01210
1	12	0.1763	0.0804	0.01210
1	10	0.1804	0.0950	0.01210
1	8	0.1872	0.1141	0.01210
1	6	0.2000	0.1422	0.01210
1	4	0.2232	0.1821	0.01210
1	2	0.2547	0.2310	0.01210

10.0PB

Value	Chroma	CIE x	CIE y	Y
9	4	0.2910	0.2850	0.7866
9	2	0.3038	0.3054	0.7866
8	8	0.2677	0.2443	0.5910
8	6	0.2792	0.2649	0.5910
8	4	0.3011	0.2848	0.5910
8	2	0.3027	0.3035	0.5910
7	12	0.2465	0.2058	0.4306
7	10	0.2563	0.2240	0.4306
7	8	0.2670	0.2425	0.4306
7	6	0.2776	0.2612	0.4306
7	4	0.2886	0.2801	0.4306
7	2	0.3005	0.3000	0.4306
6	16	0.2265	0.1671	0.3005
6	14	0.2352	0.1839	0.3005
6	12	0.2440	0.1998	0.3005
6	10	0.2540	0.2176	0.3005

6	8	0.2637	0.2352	0.3005
6	6	0.2740	0.2533	0.3005
6	4	0.2863	0.2747	0.3005
6	2	0.2988	0.2961	0.3005
5	22	0.2082	0.1225	0.1977
5	20	0.2121	0.1329	0.1977
5	18	0.2174	0.1444	0.1977
5	16	0.2224	0.1555	0.1977
5	14	0.2299	0.1698	0.1977
5	12	0.2384	0.1857	0.1977
5	10	0.2478	0.2030	0.1977
5	8	0.2572	0.2211	0.1977
5	6	0.2686	0.2412	0.1977
5	4	0.2821	0.2659	0.1977
5	2	0.2959	0.2905	0.1977
4	30	0.1952	0.0778	0.1200
4	28	0.1971	0.0840	0.1200
4	26	0.1994	0.0904	0.1200
4	24	0.2020	0.0985	0.1200
4	22	0.2048	0.1064	0.1200
4	20	0.2075	0.1140	0.1200
4	18	0.2120	0.1256	0.1200
4	16	0.2170	0.1373	0.1200
4	14	0.2220	0.1503	0.1200
4	12	0.2298	0.1659	0.1210
4	10	0.2388	0.1837	0.1210
4	8	0.2497	0.2038	0.1210
4	6	0.2618	0.2263	0.1210
4	4	0.2759	0.2522	0.1210
4	2	0.2911	0.2804	0.1210
3	34	0.1918	0.0503	0.06555
3	32	0.1926	0.0542	0.06555
3	30	0.1938	0.0599	0.06555
3	28	0.1950	0.0650	0.06555
3	26	0.1963	0.0708	0.06555
3	24	0.1982	0.0772	0.06555
3	22	0.2004	0.0847	0.06555
3	20	0.2030	0.0930	0.06555
3	18	0.2060	0.1020	0.06555
3	16	0.2092	0.1118	0.06555
3	14	0.2142	0.1250	0.06555
3	12	0.2206	0.1407	0.06555
3	10	0.2278	0.1565	0.06555
3	8	0.2387	0.1786	0.06555
3	6	0.2511	0.2031	0.06555
3	4	0.2660	0.2319	0.06555
3	2	0.2847	0.2670	0.06555
2	34	0.1911	0.0344	0.03126
2	32	0.1918	0.0379	0.03126
2	30	0.1925	0.0420	0.03126
2	28	0.1937	0.0471	0.03126
2	26	0.1949	0.0520	0.03126

2	24	0.1962	0.0578	0.03126
2	22	0.1978	0.0643	0.03126
2	20	0.1998	0.0718	0.03126
2	18	0.2021	0.0808	0.03126
2	16	0.2052	0.0910	0.03126
2	14	0.2087	0.1026	0.03126
2	12	0.2139	0.1170	0.03126
2	10	0.2200	0.1330	0.03126
2	8	0.2294	0.1551	0.03126
2	6	0.2440	0.1840	0.03126
2	4	0.2600	0.2162	0.03126
2	2	0.2803	0.2576	0.03126
1	30	0.1928	0.0240	0.01210
1	28	0.1936	0.0281	0.01210
1	26	0.1942	0.0326	0.01210
1	24	0.1952	0.0380	0.01210
1	22	0.1965	0.0436	0.01210
1	20	0.1976	0.0493	0.01210
1	18	0.1991	0.0564	0.01210
1	16	0.2008	0.0638	0.01210
1	14	0.2038	0.0745	0.01210
1	12	0.2070	0.0869	0.01210
1	10	0.2120	0.1029	0.01210
1	8	0.2190	0.1228	0.01210
1	6	0.2290	0.1470	0.01210
1	4	0.2459	0.1828	0.01210
1	2	0.2677	0.2280	0.01210

2.5P

Value	Chroma	CIE x	CIE y	Y
9	4	0.2963	0.2865	0.7866
9	2	0.3050	0.3051	0.7866
8	8	0.2800	0.2488	0.5910
8	6	0.2881	0.2671	0.5910
8	4	0.2962	0.2850	0.5910
8	2	0.3048	0.3040	0.5910
7	12	0.2664	0.2127	0.4306
7	10	0.2729	0.2289	0.4306
7	8	0.2799	0.2459	0.4306
7	6	0.2873	0.2633	0.4306
7	4	0.2950	0.2810	0.4306
7	2	0.3031	0.3000	0.4306
6	18	0.2504	0.1658	0.3005
6	16	0.2548	0.1786	0.3005
6	14	0.2593	0.1909	0.3005
6	12	0.2647	0.2052	0.3005
6	10	0.2703	0.2204	0.3005
6	8	0.2770	0.2372	0.3005
6	6	0.2842	0.2550	0.3005
6	4	0.2932	0.2759	0.3005

6	2	0.3016	0.2960	0.3005
5	26	0.2348	0.1140	0.1977
5	24	0.2372	0.1223	0.1977
5	22	0.2402	0.1315	0.1977
5	20	0.2438	0.1419	0.1977
5	18	0.2476	0.1532	0.1977
5	16	0.2515	0.1644	0.1977
5	14	0.2560	0.1774	0.1977
5	12	0.2608	0.1913	0.1977
5	10	0.2665	0.2075	0.1977
5	8	0.2728	0.2240	0.1977
5	6	0.2806	0.2444	0.1977
5	4	0.2898	0.2667	0.1977
5	2	0.3000	0.2912	0.1977
4	32	0.2265	0.0774	0.1200
4	30	0.2285	0.0847	0.1200
4	28	0.2302	0.0909	0.1200
4	26	0.2322	0.0978	0.1200
4	24	0.2348	0.1062	0.1200
4	22	0.2371	0.1143	0.1200
4	20	0.2394	0.1221	0.1200
4	18	0.2430	0.1332	0.1200
4	16	0.2467	0.1452	0.1200
4	14	0.2509	0.1585	0.1200
4	12	0.2559	0.1730	0.1200
4	10	0.2619	0.1903	0.1200
4	8	0.2685	0.2089	0.1200
4	6	0.2763	0.2300	0.1200
4	4	0.2855	0.2531	0.1200
4	2	0.2962	0.2807	0.1200
3	34	0.2230	0.0543	0.06555
3	32	0.2242	0.0587	0.06555
3	30	0.2252	0.0638	0.06555
3	28	0.2268	0.0698	0.06555
3	26	0.2286	0.0765	0.06555
3	24	0.2305	0.0832	0.06555
3	22	0.2329	0.0911	0.06555
3	20	0.2354	0.1003	0.06555
3	18	0.2380	0.1094	0.06555
3	16	0.2410	0.1198	0.06555
3	14	0.2449	0.1325	0.06555
3	12	0.2498	0.1480	0.06555
3	10	0.2548	0.1638	0.06555
3	8	0.2615	0.1845	0.06555
3	6	0.2691	0.2072	0.06555
3	4	0.2792	0.2342	0.06555
3	2	0.2922	0.2680	0.06555
2	30	0.2231	0.0432	0.03126
2	28	0.2245	0.0491	0.03126
2	26	0.2260	0.0555	0.03126
2	24	0.2277	0.0621	0.03126
2	22	0.2298	0.0696	0.03126

2	20	0.2320	0.0779	0.03126
2	18	0.2345	0.0873	0.03126
2	16	0.2372	0.0980	0.03126
2	14	0.2406	0.1100	0.03126
2	12	0.2449	0.1245	0.03126
2	10	0.2501	0.1422	0.03126
2	8	0.2570	0.1635	0.03126
2	6	0.2661	0.1921	0.03126
2	4	0.2758	0.2208	0.03126
2	2	0.2892	0.2583	0.03126
1	26	0.2251	0.0355	0.01210
1	24	0.2266	0.0418	0.01210
1	22	0.2279	0.0473	0.01210
1	20	0.2295	0.0542	0.01210
1	18	0.2312	0.0618	0.01210
1	16	0.2331	0.0696	0.01210
1	14	0.2361	0.0810	0.01210
1	12	0.2394	0.0940	0.01210
1	10	0.2441	0.1112	0.01210
1	8	0.2496	0.1303	0.01210
1	6	0.2570	0.1559	0.01210
1	4	0.2668	0.1874	0.01210
1	2	0.2808	0.2296	0.01210

5.0P

Value	Chroma	CIE x	CIE y	Y
9	4	0.3003	0.2870	0.7866
9	2	0.3067	0.3060	0.7866
8	10	0.2870	0.2380	0.5910
8	8	0.2914	0.2534	0.5910
8	6	0.2963	0.2704	0.5910
8	4	0.3012	0.2868	0.5910
8	2	0.3065	0.3047	0.5910
7	14	0.2801	0.2068	0.4306
7	12	0.2833	0.2197	0.4306
7	10	0.2872	0.2343	0.4306
7	8	0.2918	0.2504	0.4306
7	6	0.2961	0.2663	0.4306
7	4	0.3009	0.2831	0.4306
7	2	0.3059	0.3010	0.4306
6	20	0.2702	0.1621	0.3005
6	18	0.2731	0.1738	0.3005
6	16	0.2761	0.1852	0.3005
6	14	0.2794	0.1979	0.3005
6	12	0.2829	0.2121	0.3005
6	10	0.2862	0.2260	0.3005
6	8	0.2905	0.2421	0.3005
6	6	0.2950	0.2585	0.3005
6	4	0.3001	0.2778	0.3005
6	2	0.3050	0.2967	0.3005

5	28	0.2618	0.1135	0.1977
5	26	0.2635	0.1224	0.1977
5	24	0.2652	0.1304	0.1977
5	22	0.2673	0.1398	0.1977
5	20	0.2694	0.1499	0.1977
5	18	0.2718	0.1604	0.1977
5	16	0.2744	0.1718	0.1977
5	14	0.2775	0.1847	0.1977
5	12	0.2806	0.1977	0.1977
5	10	0.2845	0.2137	0.1977
5	8	0.2885	0.2296	0.1977
5	6	0.2932	0.2487	0.1977
5	4	0.2986	0.2699	0.1977
5	2	0.3045	0.2928	0.1977
4	32	0.2574	0.0833	0.1200
4	30	0.2588	0.0907	0.1200
4	28	0.2600	0.0971	0.1200
4	26	0.2618	0.1052	0.1200
4	24	0.2635	0.1132	0.1200
4	22	0.2652	0.1218	0.1200
4	20	0.2670	0.1300	0.1200
4	18	0.2693	0.1408	0.1200
4	16	0.2718	0.1520	0.1200
4	14	0.2747	0.1660	0.1200
4	12	0.2778	0.1808	0.1200
4	10	0.2814	0.1967	0.1200
4	8	0.2855	0.2150	0.1200
4	6	0.2903	0.2347	0.1200
4	4	0.2958	0.2565	0.1200
4	2	0.3022	0.2825	0.1200
3	32	0.2557	0.0630	0.06555
3	30	0.2568	0.0690	0.06555
3	28	0.2579	0.0750	0.06555
3	26	0.2590	0.0822	0.06555
3	24	0.2602	0.0891	0.06555
3	22	0.2620	0.0978	0.06555
3	20	0.2639	0.1074	0.06555
3	18	0.2657	0.1163	0.06555
3	16	0.2680	0.1272	0.06555
3	14	0.2707	0.1397	0.06555
3	12	0.2739	0.1539	0.06555
3	10	0.2772	0.1707	0.06555
3	8	0.2819	0.1910	0.06555
3	6	0.2870	0.2135	0.06555
3	4	0.2928	0.2386	0.06555
3	2	0.2997	0.2700	0.06555
2	28	0.2559	0.0525	0.03126
2	26	0.2569	0.0594	0.03126
2	24	0.2582	0.0669	0.03126
2	22	0.2597	0.0750	0.03126
2	20	0.2612	0.0838	0.03126
2	18	0.2632	0.0935	0.03126

2	16	0.2652	0.1045	0.03126
2	14	0.2676	0.1163	0.03126
2	12	0.2709	0.1320	0.03126
2	10	0.2748	0.1500	0.03126
2	8	0.2791	0.1707	0.03126
2	6	0.2850	0.1992	0.03126
2	4	0.2908	0.2261	0.03126
2	2	0.2984	0.2612	0.03126
1	22	0.2590	0.0509	0.01210
1	20	0.2601	0.0586	0.01210
1	18	0.2612	0.0667	0.01210
1	16	0.2625	0.0746	0.01210
1	14	0.2645	0.0863	0.01210
1	12	0.2670	0.1006	0.01210
1	10	0.2701	0.1178	0.01210
1	8	0.2742	0.1375	0.01210
1	6	0.2794	0.1628	0.01210
1	4	0.2854	0.1927	0.01210
1	2	0.2936	0.2330	0.01210

7.5P

Value	Chroma	CIE x	CIE y	Y
9	6	0.3120	0.2788	0.7866
9	4	0.3117	0.2928	0.7866
9	2	0.3107	0.3081	0.7866
8	12	0.3117	0.2370	0.5910
8	10	0.3116	0.2497	0.5910
8	8	0.3116	0.2626	0.5910
8	6	0.3114	0.2785	0.5910
8	4	0.3114	0.2915	0.5910
8	2	0.3107	0.3070	0.5910
7	18	0.3093	0.1962	0.4306
7	16	0.3099	0.2074	0.4306
7	14	0.3101	0.2192	0.4306
7	12	0.3104	0.2320	0.4306
7	10	0.3108	0.2442	0.4306
7	8	0.3109	0.2584	0.4306
7	6	0.3111	0.2730	0.4306
7	4	0.3111	0.2880	0.4306
7	2	0.3109	0.3037	0.4306
6	24	0.3058	0.1547	0.3005
6	22	0.3062	0.1638	0.3005
6	20	0.3069	0.1745	0.3005
6	18	0.3075	0.1870	0.3005
6	16	0.3080	0.1976	0.3005
6	14	0.3084	0.2095	0.3005
6	12	0.3090	0.2222	0.3005
6	10	0.3092	0.2350	0.3005
6	8	0.3099	0.2502	0.3005
6	6	0.3101	0.2650	0.3005

6	4	0.3107	0.2831	0.3005
6	2	0.3107	0.2993	0.3005
5	30	0.3010	0.1170	0.1977
5	28	0.3018	0.1253	0.1977
5	26	0.3022	0.1331	0.1977
5	24	0.3030	0.1423	0.1977
5	22	0.3038	0.1500	0.1977
5	20	0.3042	0.1606	0.1977
5	18	0.3052	0.1711	0.1977
5	16	0.3060	0.1830	0.1977
5	14	0.3068	0.1951	0.1977
5	12	0.3071	0.2080	0.1977
5	10	0.3080	0.2230	0.1977
5	8	0.3087	0.2375	0.1977
5	6	0.3093	0.2555	0.1977
5	4	0.3100	0.2750	0.1977
5	2	0.3103	0.2959	0.1977
4	32	0.2962	0.0906	0.1200
4	30	0.2969	0.0979	0.1200
4	28	0.2979	0.1062	0.1200
4	26	0.2986	0.1135	0.1200
4	24	0.2993	0.1225	0.1200
4	22	0.3001	0.1306	0.1200
4	20	0.3010	0.1396	0.1200
4	18	0.3016	0.1500	0.1200
4	16	0.3028	0.1621	0.1200
4	14	0.3035	0.1755	0.1200
4	12	0.3045	0.1905	0.1200
4	10	0.3056	0.2060	0.1200
4	8	0.3066	0.2228	0.1200
4	6	0.3076	0.2416	0.1200
4	4	0.3084	0.2622	0.1200
4	2	0.3093	0.2859	0.1200
3	30	0.2922	0.0750	0.06555
3	28	0.2930	0.0812	0.06555
3	26	0.2938	0.0892	0.06555
3	24	0.2944	0.0967	0.06555
3	22	0.2953	0.1057	0.06555
3	20	0.2961	0.1151	0.06555
3	18	0.2969	0.1239	0.06555
3	16	0.2981	0.1356	0.06555
3	14	0.2992	0.1475	0.06555
3	12	0.3003	0.1618	0.06555
3	10	0.3020	0.1794	0.06555
3	8	0.3037	0.1981	0.06555
3	6	0.3057	0.2208	0.06555
3	4	0.3072	0.2448	0.06555
3	2	0.3088	0.2740	0.06555
2	24	0.2882	0.0719	0.03126
2	22	0.2890	0.0799	0.03126
2	20	0.2902	0.0901	0.03126
2	18	0.2912	0.0995	0.03126

2	16	0.2922	0.1106	0.03126
2	14	0.2938	0.1235	0.03126
2	12	0.2956	0.1392	0.03126
2	10	0.2979	0.1569	0.03126
2	8	0.3000	0.1781	0.03126
2	6	0.3025	0.2058	0.03126
2	4	0.3048	0.2321	0.03126
2	2	0.3071	0.2647	0.03126
1	20	0.2831	0.0625	0.01210
1	18	0.2841	0.0706	0.01210
1	16	0.2852	0.0790	0.01210
1	14	0.2868	0.0903	0.01210
1	12	0.2884	0.1059	0.01210
1	10	0.2905	0.1229	0.01210
1	8	0.2932	0.1429	0.01210
1	6	0.2960	0.1682	0.01210
1	4	0.2991	0.1974	0.01210
1	2	0.3030	0.2361	0.01210

10.0P

Value	Chroma	CIE x	CIE y	Y
9	6	0.3218	0.2845	0.7866
9	4	0.3176	0.2966	0.7866
9	2	0.3128	0.3094	0.7866
8	14	0.3342	0.2349	0.5910
8	12	0.3312	0.2470	0.5910
8	10	0.3282	0.2582	0.5910
8	8	0.3250	0.2700	0.5910
8	6	0.3213	0.2829	0.5910
8	4	0.3175	0.2955	0.5910
8	2	0.3131	0.3084	0.5910
7	22	0.3430	0.1883	0.4306
7	20	0.3410	0.1988	0.4306
7	18	0.3391	0.2088	0.4306
7	16	0.3368	0.2192	0.4306
7	14	0.3341	0.2308	0.4306
7	12	0.3314	0.2423	0.4306
7	10	0.3288	0.2531	0.4306
7	8	0.3256	0.2654	0.4306
7	6	0.3221	0.2786	0.4306
7	4	0.3181	0.2920	0.4306
7	2	0.3138	0.3054	0.4306
6	26	0.3457	0.1604	0.3005
6	24	0.3441	0.1698	0.3005
6	22	0.3426	0.1785	0.3005
6	20	0.3409	0.1882	0.3005
6	18	0.3388	0.1995	0.3005
6	16	0.3370	0.2095	0.3005
6	14	0.3349	0.2203	0.3005
6	12	0.3321	0.2329	0.3005

6	10	0.3293	0.2450	0.3005
6	8	0.3259	0.2584	0.3005
6	6	0.3226	0.2716	0.3005
6	4	0.3181	0.2871	0.3005
6	2	0.3146	0.3018	0.3005
5	30	0.3490	0.1308	0.1977
5	28	0.3478	0.1388	0.1977
5	26	0.3468	0.1460	0.1977
5	24	0.3450	0.1555	0.1977
5	22	0.3437	0.1644	0.1977
5	20	0.3422	0.1735	0.1977
5	18	0.3401	0.1840	0.1977
5	16	0.3382	0.1951	0.1977
5	14	0.3360	0.2066	0.1977
5	12	0.3335	0.2187	0.1977
5	10	0.3308	0.2328	0.1977
5	8	0.3280	0.2464	0.1977
5	6	0.3243	0.2630	0.1977
5	4	0.3198	0.2807	0.1977
5	2	0.3148	0.2986	0.1977
4	30	0.3440	0.1080	0.1200
4	28	0.3432	0.1172	0.1200
4	26	0.3428	0.1248	0.1200
4	24	0.3421	0.1337	0.1200
4	22	0.3411	0.1424	0.1200
4	20	0.3400	0.1500	0.1200
4	18	0.3386	0.1626	0.1200
4	16	0.3370	0.1756	0.1200
4	14	0.3351	0.1875	0.1200
4	12	0.3331	0.2014	0.1200
4	10	0.3306	0.2162	0.1200
4	8	0.3280	0.2318	0.1200
4	6	0.3248	0.2493	0.1200
4	4	0.3210	0.2686	0.1200
4	2	0.3162	0.2902	0.1200
3	26	0.3343	0.0978	0.06555
3	24	0.3341	0.1055	0.06555
3	22	0.3340	0.1146	0.06555
3	20	0.3332	0.1240	0.06555
3	18	0.3329	0.1332	0.06555
3	16	0.3320	0.1456	0.06555
3	14	0.3309	0.1572	0.06555
3	12	0.3301	0.1715	0.06555
3	10	0.3286	0.1889	0.06555
3	8	0.3269	0.2075	0.06555
3	6	0.3243	0.2293	0.06555
3	4	0.3214	0.2517	0.06555
3	2	0.3170	0.2790	0.06555
2	22	0.3230	0.0861	0.03126
2	20	0.3231	0.0962	0.03126
2	18	0.3233	0.1063	0.03126
2	16	0.3235	0.1181	0.03126

2	14	0.3235	0.1317	0.03126
2	12	0.3233	0.1477	0.03126
2	10	0.3230	0.1659	0.03126
2	8	0.3219	0.1862	0.03126
2	6	0.3207	0.2132	0.03126
2	4	0.3189	0.2390	0.03126
2	2	0.3161	0.2691	0.03126
1	18	0.3069	0.0748	0.01210
1	16	0.3078	0.0839	0.01210
1	14	0.3084	0.0952	0.01210
1	12	0.3094	0.1110	0.01210
1	10	0.3102	0.1282	0.01210
1	8	0.3114	0.1481	0.01210
1	6	0.3126	0.1737	0.01210
1	4	0.3132	0.2032	0.01210
1	2	0.3132	0.2404	0.01210

2.5RP

Value	Chroma	CIE x	CIE y	Y
9	6	0.3322	0.2910	0.7866
9	4	0.3234	0.3010	0.7866
9	2	0.3149	0.3108	0.7866
8	14	0.3621	0.2496	0.5910
8	12	0.3552	0.2594	0.5910
8	10	0.3479	0.2699	0.5910
8	8	0.3406	0.2793	0.5910
8	6	0.3327	0.2898	0.5910
8	4	0.3239	0.3000	0.5910
8	2	0.3154	0.3100	0.5910
7	20	0.3811	0.2143	0.4306
7	18	0.3751	0.2241	0.4306
7	16	0.3688	0.2342	0.4306
7	14	0.3620	0.2448	0.4306
7	12	0.3555	0.2545	0.4306
7	10	0.3487	0.2648	0.4306
7	8	0.3417	0.2745	0.4306
7	6	0.3338	0.2854	0.4306
7	4	0.3254	0.2971	0.4306
7	2	0.3170	0.3076	0.4306
6	24	0.3927	0.1892	0.3005
6	22	0.3877	0.1978	0.3005
6	20	0.3833	0.2056	0.3005
6	18	0.3773	0.2158	0.3005
6	16	0.3718	0.2251	0.3005
6	14	0.3652	0.2355	0.3005
6	12	0.3582	0.2462	0.3005
6	10	0.3509	0.2578	0.3005
6	8	0.3437	0.2688	0.3005
6	6	0.3362	0.2799	0.3005
6	4	0.3272	0.2929	0.3005

6	2	0.3188	0.3048	0.3005
5	26	0.4011	0.1652	0.1977
5	24	0.3965	0.1738	0.1977
5	22	0.3924	0.1814	0.1977
5	20	0.3873	0.1909	0.1977
5	18	0.3821	0.2007	0.1977
5	16	0.3763	0.2108	0.1977
5	14	0.3703	0.2211	0.1977
5	12	0.3635	0.2325	0.1977
5	10	0.3560	0.2452	0.1977
5	8	0.3490	0.2570	0.1977
5	6	0.3396	0.2718	0.1977
5	4	0.3298	0.2869	0.1977
5	2	0.3199	0.3019	0.1977
4	26	0.4048	0.1428	0.1200
4	24	0.4011	0.1504	0.1200
4	22	0.3967	0.1593	0.1200
4	20	0.3926	0.1679	0.1200
4	18	0.3865	0.1802	0.1200
4	16	0.3807	0.1923	0.1200
4	14	0.3748	0.2039	0.1200
4	12	0.3683	0.2162	0.1200
4	10	0.3608	0.2301	0.1200
4	8	0.3533	0.2438	0.1200
4	6	0.3442	0.2595	0.1200
4	4	0.3340	0.2770	0.1200
4	2	0.3231	0.2951	0.1200
3	22	0.4018	0.1304	0.06555
3	20	0.3969	0.1413	0.06555
3	18	0.3929	0.1506	0.06555
3	16	0.3876	0.1629	0.06555
3	14	0.3818	0.1758	0.06555
3	12	0.3754	0.1898	0.06555
3	10	0.3681	0.2054	0.06555
3	8	0.3598	0.2233	0.06555
3	6	0.3501	0.2425	0.06555
3	4	0.3400	0.2624	0.06555
3	2	0.3272	0.2861	0.06555
2	20	0.3802	0.1080	0.03126
2	18	0.3778	0.1188	0.03126
2	16	0.3748	0.1310	0.03126
2	14	0.3711	0.1449	0.03126
2	12	0.3668	0.1618	0.03126
2	10	0.3617	0.1800	0.03126
2	8	0.3555	0.2003	0.03126
2	6	0.3470	0.2259	0.03126
2	4	0.3382	0.2496	0.03126
2	2	0.3279	0.2754	0.03126
1	16	0.3368	0.0902	0.01210
1	14	0.3368	0.1020	0.01210
1	12	0.3361	0.1181	0.01210
1	10	0.3354	0.1351	0.01210

1	8	0.3342	0.1551	0.01210
1	6	0.3321	0.1811	0.01210
1	4	0.3290	0.2095	0.01210
1	2	0.3240	0.2459	0.01210

5.0RP

Value	Chroma	CIE x	CIE y	Y
9	6	0.3431	0.2988	0.7866
9	4	0.3301	0.3060	0.7866
9	2	0.3172	0.3126	0.7866
8	12	0.3818	0.2742	0.5910
8	10	0.3685	0.2828	0.5910
8	8	0.3570	0.2900	0.5910
8	6	0.3440	0.2978	0.5910
8	4	0.3308	0.3052	0.5910
8	2	0.3180	0.3120	0.5910
7	18	0.4186	0.2469	0.4306
7	16	0.4076	0.2540	0.4306
7	14	0.3958	0.2628	0.4306
7	12	0.3841	0.2710	0.4306
7	10	0.3713	0.2798	0.4306
7	8	0.3603	0.2869	0.4306
7	6	0.3470	0.2949	0.4306
7	4	0.3332	0.3032	0.4306
7	2	0.3206	0.3104	0.4306
6	22	0.4449	0.2219	0.3005
6	20	0.4368	0.2283	0.3005
6	18	0.4245	0.2382	0.3005
6	16	0.4136	0.2467	0.3005
6	14	0.4023	0.2552	0.3005
6	12	0.3900	0.2646	0.3005
6	10	0.3769	0.2738	0.3005
6	8	0.3648	0.2820	0.3005
6	6	0.3520	0.2904	0.3005
6	4	0.3371	0.3001	0.3005
6	2	0.3232	0.3085	0.3005
5	24	0.4683	0.1978	0.1977
5	22	0.4581	0.2068	0.1977
5	20	0.4484	0.2150	0.1977
5	18	0.4372	0.2242	0.1977
5	16	0.4261	0.2331	0.1977
5	14	0.4142	0.2428	0.1977
5	12	0.4022	0.2523	0.1977
5	10	0.3880	0.2630	0.1977
5	8	0.3748	0.2729	0.1977
5	6	0.3585	0.2842	0.1977
5	4	0.3421	0.2954	0.1977
5	2	0.3256	0.3065	0.1977
4	22	0.4656	0.1821	0.1200
4	20	0.4571	0.1906	0.1200

4	18	0.4455	0.2023	0.1200
4	16	0.4339	0.2139	0.1200
4	14	0.4225	0.2249	0.1200
4	12	0.4104	0.2361	0.1200
4	10	0.3960	0.2489	0.1200
4	8	0.3833	0.2600	0.1200
4	6	0.3671	0.2733	0.1200
4	4	0.3491	0.2872	0.1200
4	2	0.3310	0.3010	0.1200
3	20	0.4577	0.1593	0.06555
3	18	0.4503	0.1695	0.06555
3	16	0.4418	0.1809	0.06555
3	14	0.4313	0.1944	0.06555
3	12	0.4199	0.2089	0.06555
3	10	0.4073	0.2235	0.06555
3	8	0.3930	0.2395	0.06555
3	6	0.3765	0.2569	0.06555
3	4	0.3586	0.2742	0.06555
3	2	0.3370	0.2940	0.06555
2	18	0.4338	0.1340	0.03126
2	16	0.4269	0.1454	0.03126
2	14	0.4180	0.1598	0.03126
2	12	0.4080	0.1764	0.03126
2	10	0.3971	0.1939	0.03126
2	8	0.3858	0.2140	0.03126
2	6	0.3708	0.2380	0.03126
2	4	0.3558	0.2597	0.03126
2	2	0.3383	0.2829	0.03126
1	14	0.3811	0.1138	0.01210
1	12	0.3772	0.1283	0.01210
1	10	0.3727	0.1458	0.01210
1	8	0.3660	0.1662	0.01210
1	6	0.3588	0.1920	0.01210
1	4	0.3503	0.2196	0.01210
1	2	0.3378	0.2542	0.01210

7.5RP

Value	Chroma	CIE x	CIE y	Y
9	6	0.3512	0.3052	0.7866
9	4	0.3350	0.3099	0.7866
9	2	0.3190	0.3141	0.7866
8	12	0.4002	0.2859	0.5910
8	10	0.3830	0.2930	0.5910
8	8	0.3682	0.2983	0.5910
8	6	0.3521	0.3042	0.5910
8	4	0.3360	0.3092	0.5910
8	2	0.3200	0.3136	0.5910
7	16	0.4346	0.2689	0.4306
7	14	0.4195	0.2762	0.4306
7	12	0.4040	0.2834	0.4306

7	10	0.3871	0.2906	0.4306
7	8	0.3722	0.2963	0.4306
7	6	0.3562	0.3022	0.4306
7	4	0.3389	0.3079	0.4306
7	2	0.3232	0.3125	0.4306
6	20	0.4735	0.2464	0.3005
6	18	0.4581	0.2549	0.3005
6	16	0.4448	0.2622	0.3005
6	14	0.4285	0.2705	0.3005
6	12	0.4125	0.2784	0.3005
6	10	0.3960	0.2860	0.3005
6	8	0.3791	0.2929	0.3005
6	6	0.3635	0.2987	0.3005
6	4	0.3439	0.3056	0.3005
6	2	0.3261	0.3113	0.3005
5	22	0.5045	0.2248	0.1977
5	20	0.4915	0.2330	0.1977
5	18	0.4761	0.2421	0.1977
5	16	0.4617	0.2506	0.1977
5	14	0.4454	0.2596	0.1977
5	12	0.4303	0.2675	0.1977
5	10	0.4108	0.2773	0.1977
5	8	0.3932	0.2852	0.1977
5	6	0.3726	0.2941	0.1977
5	4	0.3515	0.3024	0.1977
5	2	0.3296	0.3098	0.1977
4	20	0.5130	0.2101	0.1200
4	18	0.4965	0.2217	0.1200
4	16	0.4799	0.2329	0.1200
4	14	0.4629	0.2437	0.1200
4	12	0.4450	0.2541	0.1200
4	10	0.4259	0.2651	0.1200
4	8	0.4072	0.2750	0.1200
4	6	0.3850	0.2859	0.1200
4	4	0.3612	0.2963	0.1200
4	2	0.3371	0.3061	0.1200
3	18	0.5130	0.1893	0.06555
3	16	0.4991	0.2011	0.06555
3	14	0.4831	0.2140	0.06555
3	12	0.4654	0.2273	0.06555
3	10	0.4445	0.2419	0.06555
3	8	0.4234	0.2556	0.06555
3	6	0.3990	0.2708	0.06555
3	4	0.3739	0.2851	0.06555
3	2	0.3450	0.3001	0.06555
2	16	0.4744	0.1595	0.03126
2	14	0.4624	0.1737	0.03126
2	12	0.4481	0.1903	0.03126
2	10	0.4321	0.2082	0.03126
2	8	0.4137	0.2276	0.03126
2	6	0.3918	0.2490	0.03126
2	4	0.3702	0.2683	0.03126

2	2	0.3459	0.2892	0.03126
1	12	0.4240	0.1400	0.01210
1	10	0.4132	0.1580	0.01210
1	8	0.4005	0.1793	0.01210
1	6	0.3865	0.2036	0.01210
1	4	0.3705	0.2300	0.01210
1	2	0.3498	0.2617	0.01210

10.0RP

Value	Chroma	CIE x	CIE y	Y
9	6	0.3590	0.3118	0.7866
9	4	0.3400	0.3140	0.7866
9	2	0.3205	0.3155	0.7866
8	10	0.3983	0.3049	0.5910
8	8	0.3800	0.3082	0.5910
8	6	0.3600	0.3112	0.5910
8	4	0.3412	0.3135	0.5910
8	2	0.3218	0.3152	0.5910
7	16	0.4648	0.2878	0.4306
7	14	0.4456	0.2931	0.4306
7	12	0.4260	0.2980	0.4306
7	10	0.4040	0.3030	0.4306
7	8	0.3851	0.3067	0.4306
7	6	0.3648	0.3098	0.4306
7	4	0.3446	0.3125	0.4306
7	2	0.3258	0.3148	0.4306
6	18	0.4961	0.2751	0.3005
6	16	0.4781	0.2812	0.3005
6	14	0.4552	0.2881	0.3005
6	12	0.4360	0.2936	0.3005
6	10	0.4150	0.2989	0.3005
6	8	0.3930	0.3038	0.3005
6	6	0.3740	0.3074	0.3005
6	4	0.3508	0.3112	0.3005
6	2	0.3292	0.3141	0.3005
5	20	0.5396	0.2535	0.1977
5	18	0.5185	0.2620	0.1977
5	16	0.4986	0.2695	0.1977
5	14	0.4767	0.2776	0.1977
5	12	0.4579	0.2841	0.1977
5	10	0.4332	0.2918	0.1977
5	8	0.4105	0.2980	0.1977
5	6	0.3851	0.3039	0.1977
5	4	0.3594	0.3090	0.1977
5	2	0.3332	0.3131	0.1977
4	20	0.5674	0.2319	0.1200
4	18	0.5466	0.2424	0.1200
4	16	0.5234	0.2530	0.1200
4	14	0.5020	0.2623	0.1200
4	12	0.4789	0.2717	0.1200

4	10	0.4528	0.2811	0.1200
4	8	0.4282	0.2890	0.1200
4	6	0.3999	0.2972	0.1200
4	4	0.3715	0.3042	0.1200
4	2	0.3417	0.3106	0.1200
3	16	0.5628	0.2241	0.06555
3	14	0.5380	0.2369	0.06555
3	12	0.5139	0.2489	0.06555
3	10	0.4851	0.2618	0.06555
3	8	0.4552	0.2741	0.06555
3	6	0.4218	0.2864	0.06555
3	4	0.3889	0.2969	0.06555
3	2	0.3526	0.3068	0.06555
2	14	0.5129	0.1888	0.03126
2	12	0.4911	0.2060	0.03126
2	10	0.4678	0.2237	0.03126
2	8	0.4428	0.2419	0.03126
2	6	0.4139	0.2608	0.03126
2	4	0.3850	0.2778	0.03126
2	2	0.3532	0.2957	0.03126
1	12	0.4668	0.1514	0.01210
1	10	0.4521	0.1710	0.01210
1	8	0.4357	0.1921	0.01210
1	6	0.4151	0.2169	0.01210
1	4	0.3920	0.2423	0.01210
1	2	0.3629	0.2710	0.01210

Appendix 4: Color matching functions and cone fundamentals

Table of color matching functions, Smith-Pokorny cone fundamentals and cone chromaticity co-ordinates as a function of wavelength is given in this appendix. The first column of the table gives wavelength in nm. The next three columns give the XYZ color matching functions of the CIE 1931 Standard Observer, modified by Judd (1951)[1]. The next three columns give the L, M and S cone fundamentals respectively, calculated from the expression:

$$\begin{bmatrix} S \\ M \\ L \end{bmatrix} = \begin{bmatrix} 0.00000 & 0.00000 & 0.01608 \\ -0.15514 & 0.45684 & 0.03286 \\ 0.15514 & 0.54312 & -0.03286 \end{bmatrix} \begin{bmatrix} X \\ Y \\ Z \end{bmatrix}$$

The remaining columns give the chromaticity co-ordinates, both for the plane R+G+B = 1.0, and for the plane R+G = 1.0.

1 See Wyszecki, G. and Stiles, W. S. (1982) *Colour Science*, 2nd edition Wiley: New York, p 331.

λ (nm)	X	Y	Z	L cone	M cone	S cone	R+G+B = 1.0 plane			R+G = 1.0 plane		
							l	m	s	l	m	s
400	0.0611	0.0045	0.2799	0.00272558	0.00177424	0.00450079	0.30282163	0.19712437	0.500054	0.60570867	0.39429133	1.00021601
410	0.1267	0.0093	0.5835	0.00553344	0.00376618	0.00938268	0.29618632	0.20159094	0.50222274	0.59501778	0.40498222	1.00893068
420	0.2285	0.0175	1.0622	0.0110502	0.0074491	0.01708018	0.29064055	0.21541975	0.4939397	0.57432	0.42568	0.9760491
430	0.3081	0.0273	1.4526	0.01489937	0.01240553	0.02335781	0.29400591	0.24489416	0.46109993	0.54556666	0.45443334	0.85563159
440	0.3312	0.0379	1.6064	0.01918031	0.01871817	0.02583091	0.30096491	0.29371331	0.40532178	0.50609708	0.49390292	0.68158167
450	0.2888	0.0468	1.4717	0.02186239	0.02493574	0.02366494	0.31026732	0.35388387	0.33584881	0.46716369	0.53283631	0.50568125
460	0.2323	0.06	1.288	0.02630254	0.03369506	0.02071104	0.325895	0.4174901	0.25661491	0.43883324	0.56160676	0.34519781
470	0.1745	0.091	1.1133	0.03991281	0.05108355	0.01790186	0.36651481	0.46909441	0.16439078	0.43861987	0.56138013	0.19673165
480	0.092	0.139	0.7552	0.06495069	0.07404375	0.01214362	0.4297441	0.48990806	0.08044784	0.46728983	0.53271017	0.08736764
490	0.0318	0.208	0.4461	0.10324357	0.10474811	0.00717329	0.47983446	0.48682699	0.03333855	0.49638315	0.50361685	0.03448834
500	0.0048	0.323	0.2644	0.16748425	0.15550283	0.00425155	0.51181074	0.47519705	0.01299221	0.51854783	0.48145217	0.01316323
510	0.0093	0.503	0.1541	0.26956844	0.23341144	0.00247793	0.53331541	0.46178225	0.00490234	0.53594278	0.46405722	0.0049265
520	0.0636	0.71	0.0763	0.39297489	0.31699671	0.0012269	0.55255303	0.44572185	0.00172512	0.5535079	0.446921	0.0017281
530	0.1668	0.862	0.0412	0.49269296	0.36927256	0.0006625	0.57115344	0.42807856	0.000768	0.57715242	0.42840758	0.00076859
540	0.2926	0.954	0.02	0.56287324	0.39910886	0.0003216	0.58983364	0.40982436	0.00033701	0.59003748	0.40996252	0.00033712
550	0.4364	0.995	0.0088	0.60781833	0.38714187	0.0001415	0.61081026	0.38904754	0.0001422	0.61089713	0.38910287	0.00014222
560	0.597	0.995	0.0039	0.63289483	0.36206537	6.2712E-05	0.63060656	0.36387642	6.3026E-05	0.63610065	0.36389935	6.303E-05
570	0.7642	0.952	0.002	0.63554251	0.31641941	0.00003216	0.66759082	0.3323754	3.3782E-05	0.66761337	0.33238663	3.3783E-05
580	0.9159	0.87	0.0016	0.61455455	0.25541065	2.5728E-05	0.70639191	0.29357852	2.9573E-05	0.7064128	0.2935872	2.9574E-05
590	1.0225	0.757	0.0011	0.56973634	0.18723338	1.7688E-05	0.75263649	0.24734015	2.3366E-05	0.75265407	0.24734593	2.3367E-05
600	1.0554	0.631	0.0007	0.50642047	0.12455429	1.1256E-05	0.80258589	0.19739627	1.7839E-05	0.80260021	0.19739979	1.7839E-05
610	0.9922	0.503	0.0003	0.42710941	0.07587047	4.824E-06	0.8491499	0.15084051	9.5907E-06	0.84915804	0.15084196	9.5908E-06
620	0.8432	0.381	0.0002	0.3377362	0.04324856	3.216E-06	0.88647468	0.11351687	8.4412E-06	0.88648217	0.11351783	8.4413E-06
630	0.6327	0.265	0.0001	0.24208059	0.02290881	1.608E-06	0.91354267	0.08645127	6.0681E-06	0.91354821	0.08645179	6.0682E-06
640	0.4404	0.175	0	0.16336966	0.01162334	0	0.93357823	0.06642177	0	0.93357823	0.06642177	0
650	0.2787	0.107	0	0.10135136	0.00564436	0	0.94724684	0.05275316	0	0.94724684	0.05275316	0
660	0.1619	0.061	0	0.05824749	0.00275007	0	0.95491502	0.04508498	0	0.95491502	0.04508498	0
670	0.0838	0.032	0	0.03069085	0.00130787	0	0.95912749	0.04087251	0	0.95912749	0.04087251	0
680	0.0459	0.017	0	0.01635397	0.00064535	0	0.96203648	0.03796352	0	0.96203648	0.03796352	0
690	0.0222	0.0082	0	0.00789769	0.00030198	0	0.9631717	0.0368283	0	0.9631717	0.0368283	0
700	0.0113	0.0041	0	0.00397987	0.00011996	0	0.97073981	0.02926019	0	0.97073981	0.02926019	0

Appendix 5: Environmental ergonomics checklist

This checklist contains about 80 questions concerned with the workstation environment. Each question should be answered in the affirmative.

SECTION 1: KEYBOARD

1.1 Is the keyboard height adjustable?   YES ☐   NO ☐

    If YES:

    Are users aware of this?   YES ☐   NO ☐

1.2 Is the keyboard height between 64-84 cm?   YES ☐   NO ☐

1.3 Is the keyboard height between 71-87 cm

    above the floor?   YES ☐   NO ☐

1.4 Is the keyboard (middle row) to table edge

    10-26 cm?   YES ☐   NO ☐

1.5 If a wrist support is provided:

    (a) Is the height of the wrist support the

    same as the keyboard?   YES ☐   NO ☐

    (b) Are the edges smooth and rounded?   YES ☐   NO ☐

    (c) Is it stable in use?   YES ☐   NO ☐

1.6 If a wrist support is not provided, is there a

    free area of 6 cm in front of the keyboard?   YES ☐   NO ☐

SECTION 2: DISPLAY

2.1 Is the screen height adjustable?   YES ☐   NO ☐

    If YES:

    Are users aware of this?   YES ☐   NO ☐

2.2 Is the center of the screen between 90-115 cm

    above the floor?   YES ☐   NO ☐

2.3 Is the screen distance adjustable?   YES ☐   NO ☐

    If YES:

    Are users aware of this?   YES ☐   NO ☐

2.4 Is the screen distance from the table edge 50-

    75 cm?   YES ☐   NO ☐

2.5 Is the distance between the eye and the

    center of the screen between 61 and 93 cm? YES ☐   NO ☐

2.6 Can the screen tilt and swivel?   YES ☐   NO ☐

2.7 Is the screen angle tilted upwards between

    0-21 degrees?   YES ☐   NO ☐

2.8 Is the visual angle between the eye and

    screen center between 10^0 and 20^0 below the

    horizontal?   YES ☐   NO ☐

2.9 Are the screen controls easily accessible?   YES ☐   NO ☐

SECTION 3: WORK SURFACE

3.1 Is the work surface adjustable? YES ☐ NO ☐

    If YES:

    Are users aware of this? YES ☐ NO ☐

3.2 Is the underside of the work surface free of

    obstructions? YES ☐ NO ☐

3.3 Is the work surface reflectance between 0.4

    (optimum) and 0.6 (maximum)? YES ☐ NO ☐

3.4 Is the work surface height between 72-75 cm? YES ☐ NO ☐

3.5 Is the work surface stable? YES ☐ NO ☐

3.6 Is there adequate space for storage of the

    user's personal belongings? YES ☐ NO ☐

3.7 Is there adequate work surface for the user's

task? YES ☐ NO ☐

3.8 Is the amount of knee clearance between the

    underside of the desk and the seat of the

    chair between 17-20 cm? YES ☐ NO ☐

3.9 Is the user's field of view of the keyboard,

    screen and documents unobscured by each YES ☐ NO ☐

    other?

3.10 If the work surface has drawers, can they be

　　used without affecting its stability?　　　YES ☐　　　NO ☐

SECTION 4: SEATING

4.1 Is the seat height adjustable?　　　　　　YES ☐　　　NO ☐

　　If YES:

　　(a) are users aware of this?　　　　　　　YES ☐　　　NO ☐

　　(b) can adjustments be easily made from

　　the seated position?　　　　　　　　　YES ☐　　　NO ☐

4.2 Is the seat height between 32-55 cm?　　　YES ☐　　　NO ☐

4.3 Does the chair have a five-arm base?　　　YES ☐　　　NO ☐

4.4 Is the chair safe from tipping over?　　　　YES ☐　　　NO ☐

4.5 Is the chair mounted on castors?　　　　　YES ☐　　　NO ☐

4.6 If the chair has arm rests:

　　(a) can the chair still slide under the

　　work surface?　　　　　　　　　　　　YES ☐　　　NO ☐

　　(b) are the arm rests at least 46 cm apart

　　(inside distance)?　　　　　　　　　　YES ☐　　　NO ☐

　　(c) are the arm rests at least 5 cm wide?　YES ☐　　　NO ☐

　　(d) do they extend less than 35 cm behind

　　the back of the seat?　　　　　　　　　YES ☐　　　NO ☐

4.7 Is the seat depth less than or equal to 43 cm? YES ☐　　　NO ☐

4.8 Is the seat width greater than or equal to   YES ☐   NO ☐

 40 cm?

4.9 Is the seat backrest angle adjustable?   YES ☐   NO ☐

 If YES:

 Are users aware of this?   YES ☐   NO ☐

4.10 Is the seat backrest angle between   YES ☐   NO ☐

 95-120 degrees?

4.11 Is the seat backrest height adjustable?   YES ☐   NO ☐

 If YES:

 Are users aware of this?   YES ☐   NO ☐

4.12 Is the seat backrest height at least 23 cm?   YES ☐   NO ☐

4.13 Does the seat backrest provide lumbar

 support?   YES ☐   NO ☐

4.14 Do the chair surfaces smooth outwards?   YES ☐   NO ☐

4.15 Is the eye level above floor between 107 and

 127 cm?   YES ☐   NO ☐

4.16 Does the seat pan have a swivel/rocking

 mechanism that allows a few degrees of

 forward tilt?   YES ☐   NO ☐

SECTION 5: FOOTREST

5.1 Are the user's feet flat on the floor?   YES ☐   NO ☐

If NO:

    Is a footrest provided?   YES ☐   NO ☐

5.2 Is the footrest adjustable in height?   YES ☐   NO ☐

    If YES:

    Are users aware of this?   YES ☐   NO ☐

5.3 Is the footrest height between 0-5 cm?   YES ☐   NO ☐

5.4 Is the footrest adjustable in angle?   YES ☐   NO ☐

    If YES:

    Are users aware of this?   YES ☐   NO ☐

5.5 Is the footrest inclination between 10-15   YES ☐   NO ☐

    degrees?

5.6 Is the footrest adjustable in position?   YES ☐   NO ☐

    If YES:

    Are users aware of this?   YES ☐   NO ☐

5.7 Is the footrest stable?   YES ☐   NO ☐

5.8 Is the footrest surface non-slip?   YES ☐   NO ☐

5.9 Does the footrest cover the entire usable leg

    area?   YES ☐   NO ☐

SECTION 6: POSTURE

6.1 Is the head inclined forward at an angle of

    about 20 degrees?   YES ☐   NO ☐

6.2 Is the spine erect?   YES ☐   NO ☐

6.3 Are the upper arms vertical?   YES ☐   NO ☐

6.4 Are the forearms horizontal?   YES ☐   NO ☐

6.5 Are the thighs horizontal?   YES ☐   NO ☐

6.6 Are the lower legs vertical?   YES ☐   NO ☐

6.7 Does the user adopt a backward-leaning

    posture?   YES ☐   NO ☐

6.8 Does the design of the work station allow

    users to make postural changes?   YES ☐   NO ☐

SECTION 7: DOCUMENT HOLDER

7.1 Is a document holder provided?   YES ☐   NO ☐

7.2 Is the document holder at approximately the

    same height as the display?   YES ☐   NO ☐

7.3 Is the document holder at approximately the

    same distance as the display?   YES ☐   NO ☐

7.4 Is the document holder at an angle of 20

    degrees to the vertical?   YES ☐   NO ☐

7.5 Is the document holder stable?   YES ☐   NO ☐

7.6 Does the document holder have a row

    marker?   YES ☐   NO ☐

7.7 Is the document holder neither transparent

    nor reflective?   YES ☐   NO ☐

SECTION 8: LIGHTING

8.1 Are uplighters provided?   YES ☐   NO ☐

8.2 Is the illuminance at desk height in

    the range 300 - 500 lux?   YES ☐   NO ☐

8.3 Are the fluorescent tubes free from flicker? YES ☐   NO ☐

8.4 Is the reflectance of the walls between

    0.5 and 0.7?   YES ☐   NO ☐

8.5 Is the reflectance of partitions and screens

    between 0.4 and 0.7?   YES ☐   NO ☐

8.6 Is the reflectance of the floor between

    0.2 and 0.4?   YES ☐   NO ☐

8.7 Is the reflectance of furniture between

    0.25 and 0.45?   YES ☐   NO ☐

8.8 Is the reflectance of the desk surface between

    0.4 and 0.6?   YES ☐   NO ☐

8.9 Is the workstation positioned so that the

    operator's line of vision is

        (a) Parallel to luminaires?   YES ☐   NO ☐

        (b) Parallel to windows?   YES ☐   NO ☐

8.10 Are the windows fitted with blinds?   YES ☐   NO ☐

8.11 Is the user's field of view free of glare

    sources? (For example, from the keyboard or

    windows)   YES ☐   NO ☐

8.12 Are there any sources of direct glare on the

    display screen? (For example, from windows

    or luminaires)   YES ☐   NO ☐

8.13 Are there any sources of indirect glare on

    the display screen? (For example, from the

    desk or user's clothing)   YES ☐   NO ☐

SECTION 9: CLIMATE AND NOISE

9.1 Is the work room air conditioned?   YES ☐   NO ☐

9.2 Is the air movement between 0.1 -0.2 m/s?   YES ☐   NO ☐

9.3 Is the temperature maintained at 21 degrees

    C (winter) or 21-24 degrees C (summer)?   YES ☐   NO ☐

9.4 Is the humidity between 45%-55%?   YES ☐   NO ☐

9.5 Is the noise level between 50 dBA

    (preferable) and 55 dBA (maximum)   YES ☐   NO ☐

SECTION 10: CABLE MANAGEMENT

9.1 Are power and data cables safe from

    tripping over?   YES ☐   NO ☐

GLOSSARY

Anomalous trichromacy: A form of congenital color deficiency. In a color matching task, subjects use different proportions of the three primaries compared to normal trichromats. There are three broad classes: protanomalous, deuteranomalous and tritanomalous (see also Dichromacy).

Anomaloscope: An instrument for measuring color deficiency. Subjects view a split field, one half of which is fixed in color. Subjects adjust the color of the other half until the two halves appear to match.

Artefact: An unwanted variable. Artefacts may bias experiments and lead to incorrect or misleading inferences. Display artefacts may produce unintended visual effects. Misconvergence (*q.v.*) is an example of a display artefact.

Chromatic aberration: The term given to the fact that the lens of the human eye focuses short-wave (violet) light slightly in front of the retina and long-wave (deep red) light slightly behind the retina.

Chromaticity: A combined term referring to hue (*q.v.*) and saturation (*q.v.*).

Chromaticity diagram: A two-dimensional plane in a three-dimensional color space. A color in the three-dimensional space can be specified by its projection on the two-dimensional plane. These specifications are known as chromaticity co-ordinates.

Chromostereopsis: Saturated red and blue when presented together appear to lie in different depth planes.

CIE: Commission Internationale de l'Eclairage, a standardization body that has been responsible for specifying color spaces.

Color gamut: The limits or range of colors that can be produced by a system.

Color map: An image broken down into separate color regions denoted by an arbitrary numbering scheme. A child's 'painting by numbers' book is an example of a color map.

Color matching functions: Color matching functions are plots of the relative amounts of three primary lights required to match a monochromatic light. In other words, for any color, C_λ, color matching functions plot the values of $r(\lambda)$, $g(\lambda)$ and $b(\lambda)$ that satisfy the expression:

$$C_\lambda \equiv r(\lambda) + g(\lambda) + b(\lambda)$$

Color space: A graphical or pictorial representation of color.

Co-punctal point: The point on a chromaticity diagram where the responses of two of the three cone types are zero. These points are of major theoretical importance in constructing color spaces and in choosing colors that are likely to be confused by color deficient observers.

Crt: Cathode ray tube. An electron beam tube in which a stream of electrons may be focused at a particular and variable spatial position to produce visible light.

Dac: Digital-to-analog convertor. This device takes as input a digital value (for example, 0 - 1024) and transforms it into an analog voltage (for example, 0 - 5 volts).

Dichromats: Those subjects with congenital color deficiency that can match all colors with only two primaries. Normal trichromats require three primaries. Dichromacy is due to the fact that one of the three cone photopigments are missing. There are three types of dichromacy: protanopes (who lack the L cone pigment), deuteranopes (who lack the M cone pigment) and tritanopes (who lack the S cone pigment). (See also Anomalous Trichromats).

Dioptre: The dioptre (abbreviated D) is a measure of the refractive power of a lens. Specifically, it is equal to the reciprocal of the focal length in metres of the lens. So a lens with a focal length of 1 m has a power of 1D; and a lens with a focal length of 0.5 m has a power of 2D.

Display controler: Part of a graphics system that comprises [i] a timer to provide synchronization pulses for the monitor; [ii] the circuitry required to convert RGB (*q.v.*) values into voltages for transmission by digital-to-analog converters (*q.v.*); and [iii] look-up tables (*q.v.*).

Fovea: The region of the retina (*q.v.*) with a high density of cone cells that supports our best acuity and color vision.

Frame buffer: A section of computer memory that contains a pixel-by-pixel (*q.v.*) description of the image in digitized form.

Gamma correction: A correction factor applied to linearize the relationship between screen luminance and electron gun voltage.

Hue: The term that most closely resembles our notion of 'color', for example, red, green and blue. It is that quality of a color that cannot be accounted for by luminance (*q.v.*) or saturation (*q.v.*) differences. An objective measure of hue is provided by the dominant wavelength of that color's spectral power distribution.

Illuminance: The amount of light striking a surface from a point source. The SI units are lux.

Isomers: Two or more colors with identical spectral power distributions. *C. f.* metamer.

Look-up table (Lut): Luts are used in graphics programming for gamma correction and to translate arbitrary numbers in a color map (*q.v.*) to values for the dacs (*q.v.*).

Luminaire: A luminaire is a complete lighting unit consisting of a lamp or lamps together with the parts designed to distribute the light, to position and protect the lamps, and to connect the lamps to the power supply.

Luminance: The quality of a color that most resembles our notion of brightness. Bright colors are generally of a high luminance, and dark colors are generally of a low luminance (although there are exceptions to this). Luminance is a photometric term; the SI units are candelas per square meter (cd/m^2).

Metamers: Two or more colors that match perceptually but that have different spectral power distributions. *C.f.* isomers.

Microspectrophotometry: A method of measuring the spectral sensitivity (*q.v.*) of photoreceptors (*q.v.*). One of a pair of very small light beams, each about only 2 μm in diameter, is oriented so that it passes through the pigment-containing part of the cell; the other light beam is placed in a neighboring, but clear, area of the slide. The wavelength of the light beams is then varied through the spectrum and the absorbance of the pigment, relative to the absorbance of the neighboring area, is computed.

Misconvergence: Non-allignment of pixels in a shadow-mask crt (*q.v.*) caused by an electron gun exciting the incorrect phosphor. Misconvergence, M, is defined as:

$$M = \frac{S_2 - S_1}{S_1}$$

where S_1 is the stoke width of a perfectly converged symbol and S_2 is the stroke width of the misconverged symbol.

Monochromacy: A very rare kind of color deficiency where subjects can match all colors with only one primary, simply by adjusting the luminance (*q.v.*) of the light.

Nm: Unit of length commonly used to describe the wavelength (*q.v.*) of light. 1 nm equals 10^{-9} metres. For example, light that appears blue to us has a wavelength of about 480 nm; light that appears green to us has a wavelength of about 520 nm; and light that appears red to us has a wavelength of about 640 nm.

Optic nerve: The nerve along which all the retinal signals leave the eye and travel towards the brain. It consists of about a million separate fibres and is about 5 cm long.

Photometry: A branch of physics in which lights are characterized according to their visual effectiveness.

Photopic vision: Cone vision. This occurs at light levels in excess of 10 cd/m².

Photoreceptors: The cells of the retina (*q.v.*) that transduce light energy into electrical energy. There are two broad types of photoreceptor, rods and cones.

Pixel: The smallest discreetly addressable part of a crt.

Principle of Univariance: This principle states that the response of a photoreceptor is uni-dimensional. This means it can identify only the number of quanta absorbed; it cannot identify the wavelength of those quanta.

Quantum: The basic unit of radiant energy. When visible radiation is considered, the term is synonomous with photon.

Raster: The screen on which the image is drawn. The raster is composed of lines, up to 1024 for a high quality display.

Retina: The light receptive layer at the back of the eye, analogous to the film in a camera. As well as containing the photoreceptors (*q.v.*), the retina contains layers of cells whose business is to analyse the light signal before passing this analysed signal onto the brain via the optic nerve (*q.v.*).

RGB: A three-dimensional color space whose axes correspond to digital values passed by the display controler (*q.v.*). These values affect the red, green and blue digital-to-analog convertors (*q.v.*) and hence the color of the displayed image.

Saturation: The quality that distinguishes a hue from white. Pastel shades are desaturated, vivid colors are saturated. An objective measure of saturation is purity.

Scotopic vision: Rod or twilight vision, restricted to light levels below 10^{-3} cd/m².

Spectral sensitivity: Sensitivity as a function of wavelength.

Tristimulus values: A trio of numbers that specify a color in a three dimensional color space. In the CIE (1931) x, y system, for example, these three values are derived from color matching functions and denoted by the symbols **X**, **Y** and **Z**. The x, y and z chromaticity co-ordinates are derived from these three values by the expressions:

$$x = \frac{X}{X+Y+Z}$$

$$y = \frac{Y}{X+Y+Z}$$

$$z = \frac{Z}{X+Y+Z}$$

Vitreous humor: A transparent, jelly-like substance between the lens of the eye and the retina (*q.v.*).

Wavelength: The distance between two points (having the same phase) on a periodic waveform. The wavelength of visible light is measured in nm (*q.v.*).

SUBJECT INDEX

Page numbers in **bold** denote figures relating to that subject; *italics* indicate a glossary definition.

AUTHOR INDEX